1700

ALL NECESSARY
MEASURES

Also by Cameron Spence

Sabre Squadron

ALL NECESSARY MEASURES

CAMERON SPENCE

MICHAEL JOSEPH
LONDON

MICHAEL JOSEPH

Published by the Penguin Group
Penguin Books Ltd, 27 Wrights Lane, London w8 5 tz, England
Penguin Putnam Inc., 375 Hudson Street, New York, New York 10014, USA
Penguin Books Australia Ltd, Ringwood, Victoria, Australia
Penguin Books Canada Ltd, 10 Alcorn Avenue, Toronto, Ontario, Canada m4v 3b2
Penguin Books (NZ) Ltd, Private Bag 102902, NSMC, Auckland, New Zealand

Penguin Books Ltd, Registered Offices: Harmondsworth, Middlesex, England

First published 1998
1 3 5 7 9 10 8 6 4 2

Copyright © Cameron Spence, 1998

The moral right of the author has been asserted

Set in 12/15pt Monotype Sabon
Typeset by Rowland Phototypesetting Ltd, Bury St Edmunds, Suffolk
Printed in England by Clays Ltd, St Ives plc

A CIP catalogue record for this book is available from the British Library

Hardback ISBN 0-718-14295-0
Paperback ISBN 0-718-14375-2

To Fergie, who never made it
home (one of the best)

CONTENTS

ACKNOWLEDGEMENTS

As with *Sabre Squadron*, the list of people who've helped make this book happen is a long one. Thanks again to Nick Cook and Mark Lucas for all the work they've put in; to Paddy and Cathie Rainey, of GENRIC S.A. for their support throughout; to the ARCO project managers in Algeria, Leland, Doug, Jack, and Bon Kramm, and the two security managers, Bill and Mick, for their flexibility in helping me pursue this project properly; to the team members who stepped in at short notice to cover my periods of absence, Taff, Dave, Terry, Steve and Adam; and, of course, to the REB project staff, for which the list could be endless, but from which I should mention Mark C., Mick L., Tom O., Garry C., James B., Roger A., Winston S., Keith U., Graeme T., Bill L., Don G., Steve G., Mike Macnamara and the Texan Bill Pistol.

And last, but definitely not least, Jade, for her continued confidence, support and understanding.

PROLOGUE

I raised the binoculars and tried to steady them as my elbows sank into the deep snow. The target was lit up by high-intensity spots that had turned night into day in this desolate corner of the world. The beams were so bright they made my eyes water. The cold threatened to turn my tears to ice.

From our vantage-point, we could see the two giant wheels and the cables attached to the cages that descended to the bowels of the mine. The building that surrounded this assembly was vast, around five storeys high, and long, about seventy metres or so. It nestled in the shadow of a huge, craggy rock overhang.

To my right, I heard Keith swear. He kept it low, since the whole area was teeming with guards, but there was enough venom in it to dispatch a light curtain of condensation in the general direction of the mine. A more experienced badged member of the Regiment would have kept his mouth zipped. Keith was smart, though. He wouldn't make the same mistake twice.

I shared his frustration. Somehow, we had to get down there – past the guards, through the outer perimeter and into the heart of the complex, all under the gaze of those high-intensity lights.

To cap it all, we couldn't just plant our explosives anywhere. We needed to get them into a part of the mine where they would obliterate it – or, at the very least, put it out of action for a good long stretch. And that wasn't going to be easy with a single charge. Short of bringing a nuke with us, we were only talking one place: down the shaft itself.

I adjusted the throat-mike – two tiny microphones nestling either side of my Adam's apple – and shifted my gaze. 'Kiwi, Joe,' I whispered. 'Are you getting this?'

There was a light crackle in my right ear. I cupped my hand over the earpiece, my link to the other half of the hit-team. And then I heard what I first took to be distortion or interference. For a moment, I didn't get it, but then it shifted into a recognizable beat, as – five hundred metres away and hidden by trees and darkness – Kiwi and Joe found their rhythm.

Duh-duh-da-da-duh-duh-da-da . . .

Hearing *Mission: Impossible* tapped out on their throat-mikes sealed it for me. We'd not got this far to see our plan short-circuited by a few arc-lights.

I focused the binos on to the window of the office at the end of the large, warehouse-like building in the middle of the mine complex. Behind the condensation on the glass, a shadow moved.

Keith glanced at me. 'Is that him?'

'Who else?' I said. Seeing him, albeit in silhouette, was enough to rekindle my anger. Whatever happened, I told myself, we were going to teach that Norwegian son-of-a-bitch a lesson.

'How are we going to do this one, Cammy?' Keith asked, one hand raised to shield his eyes from the glare of the lights.

Keith was an ex-Para, lean and wiry, with a fetching haircut that went right down to the wood. He'd only recently passed Selection, but already I liked his style. He thought things through before choosing a course of action, a valuable commodity in the SAS. Because of his build, we called him the Racing Snake. He was an A Squadron grunt, the same as me. The other two, Kiwi and Joe, were B Squadron, but I don't hold that against them.

As I fought to stop the bitter, −15-degrees cold from seeping into my brain and clogging all thought, I wondered briefly if we had bitten off more than we could chew.

There were troops everywhere. We reckoned about fifty in total. We could see them patrolling the roof of the big building, around its walls and between us and the perimeter of the complex. We were wearing our 'whites' over four layers of clothing, so we were well camouflaged, but I still felt dangerously exposed.

'We lie here and watch,' I said. 'There'll be a pattern in their movements – there always is. And where there's a pattern, there's usually a gap. It just depends on where and when it materializes.'

The trick to cracking a problem like this is to search for areas of dead ground and shadow between you and the target, then link them together in a kind of join-the-dots mapping exercise.

While Keith and I worked on this, Kiwi and Joe kept their eyes peeled for signs of routine. We'd brought night-vision goggles and a big MIRA thermal-imaging system with us. We also had our KITE-sights, the light-magnification devices fixed to our Hechler and Koch MP5 sub-machine-guns. Thanks to the light, of course, we didn't need them. The target was burning enough electricity to turn night into day.

It took us a little over three hours, but by eleven o'clock, we had a plan.

The guards were sticking close to the buildings. It was cold and it had been dark for hours – in the Arctic winter, it only ever gets light for a fraction of the day – but by the end of the night it was going to get colder still. The sentries would be feeling the cold every bit as much as us, only they didn't have adrenaline on their side. And then we noticed another thing. Every so often, the guards would disappear. Somewhere, I was sure, there was a brazier or a stove; a place where a couple of men at a time were sneaking off for a chance to get a little heat into their bones. It wasn't much, but on a mission this tricky you're latching on to the merest of clues. We set off, crawling our way between shadows and the shittiest, deepest bloody snowdrifts we could find.

Suddenly there was a light crackle in my earpiece. 'Cammy. You've got a sentry real close, mate. Less than thirty metres to your right.'

Slowly, I raised my head from the drift. There he was, rubbing his hands and staring at the stars. We hadn't spotted him before. He must have wandered into the woods for a slash and just re-emerged.

Kiwi's warning had come just in time.

The commentary from Kiwi and Joe was one-way traffic, as we were now heavily into silent-running. Should we be compromised, they had instructions to detonate a couple of big home-made incendiary bombs they'd positioned on the ridge-line. These were large, petrol-filled plastic containers fixed up with detonators and command radio links.

It took Keith and me two hours to reach the first of the buildings. We stopped and took stock by a pile of big wooden sleepers. The warehouse-like structure towered above us a few dozen metres away.

Keith and I darted across the train tracks, sticking to patches of ground where the snow hadn't settled. We dived behind a large drift that had collected in the lee of the building. We lay there for a couple of minutes, catching our breath and listening for signs of compromise. Two more sentries walked right by us. Keith and I pressed back into the shadows and held our breath. The sentries walked on.

It was then that I noticed some wadding set into the brickwork a couple of metres away. It had a make-do look about it that suggested it might have been lashed there as a cover for something: a ventilation shaft, perhaps. We started to pick away at it, bit by bit.

It took about thirty minutes to get enough of it off for me to squeeze my head through the gap. The wadding turned out to be a lash-up cover for a hole in the wall, probably the result of some building work that never got finished.

I looked down and to the right and saw a metal gangway two metres below me and another two metres from the floor. It ran around the entire cavernous chamber. It must have been used for marshalling vehicles and machinery used in coal extraction.

Then I shifted my gaze and almost had a heart-attack. About thirty metres to the left, three guards were leaning against the wall having a smoke. I froze, convinced that if I moved a muscle it would prompt them to turn. The surreal sight of my head hanging from the wall like a hunting trophy might frighten them for a second, but that would have been it, game over.

Ever so gently, I inched my head back. Keith and I waited for the alarm to go up. I readied myself to give Kiwi and Joe the command to blow the incendiaries.

The seconds ticked by. Nothing happened. At least, I thought, we knew where the bastards were sneaking to get out of the cold.

Carefully, I risked another look.

The guards, thank God, had gone.

We had no idea when they would be back so we worked fast. It was decided that Keith would go ahead and scout for something that could connect us to the shaft. Provided we could get our small bomb into the subterranean area of the mine, we'd let coal-dust, accumulated gases and confined space do the rest.

Keith dropped on to the gangway and then to the floor. Within a couple of seconds, he was out of sight. I plugged the hole with my Bergen, sat back and waited, clutching the bomb to my chest. If he didn't come back within thirty minutes, I had to assume he'd been taken. Then I'd be on my own.

The minutes passed agonizingly slowly. I kept a sharp look-out for sentries. The nearest I could see was on the other side of the tracks, at least eighty metres away, checking the underside of a line of abandoned rail cars. I kept half an eye open, just in case he changed direction.

I heard a light tap on the wadding. I pulled it back and saw the Racing Snake. His face was bathed in sweat. I thought he was about to deliver bad news, but instead he told me he'd found something. Something good. I got rid of all my extraneous kit – webbing, snowsuit and Hechler and Koch – and headed for the hole.

I was still pumping adrenaline when Keith led me to the far corner of the vaulted chamber. There, just above the metal gangway, was a door set in the wall. It looked like one of those watertight jobs you get on ships, with a big, circular, twist-type lock on the outside. It was covered in rust and hadn't been touched in years.

Keith prised it open. It swung back with a muffled groan.

We waited a moment to check that nobody had heard us. My sidearm trawled the shadows, but the place was still clear.

'What do you think?' he whispered.

I probed the darkness with my penlight and found myself staring into a lift-shaft, probably a back-up access tunnel to the main shaft. The walls were bare, hewn straight from the coal. Thick wire cables dropped down the middle. Following them with the light beam, you just knew that this thing led straight down, all the way to the bottom. A thousand metres, no stops.

A concrete ledge, barely ten centimetres wide, was tacked on to the walls below the level of the hatch.

It took me a moment to figure out where Keith intended to put the bomb. Then my penlight found a recess in the far wall. It was about a metre deep and bathed in shadow. If the guards decided to do a spot-check there was every chance they wouldn't see the device. The recess it was, then.

'Perfect,' I said. 'Who gets to place it there?'

Keith smiled weakly. 'You said you'd done Everest, didn't you?'

xvi

I holstered my Browning and tugged my Bergen round so that it sat on my chest. 'No, it was Choyo, a few more down the chain.'

'What's the difference?'

'A few hundred metres, mate, that's what.'

'Well, there you bloody are, then.' He nodded in the direction of the shaft.

I looked at him squarely. 'Would you climb Everest in the sodding dark?' Before he could come back with some wise-arse reply, I told him to keep a sharp look-out, then jumped up on to the jamb of the hatchway.

This place being what it was, I knew we couldn't hang around. I had maybe two minutes to get in and out again. If I slipped, it would probably take me that long to hit the base of the shaft. My only possible let-out was the cables. But in the beam of my penlight, I noticed they were smeared with thick gobs of grease. If I grabbed them, it didn't look like being a whole lot of help.

Gingerly, I stepped down on to the ledge. It felt secure enough, but you never know with these things. The concrete was old and had probably degraded. I flattened the palm of my left hand and walked the tips of my fingers along the wall. It was freezing cold and wet.

Great. Loads of bloody condensation to contend with. And possibly some ice.

It took me a second or two to stabilize myself. I pushed my left foot as far as it would go, all the while gripping the jamb with my right. To my enormous relief, the toe of my left boot nudged up against the corner of the shaft. Gently, I transferred it to the ledge running along the adjacent wall. I scraped my toe along it, listening for silence and feeling for that momentary skate across the surface that would denote ice. The rasp of my sole on the concrete was reassuring. The bastard seemed to be clear.

I drew in a deep breath and transferred my weight, bringing my right foot along the ledge towards the corner. When I was happy that it was secure, I let go with my right hand and pressed it against the slippery wall of the shaft. In the echoing silence, it made a slight slap, like a fish hitting a slab of slate.

Now, straddling the abyss, I manoeuvred both feet, edging all the while towards the recess. The weight of the bomb on my chest was something I hadn't taken into account. I was so finely balanced, I could feel it pulling me forward. I pressed my head back into the corner and my balance returned. I let out a lungful of spent air and tried to breathe normally.

With my eyes more accustomed to the light, I could now make out the dark square on the wall opposite the hatch. I did a swift calculation and then swung out across the shaft, using my left toe as a counter-point. It was only when my foot was half-way across the abyss, my weight fully transferred to the right-hand side of my body, that a stupid thought occurred to me. What if there ain't no fucking ledge on the far wall?

I brought my right hand down sharply on the edge of the recess, fighting a pang of fear in my gullet that threatened to spoil everything.

It held, but only for a moment.

My fingers aquaplaned across the moisture. Then, they got a little bit of purchase, some unevenness on the surface where the water could not collect. I gripped hard. My right foot was still in free-fall and coming down fast. I braced my right hand, with its precarious, fingertip grip on my life, to take my entire weight. I was resigned now to the fact that there was no ledge on this side of the shaft. But then it came for me. My toe hit concrete and for a second I was thrown off balance. My face banged against the wall of the shaft.

For a moment, my nostrils filled with the bitter smell of carbon. I heard chips of coal clattering down the shaft, until the sound was swallowed by the blackness.

Then, I heard a voice. Five seconds after I should have been swallow-diving towards the Philippines, Keith had decided to find out if I was all right. 'Fine,' I mumbled. 'Just keep scanning for guards.'

Now came the interesting bit. I transferred as much weight as I could to my left and removed my right hand from the recess. Slowly I edged it towards my day-sack. I flipped open the top and grasped the bomb. I had to twist my upper body a little into the shaft, but it came out cleanly.

Careful not to make any sudden moves, I eased it into the recess.

There was no bloody way I was going back the way I came, so I called out to Keith. A moment later, he stuck his head through the hatch and I jumped. Keith grabbed my combat jacket and hauled for both our lives. I do mountaineering for fun, as well as duty, but being back on *terra firma* had never felt so good.

It took me a second to catch my breath. Then we were on the move again, retracing our steps to the hole in the wall.

Having dodged another gaggle of sentries, Keith and I pulled back a hundred metres and surveyed the scene. Nothing much had changed. The guards continued to patrol the roof of the main building and its walls. The lights in the office still burned brightly. Above, the clouds had cleared to expose an ink-black sky studded with stars. All around us, the forest was vast, dark and silent. The intense cold only added to the overall aesthetics: it was as pretty as a picture.

I almost felt a momentary stab of remorse for bringing it all to an end.

'OK, guys,' I said, speaking softly to Kiwi and Joe. 'This is it. Let's light the candles and shut the place down.'

A couple of seconds after their acknowledgement, a giant explosion flared on the skyline, promptly followed by another. I should have turned away to protect my night vision, but the sight of those billowing clouds of smoke and flame rising from the ridge-line compelled me to watch.

I glimpsed the silhouette at the window again and imagined the rising panic. *Hasta la vista*, baby.

Keith and I pulled back into the shadows. We shook hands, then turned and ran for the rendezvous (RV) where Kiwi and Joe were waiting.

ONE

Twenty-four hours later, I was back in Stirling Lines. If I thought we were going to have it easy after the success of our fun and games in the Norwegian Arctic, I was wrong. Though I didn't know it yet, I was a couple of days from heading off to another war.

Some indication of the urgency was contained in the 'warning order' that I now reread as I waited outside the OC's office in the A Squadron interest room.

I'd read it umpteen times already. Like all warning orders, it was terse and devoid of melodrama, but that didn't mean much. If you knew SAS procedure, you could spot urgency a mile off, even when it was well disguised between lines. The Third World War could have been about to bust loose and they still would have stuck to the same clipped terminology. This message was no different.

It read: 'HOPE OPERATION WENT WELL STOP FUTURE PLANS — WARNING ORDER STOP BE ADVISED DEPLOYMENT OUT OF AREA STOP PROBABLY 36–48 HOURS AFTER YOUR RETURN TO HEREFORD STOP INITIAL INT BRIEF D PLUS ONE.'

I'd shared it with the guys who'd been with me at our temporary operational headquarters. We'd been standing around, clutching our brews and shooting the shit, winding down after the exhilaration of the mission. I'd slunk off a little way from the group to read it. Toby was the first to notice the somewhat quizzical expression on my face. I showed him the piece of paper.

'Hell's bollocks,' he said, with customary Geordie emphasis. 'You mean to tell me we've been up to our necks in white vomit for the past two months and now this?'

'Right,' I said. If Toby didn't like snow, I wondered briefly what the hell he was doing in Mountain Troop. 'Knowing our luck, mate, we're headed for some more.'

By now, the rest of the group had caught wind of what was happening. Keith, Paul, Doug, Kevin and Ray started bombarding me with questions. I handed the warning order to Kevin and asked him to pass it around.

'Where are we going?' he asked, as soon as he'd cast his eyes over it.

I shrugged. 'Your guess is as good as mine, mate.'

We'd been away from base for two whole months. We always did our best to keep in touch with what was happening out there via the BBC World Service. But in a place where the sun don't shine much this time of year, it felt like current events had passed us by.

The more experienced members of the troop – Doug, Kev, Ray and Toby – started speculating on where we might be going. Before the end of the Cold War, 'out of area' usually denoted somewhere exotic, but now it could mean any place east of Calais. Somebody grabbed a four-day-old paper and ran through the columns on the foreign pages. There was the ongoing fracas in Angola, more disturbances in Somalia, some tension in the Yemen, but nothing much to write home about.

'What about Bosnia?' Paul asked. Like Toby, Paul was an ex-Para. I didn't know him that well because he'd only been with us a few months. The Arctic job had been his and Keith's first deployment.

His comment provoked a lot of tooth-sucking among the older members of the team. Paul looked a little embarrassed, like he'd dropped a real clanger or something.

As troop leader, I felt it only fair to step in. 'It couldn't be, mate,' I explained. 'D Squadron's already in Bosnia. They're the standby team. We're not due to go standby for a month or so. This has to be someplace else.'

The way the Regiment works, we always have one squadron on counter-terrorist, or CT, duties. This is the special projects, or SP, team, ready to deploy at a moment's notice to a terrorist event. Another squadron is always on 'standby' duty, which means it must be ready to leave at short notice for a 'significant event' overseas, such as the Gulf or Bosnia. A third squadron is on reserve standby duty, but in practice uses the time for training, while the fourth devotes its time exclusively to training exercises. These activities rotate among the four active-duty 'sabre squadrons' – A, B, D and G Squadrons – every six months or so.

Now, as I surveyed the walls in the warmth of our interest room at Hereford, I checked my watch. My meeting with Philip, the OC, wasn't for another forty minutes. Though big enough comfortably to seat the entire squadron – some fifty blokes – the room was empty. The TV in the corner was quietly churning out its daily diet of non-stop satellite news. I listened briefly for signs of trouble in some far-flung corner of the globe, then turned my attention to the walls. I felt pretty sure that, in the time remaining before my meeting, I would be able to crack where we were headed.

The interest room is a place where the squadron can sit around and relax, but it also tends to be its nerve centre. All four interest rooms are ranged along one side of the Quadrangle, a large building in the middle of the base complex. An interest room tends to reflect the character of the squadron as well as its achievements. Among the plaques and mementoes of a half-century of covert operations, you can also find photos of past japes and wind-ups perpetrated by, and on, various members of the squadron.

As I stood before the main noticeboard clutching my brew, I expected to see a cluster of messages relating to the warning order. To my surprise, there was nothing out of the ordinary on it: just the usual housekeeping stuff, a faded map of the Gulf and an equally scraggy-looking chart of the Balkans. I was still wondering what the fuck was going on when I heard a voice behind me.

I turned and saw Tom, a mate who'd been on my Land Rover behind Iraqi lines in '91. We exchanged insults and brought each other up to date on our respective activities.

Tom explained he'd been on a medical refresher course for the past three weeks. He was about to leave the classroom for a two-week stint in the operating theatres of a major hospital. The Regiment knows there's no substitute for practical experience and Tom was looking forward to it. Someone had told him about the local night-life and he'd already packed his glad-rags. Tom had a wardrobe that would have made John Travolta envious. But, then, as the rest of us lost no time in telling him, 1978 was a long time ago.

'Listen, mate,' he said, gesturing to the limp selection of notices on the wall, 'if it's not on the board, there isn't a drama. Relax. Old Philip's probably just winding you up.'

Just then, the O C walked in, head down and looking thoughtful. He glanced up, saw us and smiled. Philip was a major in his early thirties, around five-ten and of thinnish build. For a rupert, he was a good bloke. I'd taken him through Selection six years earlier, so I knew his strengths and weaknesses well. Fortunately, he was big on the former and distinctly lacking on the deficit side. He'd been a troop commander in D Squadron and was now A Squadron's commander.

'Give me a minute,' he said, after we had shaken hands.

4

'There's somebody I need to see first. I'll call you when I'm done.' And then he disappeared into his office.

A minute later, the 'somebody' walked in. There was a light squeak of boot rubber and a cough behind us. Tom and I turned from the noticeboard. There, framed in the doorway, was a tall bloke with a long face and a mop of fair hair. He was young, probably no more than twenty-four, and blessed with almost film-star good looks. The straightness of his bearing and the way he looked at us, while not arrogant, signalled instantly that this guy was used to giving orders, not taking them. Since the SAS doesn't set a great deal of store by rank, and especially in the paraphernalia that goes with it, such observations can be useful.

'Hi,' he said, having given the four walls of the interest room a cursory sweep. 'I'm looking for the OC's office.'

I was still taking in the public-school accent and the studied, Hugh Grant-school casualness, when Tom pointed with his mug. 'That door there, mate.'

The guy thanked us and carried on through after Philip. We waited till its door closed firmly behind him, then looked at each other.

'What the fuck was that?' I asked.

'A month's wages, that's a rupert,' Tom replied.

'I can see that, dickhead. Who is he? Any ideas?'

'None. But a pound to a penny, Cammy, that's your rupert.'

I gulped down a mouthful of coffee and almost choked. 'What do you mean?'

Tom threw open his arms and looked smug. 'Your troop's short of a rupert, isn't it? That, then, is your man. Got to be.'

I thought about this. If I hadn't been away so long, it would probably have occurred to me sooner. There are four troops per squadron: Boat, Freefall, Mobility and Mountain. Tom was Freefall, I was Mountain. Though not an officer, as a senior sergeant I'd been in charge of the troop for some time.

The Regiment tries to give each troop an officer – ruperts, as we call them – but quite often there aren't enough to go round. Of course, it's good to run your own troop, but having a rupert for a boss doesn't have to be so bad. I've always had ambitions, but climbing to the top of the Regiment had never been one of them.

I loved my job and had been lucky enough in my eleven years with the SAS to have done some interesting things. With less than two years to go before I was scheduled to leave both the Regiment and the Army, I had to concede that I was probably overdue a rupert as boss of the troop.

Tom clapped a hand on my shoulder. ''Ere, Cammy, don't worry about it, mate. Think, with a rupert in charge, you can book into fancy hotels on officer's rates.'

I smiled. This was true. Officers got a sixty-pound allowance from the Army towards their hotel bill whenever we spent a night away on official business. As an other rank, or OR, however, I was only entitled to spend thirty pounds of the MoD's money on my gaff. But with an officer in tow, our perks became one and the same.

I was still chewing this over, when Phil stuck his head around the door and called me in.

Philip has two doors to his office, one that opens directly on to the interest room, another that leads to and from the corridor. I was surprised, therefore, to see that the rupert was still there. I thought he'd left the other way, but there he was, large as bloody life, in one of the chairs in front of the OC's desk. Now, I knew that Tom was right. This was the big introduction, no question. I was about to be teamed with a Hollywood fucking matinée idol. But I didn't know the half of it yet.

'Sit down,' Philip said, rolling the words into one. He settled himself behind the desk, took a pull at his coffee, and turned to the rupert. 'Cammy, I'd like you to meet Charlie Hyde. Charlie, this is Cameron Spence, the guy I was telling you about. Charlie's your new troop commander, Cammy. He's just passed Selection. The idea at the moment is for him to head up Mountain Troop for the next couple of years. So, it looks like he'll be seeing you into retirement.'

We shook hands. The grip, I was glad to note, was firm. He gave me a kind of self-deprecating nod. Very Hugh Grant. My Mel Gibson's a bit rusty, so I mumbled something suitably polite and sat down again.

OK, I thought. That's one little mystery cleared up. Now let's cut to the chase.

'Welcome back, Cammy,' Philip said, as soon as we'd taken out seats again. 'Nice work, by the way.'

'Thanks, boss. It was a good little workout, no mistake.'

'I'll get the details later,' the OC replied. 'As you know, something's come up. Something rather urgent.'

He paused and looked at both of us. 'You're going to Bosnia. We're looking at getting you there in the next thirty-six hours. You'll be going in under cover as part of the Signals Regiment. I'm not going to get into the nitty-gritty now – you'll be given all that when you arrive at British Army headquarters in Split. You'll be working under the command of D Squadron over there, but that shouldn't give you too many problems, should it?'

I shook my head. Right now, working with D Squadron was the least of my concerns.

'Good. Then I'll leave you two to get acquainted and to tie up the admin. Remember, you're going to be a green army unit operating under the banner of the UN, so make sure you get all the right uniform and insignia from Stores, not to mention kit and equipment.'

He shuffled some papers from his desk, then looked up. 'Any questions?'

'Yes, boss,' I said. 'What the fuck are we doing over there?'

I knew Philip wanted to keep it tight, but this was ridiculous.

I'd read the headlines over the past two years, trying to make sense of them like everyone else. At first, it had all seemed a long way off. But as the Balkan war had shifted from Slovenia to Croatia and from there into Bosnia, it had all got a lot closer to home, mainly thanks to the coverage it had got on television.

As things stood, the Croats, Bosnian Muslims and Bosnian Serbs were still knocking seven bells out of each other. For the beleaguered UN, whose forces were there on the ground, it was like trying to deal with a rash of brush-fires. No sooner did the conflict die out in one area than it flared in another. Sometimes it was the Serbs and the Croatians trying to kill each other, other times it was Muslims against Serbs or Croats against Muslims. And sometimes two of them teamed up against the other. It was all very perplexing and I didn't pretend to understand it.

All I knew for sure was that people – mainly Muslims – were still starving to death in places like Maglaj, Srebrenica and Gorazde. The siege of Sarajevo, the Muslim capital, had recently been lifted, but nobody was holding their breath. Death was still very much a part of everyday life in Bosnia-Herzegovina. And, as far as I could tell, not a whole lot was being done about it.

In the end, there wasn't a bloke in camp who hadn't been moved by TV pictures of civilians being driven from their homes, or women and children lying dead in the streets, all in the name of that barbarously understated act, ethnic cleansing. In the confusing picture that had developed, it was the Serbs who had emerged as the main aggressor. I hoped, therefore, that Phil was about to give us some juicy tasking to take out a local Serbian warlord or an arms dump crucial to the Serb war effort.

I should have known, though, that the pitch wasn't going to be that simple. Nothing about the next few months would be.

Phil got up and tapped a map on the wall behind him. It showed the Yugoslav theatre of operations. 'As you probably know,' he began, 'there's been a breakthrough in the picture over there. The Croats and the Muslims have agreed to recognize each other's borders in Bosnia and call a ceasefire if – and I repeat if – we can get their lines mapped and a settlement agreed by the twelfth of April, a little over a month from today.'

I frowned. I had been dimly aware of this during our time in the Arctic. However, like I'd told the boys when we first got the warning order, it was a situation I thought that we, the Regiment, had got covered.

I put it to Phil. 'What's D Squadron doing out there, then?'

'They're up to their ears in it,' he replied. 'There's a fuck of a lot to do, Cammy, and the clock's ticking. I don't need to tell you how high the stakes are. General Rose has called upon us because he knows how we work. If the job's not done in time there'll be no peace between the Muslims and the Croats and the war could drift on for years, a decade – who the hell knows?'

I nodded. General Sir Michael Rose, the head of the United Nations Protection Force (UNPROFOR) in Bosnia, was ex-Regiment, one of us.

'How long will we be gone?' I asked.

'Put it this way, you're going to need more than an overnight bag. Preparing for the ceasefire is merely the primary task. There's a lot more to it. Rose wants you to be his eyes and ears in the Balkans. There's a shed-load of confusion over there, a lot of bullshit that needs sifting. The picture's changing by the day. What Rose needs is good intel, particularly from the siege cities, so you could be deploying to places that haven't seen a blue beret in years. D Squadron, however, will put you in the picture as soon as you get to Split.'

'Who do I – who do we – get to take with us?' I asked, glancing at Charlie.

'You'll take your own troop plus Fergie to make up numbers. Ferguson's a good man,' Phil explained to Charlie, 'and he speaks a bit of Serbo-Croat.'

Phil slapped his hands on the desk and got to his feet. 'This is detail stuff,' he said, looking at both of us in turn. 'I'm sure you two have got a lot to talk about, so I'll let you get on.'

I thought back to the events of 1990, when we'd been preparing to ship to the Gulf. There, we'd been going in to do a job that the SAS had been trained to carry out ever since its formation. Here, now, I was being assigned a role none of us had ever considered before. But things had moved rapidly since the fall of the Wall and this was the living proof of it.

Back in the interest room, Tom had disappeared and things were still quiet. Since we didn't have a whole lot of time, I thought it best if we settled down and talked brass tacks. I made Charlie a coffee, grabbed a tea for myself, and plonked down on one of the tatty settees. I half expected the new rupert to get out a hankie and dust the cushions down but, to his credit, he didn't. He perched on the arm of the next-door chair and sipped his brew thoughtfully as he gave the room a quick once-over. For a new guy, it's all a bit baffling, but it tells pretty much the whole story: from David Stirling's Long Range Desert Group in the Second World War, to Malaya, Borneo, Oman, the Falklands and the Gulf. If you've lived with it for a while it's easy to take it all for granted. But it's impressive stuff, especially to a guy who's just sweated bullets to get through Selection.

Charlie, it turned out, had arrived back in Hereford that day. He was a captain, ex-Light Division, who'd been through Selection with Keith and Paul but had taken a little longer to escape Aldershot. I'd seen a lot of ruperts in my time, both in and out of the Regiment. Some were good and some were bad. During our six weeks behind enemy lines in the Gulf War we'd been commanded by a real peach – a guy so bereft of the right stuff, as it turned out, that he ended up getting pulled out of Iraq in the middle of our anti-Scud campaign.

That, it has to be said, is the exception not the rule, but it doesn't help endear the officer corps to the likes of us senior

NCOs. The unspoken truth – as true in the SAS as it is anywhere else in the Army – is that these guys have to earn our respect long before we give it to them; and Charlie, whose appearance said he'd been cast from the classic officer mould, would have to earn it harder than most.

The first thing I needed to brief him on was the troop order of battle, or orbat. We decided it was best to split the troop into two patrols. Charlie would lead one, while I'd take the other. Because there was more than the average number of new intakes in the troop, we'd have to be careful how we constructed the patrols, I explained. We were already short of two old hands, Taff and Dean, who were off on a demolition course. Recruiting Fergie would help, but we were still low on experience. It would be wisest, I went on, if we loaded most of the old sweats into Charlie's patrol, while I took a disproportionate number of new hands. I looked at Charlie to see if he'd taken offence at this suggestion, but he nodded genially. So far, I thought, so good.

'So tell me about these guys,' he said.

I gave him the rundown, starting with the people in his own patrol.

First, there was Ray, a quietish sort of bloke in his early thirties, who was a handy forward air controller and fully trained in all the bits of kit that went with it. Ray was a 'crap hat' like me, which meant his parent regiment was infantry. The Paras escaped this dubious moniker on account of their sporty red berets, which a lot of people think make them look like poofs. The Regiment tends to be split down the middle between these two camps, a division that results in endless insults and occasionally even fisticuffs.

Next up was Dave, an ex-Para in his late twenties, of not dissimilar build to me, though bigger in the biceps department because of his keenness for weight-training. He had been in the troop for quite a spell and was a quietly switched-on kind of bloke.

Then there was Fergie, six foot two and built like Arnie. Another ex-Para, Fergie was a great guy with a keen sense of humour. He also had a lot of credibility as a soldier. With that little bit of Serbo-Croat under his belt, too, I figured he'd be a hell of an asset for this mission. Charlie seemed to take this on board.

Last, but not least, in Charlie's patrol, was Toby. Though a Geordie, Toby reminded me greatly of my old mate Taff, the Welshman who had taken the brunt – and been the originator – of so many wind-ups during the Gulf War. Like Taff, Toby was stocky and a perpetrator of the most appalling practical jokes. As with Ray and Dave, he was married with young kids.

My patrol would contain two old hands and two new ones. There was Doug, an ex-Royal Corps of Transport jock, who'd also gone behind the lines in '91. Despite our shared experiences of Iraq, we didn't know each other that well, mainly because we hung out with different crowds. He was small, but strong as an ox. He was also an amusing bloke, brimming with Billy Connolly humour.

Much the same could be said for Kevin, another Gulf vet. Kev was a great guy, who also liked to have a bit of a laugh, but strange in other respects, most notably in his eating habits. I'm renowned for treating food as fuel, but Kev took this to extremes. His favourite nosh was the hard-tack biscuits we get on exercise and deployments to supplement our rations. Kev actually went out of his way to acquire these things. Several times in Iraq I caught him swapping his main meal for a handful of dog biscuits. Weird, like I say, is our Kev, but a first-rate bloke. He was also our main medic, having done enough time in operating theatres virtually to qualify as a real doc.

Keith, of course, I'd got to know pretty well in Norway. Paul, his mate from Selection, was about the same age. A stocky Londoner, he wouldn't have looked out of place running a veg stall down the East End. Though I didn't know him that well, people said he had a genuine desire to help; the sort of bloke who'd peel the shirt off his back for someone in need. Bosnia, I figured, should bring out the best in him.

Next, I briefed Charlie on the things we were going to have to take with us. It was now around four o'clock, too late to make much of a dent in our preparations that day. We had one full day left before we drove down to RAF Lyneham to catch our C-130 to Split. The next day, I told him, was going to be busy. We had to make sure we had our Signals Regiment and UN kit squared away, plus all the other trappings.

The principal item here was the SA-80 assault rifle, a gun with a dodgy reputation that the SAS had managed to avoid like the plague, but for everyday duties in Bosnia we wouldn't be allowed the luxury of our regular weapons since they'd finger us instantly as Regiment. At the same time, I pointed out to Charlie, we couldn't ignore them. We'd have to take our regular kit in with us in case the shit hit the fan.

'Talk me through it,' Charlie said.

I was impressed by this. It would have been all too easy for him to have sat back and let me sort out the logistics, but I could see that that wasn't good enough for him.

'Well,' I began, 'we're going to have to take our M16s and maybe our MP5s. We'll keep them out of sight but, frankly, I wouldn't go into a place like Bosnia without at least one of them. We'll also need our FAC and LTD kit in the unlikely event the politicians give the nod to air strikes.'

From the little I did know, several Nato-imposed deadlines against the Serbs had come and gone with no sign of a US or RAF jet being scrambled against their artillery. The Bosnian-Serb Army was still shelling the so-called 'safe havens' as if the UN or Nato never existed.

But that didn't mean that things wouldn't change. And if they did, we'd need to be there with our laser target designators (LTDs). These were vital for ensuring that bombs fell on their designated targets, as were the specialized ground-to-air comms that we also used for forward air control (FAC).

It was close to five o'clock when we finally wrapped things up. We agreed to rendezvous at eight thirty the following morning so that he could meet the troop prior to us cracking on with our preparations for departure. Top of the list was getting our SA-80s 'zeroed' down at the range.

'Is there anything else, boss? I asked, as I clambered to my feet.

'No, I'll leave it up to you,' he replied levelly.

I made to go, but he called me back. 'Cammy, I'm not going to pretend that this isn't horribly new to me. If it weren't so vital that we get this right, I might just have a stab at muddling through. I've got a lot to learn and I need your help. All I'm asking is that you lead me by the hand till I get my feet under the table. What do you say?'

I studied those open features again and saw Charlie in an altogether different light. I realized, even then, that throughout our short encounter I had been the one with the prejudices and preconceptions.

Charlie was right. He did need my help. I'd been in the Regiment for eleven long years. My time was almost up. This would be my last big operation, I felt sure of that. A decade of special-forces experience had to count for something. I resolved there and then to give him all the assistance he required, but something told me that in next to no time Charlie wouldn't need to call on it. 'Hey, boss, we're all in the same boat. We sink and swim together on this,' I said.

We shook hands. As I watched him go, a voice at the back of my head told me Charlie Hyde was someone I could do business with.

The following morning, I introduced Charlie to the troop. If the boys shared any of my original misgivings about having a new rupert as a boss they did not show it. The warning order overshadowed everything. The lads still did not know where we were headed, so it was only fair that Charlie put them out of their misery quickly.

I handed things over and he broke the news. The interest room filled with an air of expectation, tinged with something else; a little humility, maybe. We weren't going to Bosnia to start a war, but to finish one. It was a different kind of mission, but I think everyone knew the stakes.

As soon as he was done, Charlie relinquished the remaining proceedings to me. I made a brief play on the fact that we were going into the Bosnian theatre of ops covertly, under green army cover. 'Some of you Paras have been waiting for years to get your hands on a decent beret,' I said, 'so now you've got your chance.'

Before I met my death under a barrage of coffee-cups, I handed everyone their assignments for the day. Ray and Toby had to get down to the LTD store to break out the laser and comms kit; Kev to the infirmary to lay his hands on the trauma packs and other medical items we'd need. The rest, I said, were coming with me to Squadron Stores. The idea was to RV at midday, shortly before heading down to the firing range.

Squadron Stores are downstairs. Here we keep what are called 'starred items' – bits of kit we use regularly or cost a lot. These include binoculars, watches, KITE sights, passive night-vision goggles (PNGs) and our global positioning system (GPS) hand-held navigation sets, as well as such diverse consumables as candles, spare batteries and anti-mosquito coils.

When we got there, the squadron quartermaster, who'd pre-viously been warned of our requirements, thumped down the first set of UN gear on the waist-high bench that divided us from him and his precious kit. I'd never seen so much light blue in my bloody life. 'Here's the latest fashion, fellers,' he said, pointing to the beret, the badges, the armbands, the Kevlar helmet and full, blue body armour. Among it all, looking slightly pitiful, was the black crap-hat beret of the Signals Regiment with the badge already sewn on.

While everyone else grabbed their new uniform, I made sure that we had all the gadgets we needed. I checked off the Swift scopes – small but powerful ×20 binos – compasses, GPS sets, sights and weapon brackets. Stuff that needed batteries, like the little 'fireflies' – strobe lights that come with an optional infra-red filter – was all checked and double-checked. The firefly's IR filter allows a chopper pilot wearing PNGs to spot the beacon while it remains invisible to people not so equipped. It can be a useful bit of kit, especially for covert extractions in shitty weather.

I dashed outside for a quick meeting with Ray, Toby and Kevin. They had managed to find the things they needed and were now packing the FAC/LTD gear and medical supplies into boxes that would shortly be shipped, along with the rest of our kit, down to Lyneham ready for loading on to the C-130.

Kev, meanwhile, had grabbed two full trauma packs and was administering a final check of their contents before loading them into the crate. A trauma pack is a pretty heavy-duty item that allows you to perform anything up to major surgery in the field. The main constituents are a saline drip, splints, tubes, surgical tools, scalpel blades, creams, drugs, needles and catgut. Kev told me he'd also packed some extra saline drips for good measure. These things are worth their weight in gold. I left them to it and went back to the quartermaster's stores. While our UN and green army aliases were packed away and loaded up, I took Keith and Paul, the two new blokes in my patrol, down to the armoury. If they hadn't seen it yet, I figured now was the time. It would also serve as a suitable moment to introduce them to Mac.

The armoury resides in the most secure part of Stirling Lines, a hundred metres or so from the Quadrangle. It's guarded by

Ministry of Defence police night and day and ringed with sensors and trip systems. Heaven help us if any bad guys ever get into the place. It's stuffed full of enough weapons to start – and finish – a war.

I stood before the thick metal door and rang the bell. Someone buzzed the door from within. Keith, Paul and I stepped inside. To me, of course, it was all second nature, but I could see the two new blokes looking around, taking it all in.

We stepped into a cage and the door closed behind us.

Each squadron has its own armoury, with a room about four metres square leading off it. This is the armourer's workshop, a place filled with bizarre bench-top tools and clamps, where 'routine' maintenance and alterations are carried out on all the weapons we use. This was Mac's domain, his kingdom, and there was nothing routine about it at all.

The three of us checked into the A Squadron armoury and closed the door. Under the glare of the high-intensity lights, the weapons ranged along the walls gleamed like polished sentries. The tang of gun-oil and cordite was an intrinsic part of the place, fundamental to its character. I loved it.

Keith and Paul did a quick 360 in the confined space. There were four rows of M16s along one wall, with general-purpose machine-guns (GPMGs) ranged on the floor in front of them. The remaining floor space bristled with mortars and other heavy support weapons like the Mk19 grenade launchers and heavy Browning ·50 machine-guns that we took with us into Iraq.

The M16 is our standard assault weapon, a versatile beast as much at home in the jungles of Indonesia as it is in the desert. Combined with the 203 grenade launcher it is truly awesome. This combo was one of the items that I now earmarked to go with us.

Adjacent to them was a row of Hechler and Koch MP5 sub-machine-guns. This is a very reliable weapon with a high rate of fire that we use mainly for CT work. However, in the theatre to which we were headed, I didn't know what kind of contingencies might lie ahead so I asked the boys to box us up a dozen.

While they were doing this, I nipped down the corridor to see Mac.

I'd got to know Mac during my stints as orderly officer when, once a month, on a rota basis, you had to take time out to do a spot-check on the squadron's weapons inventory. Depending on how the dice fell meant the difference between a quantity tally, which was a piece of piss, and matching individual weapons to their registration numbers, which was a complete fucking pain in the arse. This latter task required a lot of concentration, relieved periodically by brews and smokes. It was here that Mac came into his own.

I pushed the door of the armourer's workshop. It swung back with a creak that would have warmed the heart of any Spanish inquisitor.

At first, I couldn't see for the layer of smoke that hung at head-height throughout the room, filtering out the light from the bare bulb that dangled from the centre of the low ceiling. Moments later, I was hit with a cocktail of smells, some associated with weaponry, which was OK, others less identifiable, but with a vaguely visceral whiff about them and altogether less palatable.

'Who the fuck's that?' a voice called out from the smoke.

'It's me, Mac. Cammy.'

'Well, shut the fucking door, will you? I'm getting a rush of cold air up the trouser-legs and my testicles don't bloody like it.'

I did as he asked and said goodbye for the next ten minutes to the delicate balance of gases that have sustained life on this planet since the dawn of time. Mac and I get on well, and I hadn't seen him for about two months. It was good to note that he hadn't succumbed to sentiment in the intervening period.

Mac was a crusty old sod who lived and breathed – if anyone could in this place – for his work. He was only about forty-five but looked fifteen years older, mainly, I suspect, because of the amount of fags he smoked. I enjoy the odd tab – twenty or thirty a day, in fact – but Mac smoked for ten men. He smoked, in fact, whatever he could get his hands on. This occasionally had its advantages for me, since I could always rely on him for a nicotine fix if I ran out of Silk Cut. Since beggars can't be choosers, I never questioned his generosity, but from the taste of some of the smokes he passed my way I think he was dipping them in gun-oil.

The draught split the curtain of smoke and revealed Mac's world in all its glory: a pock-marked wooden workbench studded with clamps and vices and other specialized tools. Any space not taken up with bits of weaponry was filled with exotic and noxious-looking glues, some of which had stuck to Mac's fingers like a second skin.

Normally, he worked with a couple of cronies of long standing who, like him, had been seconded to the Regiment from the REME, the Royal Electrical and Mechanical Engineers. Today, however, he was on his own. I figured the solitude had made him especially tetchy, since there's nothing Mac likes better than nattering and smoking with his mates.

I lit up a Silk Cut and watched him work. He was squinting down the barrel of an MP5 through his thick-rimmed glasses. From what I could see, he was zeroing an overhead torch to the weapon. This was important for CT work, where the torch/MP5 combination comes into its own. If the torch wasn't aligned exactly with the barrel, you could point the beam at a terrorist and shoot the hostage he was holding instead.

He looked up and beamed me a smile. 'What are you doing here, mate?' he asked. An inch of ash dislodged from the end of his cigarette and tumbled into his coffee. 'You haven't gone and bloody broken something again, have you?'

'Not yet,' I said. 'Give me time, though.'

'Where are you off to?' he asked.

I told him about Bosnia and he nodded sagely, pausing only to down a slug of coffee before I could warn him about the ash. 'That bloody place needs sorting out and no mistake. I was telling the wife the same thing just the other day. Who you going with?'

I reeled off the names of the usual suspects and then came to Charlie, Keith and Paul.

'Don't think I know them, do I?'

'No, mate, they're new.'

Mac frowned. 'That wise,' he asked, 'sending in a bunch of rookies to a place like that?'

'Bah, come on, Mac, it'll be a piece of piss,' I said, not sure who I was trying to kid here. 'Besides, they're good blokes.'

'It'll be your last shout, won't it? You're up for retirement soon, eh?'

'Soon enough,' I acknowledged, trying to steer him off this unwelcome subject. I still hadn't a fucking clue what I was going to do when I left the Regiment. In truth, I found it hard to think about, something best left on one side for the time being.

Just then, there was a knock on the door. Mac cursed under his breath at this second intrusion. I turned and saw Keith and Paul. They were both pulling that bad-smell face that, years ago, had made Clint famous. Keith and Paul were fitness freaks. For them, Mac's lifestyle must have been some incarnation of the furthest reach of hell.

'Guys, meet Mac,' I said. 'If ever you've got a problem with a weapon, remember him.'

Mac looked up from his bench and studied the new arrivals over the top of his Coke-bottle-bottom specs. 'Shut the fucking door or piss off,' he said, with customary good humour.

We made our excuses and left, shutting the door firmly on Mac's bizarre troglodyte existence.

'Good bloke is Mac,' I said, as we marched back to the squadron armoury. Keith and Paul looked unconvinced.

They showed me the box they'd packed and I chucked in a bunch of Walther PPK and Sig Sauer 9mm pistols for good measure, as well as a couple of MP5 Suppresseds – silenced versions of the Hechler and Koch. I also thought it wise to bring along a lone example of that mother of all sniper rifles, the Parker L52, which was accurate enough to dispatch a mouse with a mega ·50 slug over a distance of a mile.

Now, on the weapons side, at least, we were almost ready.

Shortly before we headed for the range, Charlie and Toby showed up with the comms gear. This comprised our satcom set, a couple of 319 HF burst frequency radios, several smaller 349 personal one-to-one radios, special encoding key-pads, all our regular codes and a fancy little device called a 'fill-gun'. This is a box of tricks that contains a set of preloaded codes that tally with other radios fitted with an identical device. For as long as the fill-guns feed their electrical codes into the radios, the participants can all talk quite securely. Remove it, and the radio reverts to its non-secure mode.

There's nothing as clever about the other stuff. Provided you have plenty of aerial, the 319 has enough power to reach Hereford from pretty much anywhere on the globe. The satcom, similar to those used by any self-respecting foreign correspondent, is normally non-secure, but ideal for transmitting routine information.

We weren't too weight-constrained – unlike in the Gulf, where every ounce counted – so we packed a range of different satellite dishes: from the big buggers that look like they could reach ET to smaller, man-portable sets that fold away into your Bergen.

The last item that Charlie and Toby checked off was the

encoding device that gives us access to the high-accuracy GPS navigational data – good to the order of a few tens of centimetres – that the Pentagon reserves for its own special forces and a few close friends. Twenty-centimetre-error probability from a satellite in geo-stationary orbit several thousand kilometres above the earth ain't too fucking bad in my neck of the woods.

We have a close range in camp but, as the name suggests, it's only thirty metres long and really only good for a bit of pistol practice. For rifles, we have to head to a place about thirty minutes' drive from camp. It's so discreet you could live a few hundred metres from the thing and never even know it's there. It's ideal for 'checking zero' on any sizeable hand-held weapon. By early afternoon, we were all banging away on our SA-80s and, this time, you could have heard the curses for miles.

The SA-80 is not a greatly loved weapon, but it has been the standard British Army assault rifle since the mid-1980s. Zeroing weapons is second nature to us, or supposed to be. The way a gun shoots depends largely on your eyesight and how you hold it. You check zero by firing off a bunch of rounds, assessing how the gun is shooting and then making the necessary corrections with a twist of the foresight here and a click of the backsight there. When you think you've got it right, you go back and take a few pot-shots at a target a hundred metres away. If the weapon is correctly zeroed, you should be grouping approximately 100 millimetres above and to the right of the bullseye. When you translate this to a 300-metre shot – an average sort of engagement distance for an infantryman – the physics of ballistics and trajectory should result in you being smack-on.

That was all well and good, but when we tried this with the SA-80, it seemed to have a life of its own. Every weapon has its unique zeroing characteristics. I can zero an M16 or an MP5 in the dark, but had no knowledge at all of this bizarre green army instrument. I might just as well have been dicking around with Captain Kirk's Phaser. The same went for the rest of the old hands. Not having seen an SA-80 in years – at least, that was my excuse – we were hopeless. I figured that if the Serbs ever came for us in anger we'd be better off throwing our SA-80s at them than trying to hit them with bullets.

We were rescued by Keith and Paul, our two newest recruits: they'd been sleeping with the bloody SA-80 right up to a couple of months earlier. With patience and humility, they took us through it until, after a few clicks here and there, we were pretty well proficient. This, of course, didn't stop the complaints from some of the old hands, who, what with one thing and another, were now beginning to feel seriously invaded by green-army practices.

'It's bad enough having a fuckin' crap-hat to wear,' Fergie said, as he squinted down the open sights of his rifle, 'but this gun takes the bloody biscuit.'

'Piss off,' said Doug, from his prone shooting position next in line, 'everyone knows you Paras can't hit battleships with bazookas. It's got nothing to do with that wee rifle you're holding there. Face the facts, man.'

'Oh, and I suppose you'd know,' said Toby, a bit to his right.

'And what's that supposed tae mean?' Dougie said, turning to the wee Geordie.

'It means,' said Toby, sticking up for his Para brothers-in-arms, 'that all you did before coming here was drive a few trucks around the place. What could you possibly know about firing a rifle?'

'Hey, Tobe,' Ray chipped in, 'at least you wouldn't find no self-respecting crap-hat being so under the thumb of his missus that he doesn't dare tell her they're not going on that all-inclusive package to the Costa del Sol together.'

Blimey, I thought. It takes a lot to get old Ray hot under the collar. He kept pretty much to himself most of the time. The last time I'd heard him string so many words together in a single sentence had been in 1992. It was true, though. Toby's first thought when we told him about the Bosnia trip was big-time concern over what he was going to tell his wife about their long-booked Spanish holiday.

'Have you told her yet?' I asked.

'Er, not yet, no,' Toby said, staring desperately down the KITE-sight of his weapon for inspiration.

'Are you going to?' I probed.

Toby shot a round off down the range, then put the gun down and turned to look at me. 'If you must know,' he said, 'I figure I'm safer off in Bosnia when she finds out.'

While ex-Paras and crap-hats alike collapsed laughing, I did a quick head-count and realized that us crap-hats were hopelessly outnumbered on this one. It was seven against three, some of the worst odds on a long deployment that I could remember.

Charlie gave me a vaguely concerned look. It was his first real experience of the never-ending Para versus infantryman struggle that characterizes most of the regimental banter. I merely shrugged. 'Is it always like this?' he asked, taking me to one side.

'Pretty much,' I replied. 'Don't worry about it. Wasn't it Napoleon who said he didn't know how much his own men frightened the enemy, but they sure as fuck frightened him?'

'It was Wellington, actually,' Charlie said, embarrassed, I could see, that he had to correct me.

'Whatever, boss. Bottom line is, they're ready. We're ready. We should quit while we're ahead.'

'They seem like a good bunch of blokes,' Charlie said, casting his eye up and down the firing line one last time.

I nodded. They *were* a good bunch of blokes. A mixed bag, to be sure – and some a little low on experience, perhaps, for a war-zone – but a good bunch, none the less. It wasn't as if we were heading off for another ding-dong against Saddam. Then, we'd all been on edge. We'd said our goodbyes to our wives, girlfriends and families, told them how much we loved them and meant it. Christmas 1990, we'd all left Hereford knowing what a tough nut the Iraqi regime would be to crack. We knew – indeed, we'd been told by our superiors – that several of us, many even, wouldn't be coming back. A half-dozen fresh headstones in the Regiment's cemetery had most regrettably proved them right.

But this was different. We were going into Bosnia as policemen and peacekeepers. The threat level was high, but not specifically against us. The warring factions were so hell-bent on kicking the crap out of each other that they had little time for anybody else. At least, that was what we had been told.

So, why did I have this strange feeling in the pit of my stomach? I hadn't lied to Charlie. We were ready. The guys were gelling nicely. It was a lovely early-spring morning in England and we were off to do a real job.

What could be better?

I surveyed the troop one more time as they gathered their rifles and headed for the vehicles that would take us back to camp. The sun broke through the clouds and raced across the hills, passing briefly across us as it moved westwards towards the Welsh border. There was still a lot of laughter in the air, a lot of banter.

That was it, I thought. This is all too normal. Bosnia was Europe, for Christ's sake. An hour's time-zone from GMT. It shouldn't be possible to jump on a plane and two hours later be caught up in the middle of some sideshow scene from Armageddon. Two hours on a plane got you a holiday in the Balearics, or Portugal or Corfu. Not a fucking war-zone.

It was only the merest feeling, nothing you could hang a hat on. But I should have examined it a little more closely as we left the range and turned back towards camp. A decade of instinct in the UK's premier special-forces outfit was trying to tell me something that day, but, like so many other people caught in the Bosnian maelstrom, I didn't quite read the message right.

Bosnia was about to cost us dear.

TWO

Lowering through the clag on short finals into Split, there was nothing overtly tactical about our descent, no stomach-churning, near-vertical Khe Sanh approach of the type developed by US C-130 pilots in Vietnam for dodging lock-ons by Vietcong SAM crews. In fact, I was just beginning to wonder if we'd got the right country altogether when a series of searing bright flashes exploded off our right wing-tip.

Now, at least, I knew we were over the former Yugoslavia. This was our cheery Royal Air Force flight crew popping off anti-missile flares as our C-130 hit a flight level technically within range of offensive SAM (surface-to-air missile) systems.

I watched the flares fall gently away towards the patchwork of rocks and fields that made up the jagged Dalmatian coastline. In my early days with the Regiment, RAF crews used to chuck Nato-standard sick-bags full of chaff – powder-like metal filings designed to spoof the radar guidance systems of enemy missiles – out of the back of the aircraft and pray for the best. Now, at least, the whole thing was a little better organized.

Only the previous year an Italian transport aircraft had been shot down by a Serbian shoulder-launched SAM as it banked on to its final approach towards Sarajevo. The poor Eyeties never even saw the thing coming, and even if they had it wouldn't have done them any good. Their twin-engined G222 was devoid of any self-protection systems, allowing the infrared-guided SA-7 to home unswervingly on to one of its hot engine exhausts, blowing its wing off in mid-air.

Within forty-five minutes of this, or so I heard, the Italian MoD had contacted every manufacturer of IR-jamming gear in the business and asked them for quotes. War is hell, but that doesn't stop some people doing nicely out of it, thank you very much.

Thirty seconds later, the Hercules thumped down on the tarmac. I looked out of the window again and thought we'd landed in Russia. Split looked drab and cold. I wondered how in hell the Croatians had ever made it a tourist destination.

'Got your skiing kit?' I said to Keith, poking him in the ribs to make sure he was awake.

'I told you,' he replied, 'after the last place I never want to see any fucking snow again for as long as I live.'

There's gratitude for you.

Looking as nonchalant as we could, we hit Immigration – and a large, sweating Croatian border official who did a first-rate impersonation of the Turkish guard in *Midnight Express*, the really unpleasant bastard with the hairy ears who gives Billy Hayes such a hard time for trying to smuggle a shed-load of ganja on a flight out of Istanbul.

'Passport, passport,' he barked at a startled-looking Ray, who was head of the queue.

Ray frowned, shrugged and produced his UN travel documents.

This brought forth a flurry of tsks and clucks from the border Nazi, who promptly went into a fist-banging routine with ever-shriller demands for Ray's passport.

The fact is, you never produce a passport when you're on one of these jaunts. A Nato ID pass maybe; a UK MoD travel document, perhaps. But never a passport. It's just the way things are, wherever you go: Singapore, Saudi, the States, it really doesn't matter. Of course, you always take your passport with you, just in case you need to fly home in a hurry on a civvy airline or you run into old Hairy Ears' long-lost cousin.

After a bit of a search rigmarole – some of it put on, I'm sure – Ray duly produced his. With an exaggerated stamp and a smile that exposed several missing teeth, the border Nazi bid Ray and the rest of us a sunny welcome to Croatia.

After clearing Passport Control, we were met by James, the captain 2i/c for the D Squadron mob out here. I hardly knew him at all, but the D Squadron lads rated him so that made him OK in my book.

'Bloody hell,' I said, as we shook hands, 'are they always like that?' I jabbed a thumb in the direction of Passport Control.

James was tall, well built and thinning on top. A friendly sort of bloke. 'You caught them on a good day.' He smiled.

It set the tone for much of what followed.

Our priority was to get everything loaded and into the ex-Croatian Army barracks that made up BRITFOR HQ, the headquarters of the UN British Forces contingent in Bosnia-Herzegovina. Since we weren't talking another Gulf-type deployment, I was looking forward to getting the whole thing wrapped in an hour or two.

It didn't pay to be too hasty. Not so long ago, a B Squadron bloke had lost a hessian roll with five MP5s wrapped inside it on a deployment to the Middle East. No one ever determined what happened to it. It simply never turned up. This resulted in the guy getting a whopping fine and a serious disciplinary charge. Since I was pretty sure the Croatians wouldn't say no to a bit of new weaponry, I made a mental note to watch everything.

We left James and made our way to a hangar where we waited for our freight to turn up. After Immigration, I should have known that all the right manifests in the world wouldn't have made any difference. Customs made Passport Control seem like a day out at Alton Towers.

As soon as the crates showed, Croatian Customs were on them like flies. Nor was it enough to open them up and show them the contents. We had to unscrew all the brackets and clamps that held the weapons, then get them out and match each piece to its serial number.

This went on for several hours.

At first, we were meek as you like. But then, and quite suddenly, Doug lost it. 'What the fuck do you think you're doing?' he demanded, of one particularly officious Croatian as we moved into the third tortuous hour.

Since I was barely able to decipher this burst transmission of Gorbals Glaswegian, the Croatian must have been really struggling – which, considering Dougie's turn of phrase, was probably just as well.

'We've come out here to help you solve this shite-awful mess you've got yourselves intae,' Dougie ranted on. 'So, what's wi' the bloody hassle?'

The Croatian gave him a bored look and went back to his clip-file. I thought Dougie might explode, he'd gone so puce. Fortunately, though, he managed to hang on to it.

When we finally caught up with James outside, I put the same question to him.

'Don't, for Christ's sake, labour under the belief these people might be grateful for what we're doing here,' he said. 'They either think we got here too late or we're bloody interferers who shouldn't be here at all.'

'Then what the fuck *are* we doing here?' I asked.

James sucked in some cold, moisture-laden air off the Adriatic and held it down for a moment. 'Do you know anything about the former Yugoslavia?' he said.

I was about to stammer some half-arsed excuse about being

on deployment for the past four months, but the words died in my throat. 'Not a whole lot, no,' I managed.

'Then save your comments for the int briefers,' James replied tersely.

He sounded tired or disillusioned, or maybe both. It's unsettling to see a guy from the Regiment like this. I figured maybe he'd been spending too much time in the company of paper-shufflers and not enough at the sharp end of things. Split had all the makings of an administrative black hole, a place where even a modicum of talent was absorbed and crushed by sheer bloody inertia. It was enough to get any sane man down. I vowed to get out of the place as quickly as we could. I asked James when that might be.

'The plan is for you to get four or five days' worth of indoctrination from Green Slime before you move out on your first assignment.'

Green Slime was local slang for the Intelligence Corps. We have a mixed relationship with these people. On the one hand, of course, they are invaluable. Their briefings, along with the intel they routinely collect, are a vital prerequisite to our undertaking any new job. But the bastards can never win, because their intelligence often fails to reflect – not unnaturally, some might concede – the reality of the situation on the ground.

Still, appreciating the difficulties of their job didn't make me feel any better about four or five days' worth of briefings from the Slime. I wanted to get out there, into the hills. I wanted to start poking around.

We hit the barracks at about seven and set about unpacking our kit from the four-tonne lorries that had brought us from the airport. The barracks reminded me of some of the military architecture you come across in Germany: a big, austere-looking thing surrounded by acres of parade-grounds. It had belonged to the Croatian Army until the UN had shown up. Now, as

BRITFOR HQ, it was home to an army of pen-pushers and a host of other pale-skinned life-forms that you usually find in the nether world of British military bureaucracy.

We were shown to a bare room off a long corridor where we settled down and offloaded our Bergens. Because the Regiment was already in Bosnia, we hadn't needed to bring much with us; just our combats, waterproofs, cold-weather gear and the odd cooking implement. I was slightly conscious, however, that, despite our black berets, we didn't exactly look like green army. Each man had his own little idiosyncrasies and these now stood out. It might have been a non-standard boot – bought from a mountaineering shop, perhaps – or hair that was a little longer than regulation length.

After a quick talk from James about the dos and don'ts of BRITFOR, I decided to wander off and take a look for myself. Keith and Paul came with me.

If I hadn't still been seething about the third degree we'd got at the airport, I might have been a little more alert to the hazard area we'd all just walked into. It may sound a touch arrogant, but after a while in the Regiment you forgot about the ways of the green army.

'You there!' a voice boomed behind us, as we strolled across the parade-ground looking for the scoff house. Before turning, I took the fag out of my mouth and scrolled back through my subconscious. In my mind's eye now, I saw them: a major and a captain, all spit and polish and creases in the right places. They were walking towards us, the expressions on their faces changing as they tagged our slightly unconventional appearance. Keith and Paul had dutifully snapped to attention, but I hadn't even thought about it.

The last thing I recalled now was a sneer on the captain's face.

I turned and confronted the Army's finest. He was about my size – not that big – and sported a dandy clipped moustache.

'Don't you bloody salute officers where you come from?' he inquired testily.

We don't do much saluting at Stirling Lines because in the intense environment in which the Regiment operates someone took a decision a long time ago that life by the book simply isn't applicable. The last person I'd saluted was this small but impressive-looking man I damn near collided with in the corridor outside the A Squadron interest room. It had turned out to be the King of a Middle-Eastern country.

Split, of course, was full of people who hadn't done any real soldiering in years. And it's always these people, in my experience, who make the most noise when it comes to the rules.

'Yeah, boss,' I replied with all the deference I could muster, 'but I'm smoking. I can't do two things at once.'

The words tumbled before I'd really had a chance to sort them out in my head. I heard a sharp intake of breath from Paul and a kind of choke from Keith. The captain drew breath to deliver the neutron bomb of all bollockings, but suddenly changed his mind. 'Well, in future, look a little sharper,' was all he said, before the two of them turned and walked off. As they did, I noticed them exchange comments and give a quick rearward glance.

They'd sussed us all right, which was probably just as well for me. We were already conspicuous by our lack of dress code. The green army always dresses the same. Keith and Paul were wearing German army alpine boots and smocks a little bigger than the Army standard DPM. Mine was an alpine DPM with big pockets and a larger than average hood. In a sea of uniformity, these subtleties stood out, particularly to sticklers for the rules. That, and the fact our faces didn't quite fit in this place, had earmarked us for special attention. I made a mental note to try in future to merge a little better with my surroundings.

Keith and Paul, youthful as they were, were still gob smacked by the exchange.

'Jesus,' Keith said, 'I'd have got twenty-eight days for that six months ago.'

'Fuck it,' I said, watching them go. 'If they get uptight about waving at them, then they're obviously dickheads. Spence's rule number one: never salute a dickhead.'

Paul looked puzzled. 'You get to tell which ones are dickheads before you've even spoken to them?'

'Sure.' I smiled.

'How?'

'Don't salute and see how they react.' I took a drag on my cigarette and pulled a face. Instead of the watered-down smoke of a Silk Cut, I got a whole load of stale air. Paul, meanwhile, was intent on pursuing this mindless Q and A session.

Before he could get the next question in, I stopped him. 'I tell you what, mate,' I said. 'Would you go back and ask them for a light? My bloody fag's gone out.'

I honestly think he would have done it. Luckily, Keith called him back.

For a brief moment, a strange feeling washed over me. I thought I knew how it must feel to be Sergeant Bilko.

The following day, the ten of us went into the classroom for a heavy overdose of intelligence briefings. Our briefers were many and various; each was knowledgeable in a different specialization. We started from the bottom – history class – and worked our way up to threat-briefs on weapons. It was like going back to school, only this time knowledge could mean the difference between life and death. There was a hell of a lot to learn. We listened up.

To say that the former Yugoslavia was totally screwed up and always had been was an understatement. The various factions had been killing each other since the dawn of time. Like clinical madness, it was in the genes. It was only when Tito, the wartime Communist partisan leader, showed up after the

Germans had been driven out in 1945 that the Balkans ever enjoyed any semblance of order and normality. But when he died in 1980, Yugoslavia began to revert to type. Thirty-five years of peace had simply been too much for it to handle. By 1991, the place was ready to bust wide open again and when Slovenia and Croatia declared independence in June of that year, it did just that. The real problem was in Bosnia where, it seemed, every kind of ethnic and religious group that had ever been in the former Yugoslavia came together in a heavy and mutually suspicious mix. In 1992, the uneasy tension between ethnic Serbs, Croats and Muslims erupted in an orgy of violence. By the time the rest of Europe had woken up to what was happening, men, women and kids on all sides were being butchered, raped and maimed in daily acts of barbarity. To outsiders, the war was made all the more senseless by its apparent randomness. One day, the Croats and the Muslims teamed up to fight the Serbs, the next it was the Serbs and the Croats against the Muslims. Any and all combinations could be mixed and matched in the name of violence. The perpetrators of the killing were just as likely to be former dentists or car-park attendants as soldiers. And it was this fact, apparently – the sense that the devil was throwing a party and any sad sicko with or without military experience was welcome to come on down and get down – that drew mercenaries from all over the world to fight for the highest bidder or the side that offered the most gratuitous entertainment. I say entertainment because I'd seen these fun-seekers around in other theatres – faraway shit-holes in Africa and Asia, mainly – and the dumb, happy expressions on their faces were usually the same. In Africa, you're lucky if the mad despot for whom you're fighting gives you so much as an AK-47. Here, thanks to the super-well-armed Yugoslav Federal Army, whose weapons were now scattered across the Balkans, you could get your hands on whatever you liked. A tank? No problem. A quad anti-aircraft gun system for clearing trenches? Piece of cake. What it all amounted to was a picture in which everybody was a potential enemy – both to each other and to the UN, which, for the past two years, had been trying to keep the factions apart but mostly failing miserably. Only now, with the arrival of General Sir Michael Rose, the no-nonsense fifty-four-year-old former SAS veteran and head of UNPROFOR, the UN Protection Force in Bosnia, did it seem like peace might get a chance.

The glimmer of hope was the brokering of the deal the previous month between the ethnic Croats and the Muslims. The resultant Muslim-Croat Federation, which would only be ratified when new frontiers between the two groups could be mapped and agreed, was half the reason for our coming to Bosnia. Rose needed us, the Regiment, to chivvy the process along, to make sure that the agreement was signed, as scheduled, on 12 April. We were to give this our maximum attention, our briefers told us, when the call came for us to get stuck in. In the meantime, we'd be Rose's eyes and ears in Bosnia, a roaming force of covert intelligence gatherers with a special brief to get information out of the siege cities; places like Bihac, Maglaj, Gorazde and Zepce. Information was power, of course, and with it Rose knew that he could force the aggressors to stand down.

On the fourth day, when our brains could absorb no more, James appeared in the classroom. As the picture of our mission had built up, it was clear to me, Charlie and the rest of the lads that there was one very obvious flaw in our cover story.

All the other units operating within Bosnia had a TAOR – their own tactical area of operations responsibility – while we were expected to roam throughout the province without any awkward questions being asked. This struck me as untenable. People would become suspicious. There was no way that a bunch of signallers – especially as the bulk of us were NCOs and other ranks – would normally acquire such responsibility.

I put this to James.

'Ah,' he said with characteristic aplomb, 'I was coming to that. A special unit has been created for you. We're calling it the UKLO. You are henceforth United Kingdom Liaison Officers, with direct responsibility to General Rose.'

'What is the UKLO?' Charlie asked.

'Your brief is province-wide, but you won't have any papers to that effect, I'm afraid. The Regiment's involvement is too sensitive for you to carry official documentation. If you get any bullshit, any obstruction, then get them to call Rose's forward HQ in Sarajevo directly. Our guys there will sort things out. Of course, a lot of people on the ground will twig that the UKLO is some kind of special-ops unit, but the essential point is they'll lack proof. The same goes for the media.'

'The media? What's the media got to do with any of this?' I asked.

James rubbed the back of his neck thoughtfully. 'Fleet Street has got the sniff that we're here, but so far they've got nothing they can hang a hat on. If any journalists confront you, stick to the story. If they press you for your affiliation, ask you if you're Regiment and all that, don't lie, simply give them the name of your parent regiment and make yourself scarce as quick as you can.'

I liked what I heard. Unlike the rest of the UN, it looked like we at least were being given some teeth.

'So, what's our first move?' Charlie asked.

James turned to the map on the wall behind him. 'You're to move out to BRITBAT HQ in Gornji Vakuf – GV, as we call it here. There's a Navy Sea King leaving the day after tomorrow with six spare seats on it. I'll leave you to sort out who takes the high road and who drives. For those of you going by road, there's a white UN Land Rover waiting for you in the vehicle park. I suggest that an advance guard heads up by road tomorrow. The rest of you can follow the next day in the helicopter.'

We'd learned about GV. It was the garrison headquarters of the Brits' battalion of Guards, around five hundred fighting men and their armoured vehicles, with perhaps another thousand people within the camp for logistics and admin. GV was on the Muslim and Bosnian-Croat front line.

To get there you had to drive along the main supply route into the interior. From Split to Tomislavgrad, a leg of around eighty kilometres, the journey was relatively simple: an all-weather metalled main road the whole way. Thereafter, however, the route became more challenging. On the next stage, to a place called Prozer, you had to take a mountain log-track, known locally as the Ho Chi Minh Trail. This was slow-going, twisty and climbing, rising to around two thousand metres. It was the route taken by most of the aid convoys operated by the UN High Commission for Refugees (UNHCR).

After so many days in the classroom I felt a burning need to tune into my surroundings. I could think of no better way of doing this than by going in overland. I checked with Charlie. We agreed I'd lead the Land Rovers to GV and that I'd take Dougie, Keith and Paul with me. The rest would take the chopper.

'Fine.' James nodded. 'When you arrive you should track down the D Squadron lads. They'll introduce you to the set-up there. The ops room at GV will serve as your RHQ for the duration. Your first and all future directives will come from there.' He looked down at the piece of paper he was holding in his hands. 'The weather for tomorrow looks pretty good. There's some mild shelling around Tuzla, some mortar-fire coming down on Bihac, a little light artillery around Vitez, but nothing in the GV area. Have a nice and pleasant day.'

At first light, we checked in with GV on the 319 radio and got the all-clear to move. All being well, they said, we'd see them in six to eight hours. Dougie elected to drive. With his RCT experience, the Great Scots Git was a natural with vehicles. If he hadn't been nabbed by Mountain Troop he'd have made it easy in Mobility. I sat up front beside him, clutching a map, and tried to familiarize myself with the place-names. As we left, James came and waved us off.

'Give us a call when you get to GV,' he said merrily. 'Oh, and one last thing. The locals have a funny habit of turning all the road signs round the wrong way. You'll have to watch for that. It can make life interesting.'

'Fucking great,' Keith said from the back, as we watched the barracks recede into the distance.

'Just make sure you keep your eye on that trailer,' I told him and Paul.

One other nice little piece of advice we'd been given was the adeptness of the locals – kids, mainly – at jumping on the back of UN lorries and trailers when the vehicles slowed for hairpin bends. By the time the driver had begun to accelerate again, there could be half a tonne of kit missing out the back and the first you'd know about it was when you got to the other end. This coupled with the dodgy signposts made for an interesting journey. If for any reason we strayed off the Ho Chi Minh Trail – officially known as Diamond Route – we could blunder into Serb-controlled territory. This was classified as a big bloody drama, as they'd probably start shooting at us. Provoking conflict was about as deadly a sin in these parts as you could dream of. The whole region was on enough of a hair-trigger as it was.

Then there were the mines, which were all around us just beyond the edge of the road. But you never really knew if some joker had decided to move them back on for the hell of it. And finally, if we survived everything else, there was always the prospect that some guy with a rifle who was bored out of his skull that day might just indulge in a bit of sniping against the UN to pass the time.

'What are you bloody beamin' about?' Doug asked me. 'You've got that fuckin' happy face of yours on.'

I wasn't conscious that I had. 'It's just good to get out of the classroom, I guess,' I replied, taking the rarefied air of a Silk Cut down deep.

'You keep one eye on that map and the other on the look-out for bloody mines,' Dougie said. 'You might be havin' a good time here, but the rest of us want to hang on to our bollocks.'

We pulled out of Split's suburbs. The sun was just breaking above the mountains ahead. We were on the road. Dougie was in fine foul-mouthed form. The more distance we put between us and UN middle management the better I felt.

We hitched up with a string of trucks and lorries winding their way slowly into the interior. The only unusual feature of the opening stages of the journey was the number of isolated houses gutted by fire. In any other country, you'd drive past, maybe speculate a little on how you thought the blaze had started, express the hope that there hadn't been any casualties and then perhaps make a gentle observation about twists of fate or the grace of God. If it hadn't been for the increasing number of these homes that we saw now, we might almost have concluded the same thing here – that perhaps, by a bizarre coincidence, these properties had been struck down in a series of multiple domestic incidents at or around the same time.

But little by little it dawned on us that these were the homes of families who found themselves part of the ethnic minority in this region. There was no evidence of battle here: no bullet-spattered walls or gaping holes in the brickwork to mark the brutal passage of a high-velocity shell. This was simply the work of local Croats rising up to take their own action after quiet years of pent-up prejudice.

It was chilling. The houses looked so bloody normal. The countryside looked so normal. It wasn't exactly England, but I'd seen immaculate little two-up, two-downs like these with their quaint chalet-style terracotta roofs in the alpine resorts of Switzerland, Austria and France. Places I'd gone for a good time. It didn't bear thinking what might have happened to the occupants, only you couldn't help it. On several occasions, I noticed the charred remains of a tricycle, a swing or a slide.

Blink, and you rounded a bend and were once again in the kind of quiet rural scene you'd expect to see anywhere in central or eastern Europe. The next house was fine, and the next one and the one after that. Children were playing on identical tricycles, swings and slides. Men and women were out and about, smiling, chatting, walking with their kids. I'd seen some of this, of course, in Northern Ireland, but it wasn't the same. In Ireland, sectarian murder was a crime. Here, ethnic purging was an activity towards which everyone but the UN turned a blind eye.

As we pressed on, I concentrated on the map and on the topography, and Dougie kept his eye on his rear-view mirror as we slowed to take the hairpin bends that allowed Diamond Route to climb into the mountains.

The countryside was changing by the minute now. Soon, the rolling pastures of the hinterland were nothing but a hazy patchwork behind us. In their place, the road became narrower and bordered by steep-sided rock cliffs on one side, an ever more precipitous drop on the other.

As the gradient increased, so the lorries that we'd started with were forced to slow. Vehicle by vehicle, we overtook them, until suddenly we found ourselves alone on an open road, surrounded by pine trees, steel-grey, snow-capped peaks above us. Closer to hand, the last of the seasonal snow – bulldozed in dirty piles by the side of the road – was running off in rivulets of melt-water, disguising the pot-holes.

It was in countryside such as this, under a clear sky, that we crossed the frontier into Bosnia-Herzegovina.

*

We stopped around half-way on our journey at a small hamlet on the shores of Lake Busko Jezero. We bought some coffee from a bloke who'd set up a stand by the side of the road and who was now scratching a meagre living from the aid convoys that trundled daily into and back from the interior. The coffee was the same shit stuff I'd found in backwaters of the Middle East – a bitter, grainy brew that was close to undrinkable – so we elected quickly to saddle up and continue on our way.

We lumbered on until we reached Prozer. This was a main garrison for the Bosnian-Croats. After the deceptive tranquillity of Croatia proper, Prozer was a real eye-opener. For a start, it was a shit-heap. Rubbish was piled high in dumps beside the road, and where it wasn't, bits of paper and plastic blew across the street like tumbleweed.

There were soldiers everywhere. Most wore the standard uniform of the HVO, a camouflaged two-piece with a green beret. Against this, different unit patches stood out strongly. Our briefers had urged us to practise our recognition whenever and wherever we could, so I treated Prozer as a kind of practical exam.

HVO uniform insignia was characterized by a shield symbol partly given over to the red and white check emblem of Croatia, the rest being taken up by a local unit motif. Judging by the variety of different badges around us, Prozer looked like a cross between an annual regimental get-together and a heavy chapter-meet of Eastern Europe's Hell's Angels.

It wasn't just the guys in uniform who had weapons. Blokes in their sixties and older, right down to pock-faced youths, were walking around, chatting and smoking and clutching their pieces. There was more than a whiff of insanity in the air. It looked like a place that had just fallen to an invading army, the moment before law and order broke down completely and the raping and pillaging began. If this was their own town, I hated to think what they'd do to some place they'd just captured.

The whole of Prozer was like some walk-in arms bazaar. Russian infantry guns competed for the upper hand with an assortment of Western kit. I saw Browning heavy machine-guns and MG42 general-purpose machine-guns. Both had seen service in the Second World War, the former with the Allies, the latter with the Wehrmacht. Elsewhere, I clocked a rare kind of Dragunov sniper rifle – the kind used by Spetsnaz's hottest marksmen during the Cold War – and the unusual-looking Ultimax lightweight machine-gun, a Singaporean weapon fitted with two quick-change barrels.

'Bloody hell,' Dougie announced suddenly. 'Would you look at that?'

I peered through the windscreen. At first, all I saw was a mound of humanity, a collection of soldiers lolling on something in the middle of the town square. Only as we trundled past did I realize that their perch was an old M4 Sherman medium tank of D-Day fame. The last place I'd seen one was in the movie *Kelly's Heroes*.

Prozer was a sort of R and R resort for troops down from the front. The cafés were stuffed full. The menfolk were sitting around tables, laughing over card games and, no doubt, stories of their achievements in battle. Large quantities of slivovitz were being consumed – you could almost smell the stuff as you drove by.

If you didn't have an AK-47 or some other assault rifle slung over your shoulder, you were seriously out of touch with fashion. The blokes came from a curious genetic brew of Medallion Man and any of the Mohican-haired maniacs that crop up in the *Mad Max* movies. The women weren't a whole lot better.

As we drove through the town, I caught the stares and felt the hatred. In the heartland of Herceg-Bosnia, the self-proclaimed Croat state within Bosnia, the blue beret was nothing but an encumbrance to the military objectives of the local warlords. During the Second world War, I remembered from our int briefs, the Croatians had done things that had even unsettled their allies, the Nazis.

The Germans' conduct during their five-year occupation of Yugoslavia took some beating, but the Croats gave it their best shot. During the war, Bosnia was part of the independent state of Croatia. The Croats modelled their military and police forces along the lines of the Wehrmacht and the SS. Any group that didn't fit in was systematically liquidated. They started with the Serbs, moved on to the Jews (to please the Nazis), then set about the Communists. Finally, it became the turn of the Greek Orthodox Christians. The Ustase, or Croat secret police, made the burning of churches, complete with their congregations, a speciality. And – in a telling indication that nothing much had changed over the past half-century – their unlikely bedfellows in all of this? None other than the Muslims, who were also supported by the Germans in the collective fight against the mostly Communist Serbs.

All change, please.

As we crawled through the town, Dougie voiced what I knew both of us were thinking. 'Shite. Suppose they do a spot-check on the vehicle?'

We'd buried our specialist gear under as much routine kit as we could pile in the back. If they did stop us and find it, at first glance it wouldn't be much: just a bunch of comms and satnav equipment. But it might attract attention from the unduly curious. And even if they didn't clock that we were special forces, they might just elect to pinch it, lock, stock and barrel.

Out of the corner of my eye, I could see Dougie looking at me, still hoping for an answer. 'We'll cross that bridge when we get there,' I replied.

Dougie looked doubtful, and I couldn't say I blamed him. Beyond the windscreen we were getting some attention from a bunch of teenagers dressed in a rag-tag selection of combats.

Their bandaleros and stick-grenades had the appearance of fashion accessories.

We'd stopped in a line of vehicles at a junction. The youths were lounging on the corner, striking the pose. I was beginning to familiarize myself with this: it consisted of a surly stare, gun held at a macho, jaunty angle, a cigarette clamped between the teeth and a red and white check bandana to top off the look. In the UK, this lot would have been members of a gang in some shitty part of London, Newcastle or Manchester. Here, they got their kicks of an afternoon by wandering up to the front line and picking off a Muslim with a high-powered sniper's rifle.

There's something particularly repugnant about war fought this way. I couldn't quite put my finger on it, but it was accentuated by the proximity of people's homes and streets full of shops. For civilians, it meant a relentless diet of terror, injury and death, reinforced by shells, bullets and torture. For the aggressor, it was war in the morning and home in time for tea. And so it went on, day after day.

I was overcome with a desire to grab the little bastards by the scruff, give them a kick up the pants and tell them to get back to Mama.

Fortunately, a militiaman directed us to move on before the youths could swagger over and start hassling us. If there's one thing that scares me shitless it's an army without discipline. Fuelled by slivovitz and dope, those kids wouldn't have thought twice about spraying our Land Rover with bullets.

I had the feeling, for that matter, that anybody in Prozer would have slotted us if they'd thought they could get away with it. It was that kind of a place.

'Well,' Keith announced, 'if that's where the HVO goes to get away from it all, I can't wait till we reach the front line.'

We arrived at a UN checkpoint. We'd passed through something similar to get on to Diamond Route. Now we had to report in again to let them know we'd negotiated the journey safely. Dougie and I got out of the vehicle and walked over to a tent that served as the admin area. Inside, we were confronted by a couple of British Army military policemen sitting behind a table.

I was about to say something cheery when one of them asked me where my beret was. After six hours on the road, and with GV just ahead of us, I hadn't been thinking about my appearance. I told him it was either in the back of the wagon or maybe in the bottom of my Bergen.

The sergeant MP's expression darkened. 'What fucking unit are you from?' he asked me.

I felt my hackles rising, but I checked my reaction. This was going to be our first test of the *carte blanche* alias that we'd been given by General Rose.

'We're UKLO,' I said firmly. 'United Kingdom Liaison Officers.'

I could see the MP weighing up whether or not to deliver a withering response when his mate tapped the clipboard in front of him. The sergeant's lips mouthed each syllable of a directive neither Doug nor I could see, then he looked at us and double-checked his manifest. Finally, without saying a word, he waved us on our way.

When we got back to the vehicle Dougie told Keith and Paul what had happened. They listened agog before rubbing their hands with glee at the way the MPs had been forced to wind their necks in. After my set-to with the two officers in Split on our first night, the two new Regimental recruits clearly thought they'd arrived in military heaven.

'Shit,' Paul said gleefully, 'this is what we came for. Cut the bullshit and get on with the fucking job, that's what I say.'

Ahead, in the distance, nestling in a valley far below us, I caught my first glimpse of Gornji Vakuf. Due to the muslin effect of the evening mist, it looked like any normal mid-sized town. I knew, though, that this was illusory. The people back in Split had told us in graphic detail how much G V had endured these past couple of years. It was partly this, partly some nagging thought at the back of my head about what Paul had just said, that left me feeling unsettled.

'Hey, fellers,' I said, keeping my eyes on the town, 'if you're going to make a stand, make sure it's a winnable one.'

I hadn't wanted to put a total dampener on things, but we descended the mountain in silence.

THREE

Most of us have seen pictures of Berlin at the end of the Second World War. That's as close a template as I can conjure for what we saw when we pulled into the suburbs of GV. From a distance the damage wasn't visible, but the closer we got, the more details moved into focus. Eventually, as we hit the outskirts, we knew that the destruction wasn't random or isolated. It was everywhere.

There wasn't a building that hadn't been hit. Yet, for all the carnage that had rained down on the 20,000-strong Muslim population from HVO positions in the surrounding hills, this wasn't what struck me most about GV. It was the silence.

Doug drove slowly to allow the rest of us to look for land-marks. The British battalion, or BRITBAT, garrison was on the far side of town.

We passed an old woman hobbling between the craters. In her grasp was a meagre day's foraging, a piece of wood and some rubbish that would buy maybe a few minutes' warmth on a fire. Otherwise, we saw no one; not even in the ruins. Yet, our briefers had told us there were people here – hundreds of them.

'Shit,' Keith said, 'there's nothing left. Nobody's won. This place is beyond occupation or liberation or whatever the fuck the Croats call it. What's the point?'

None of us said anything. Anybody who thought they were liberating the place was insane. The only way to make sense of Gornji Vakuf was to get in a fleet of bulldozers and start all over again.

With the light closing in, the garrison loomed through the gathering gloom like a squat battleship in a blitzed naval yard. First I made out the observation towers and the communications masts, then the corrugated-iron fencing and the razor-wire. It was depressingly familiar. If I half closed my eyes I could have been back in Northern Ireland. At least the Brits had a template for this operation, I thought, as we swung on to the approach road.

The evidence of the British Army's experience 'across the water' against the Provisional IRA-or 'Pira', as they're known to us – was all around us as we drove up to the gates. We produced our passes and were waved through the checkpoint. We bumped over sleeping policemen and manoeuvred through chicanes, features that were designed to obstruct the path of a terrorist in a truck with a suicide bomb in the back. Either side of the approach road was clear land, an exclusion zone in which anyone trying to sneak up to the perimeter would stand out like a sore thumb. At least, that was the idea.

The walls themselves were several metres high and made of corrugated iron. There were watch-towers in each corner of the compound, which was roughly the size of a half-decent football stadium. Off to the right, just beyond the walls, I could see a clutch of helicopters lined up under a wind-sock.

We pulled up at the guardroom and presented our credentials again. A couple of minutes later, the great gates swung inwards and we drove inside.

'Oh, God,' Dougie announced, 'what a shite-hole.'

It was as if a modern building site had gone back in time to the Western Front. There was mud everywhere. And where it wasn't muddy, there was water. Ahead of us I could see what was clearly the main working and living area. It had the appearance of a large covered market, much like the old Covent Garden, with ramps leading up to loading bays around the outside and a quadrangle of sorts inside under the eaves. To the left of it was a big parking area full of military vehicles: four-tonne trucks, ten-tonners, Land Rovers, armoured personnel carriers and Scimitar and Warrior fighting vehicles. Their white UN livery was fashionably mud-spattered. Immediately to the left was a heavy plant vehicle assembly area, wall-to-wall with diggers and tractors.

The rest of the space was taken up with sandbags and high-power lighting emplacements. At night the base was most likely illuminated like a travelling fairground so as to discourage pilferers. To the outside world it would have looked unreal: a multi-kilowatt oasis in a town given over almost exclusively to candle-power.

We parked up and walked over to a loading bay set into the main working and accommodation block. Somebody had thoughtfully provided duckboards to keep us from drowning. We strolled past soldiers engrossed in offloading supplies from a bevy of trucks that had reversed into the bay. We carried our SA-80s with us as we didn't want to leave them unattended in the Land Rover. Elsewhere, the fashion was a mix of camouflaged combats and the dark green coveralls of the REME.

We jumped up on to the loading bay and dived through a set of double doors. Immediately, I was hit by a mixture of smells I had come to know well after twenty years of soldiering. Here, however, it was heavily accentuated by the cramped confines of the place and the bittersweet tang of men working round the clock under near-combat conditions.

'Mmm,' Dougie said, taking this rich perfume down through his nose, 'nice.'

Among this plethora of odours, I caught the unmistakable whiff of the cookhouse. Since we were looking to make contact with the lads from D Squadron and didn't really know where to begin, I figured this might be the place to start. We followed the clues along a dark corridor and soon found ourselves in the mess hall. It was very basic, with long tables set in rows in front of a kitchen, in which a bunch of sweaty-arsed cooks were wrestling with an assortment of steaming vats and dishes. I'd seen better noshing facilities in Army facilities in Northern Ireland – and that, sadly, was saying something.

'Looks like we'll be dining out, then,' Keith said. 'Any sign of them?'

We did a quick tally of a gathering of fresh-faced squaddies who'd sat down to eat a particularly unappetizing-looking slop, redeemed only by some averagely crispy chips.

I shook my head. 'Nope. Let's keep looking.'

Anxious to avoid the 'who the hell are you?' routine, we had little choice but to search the place for our colleagues without recourse to directions. It's difficult, in any case, asking for a bunch of people who don't officially exist.

We left by a different door and carried on down another long corridor, which fanned out into an open area divided by dark hessian curtains hanging from the roof. From the power cables running along the floor, I knew we had entered an operations area. I pulled back the first curtain and found myself confronted by the angry stares of two Coldstream Guardsmen. I mumbled an apology and carried on.

The next compartment was the ops room for the UN's Military Observers (UNMOs). Like the previous one, it was packed with tactical radios and staffed by a couple of geeky-looking blokes who were monitoring the airwaves. The next one was temporarily deserted, but clearly belonged to some intelligence outfit – aside from the obligatory radios, there were maps pinned to the walls, a bunch of intel on threat equipment and UN unit reports on the fighting across Bosnia.

Just when I thought we were never going to find our guys, I pulled back another curtain and found a refreshingly familiar scene. The area was small and bathed in semi-darkness – most of the light came from the diodes and LEDs of the electronics – but it was packed: 319 receivers, battery boosters and spare patrol radios under charge jostled for space. A steady static mush from radios on standby filled the air. Other stuff drifted into focus: charts on the walls with frequencies I knew all too well, a big hot-water boiler for brews, a general-service table littered with papers.

In the far corner there were two safes. One of these had been improvised out of pieces of a steel grille and welded together. The decent safe, built from slabs of best fuck-off Sheffield steel, would be full of crypto, the codes we used for encrypting and decrypting the signals that come and go between Regimental units and Hereford. Inside the grille safe were a line of MP5s. If I'd had any doubts before, these weapons confirmed that I was in the right place.

With my eyes accustomed to the light, I now noticed two vital features of the place that I had not initially clocked: a couple of 'scalies' sitting behind the GS table.

A scaly, sometimes known as an REMF, or rear-echelon mother-fucker, plays a vital, but largely unsung, role in the Regiment's operations. These particular characters were signallers from 264 Signals Unit, an outfit specifically attached to the SAS. These guys are a cut above your normal signaller, who more often than not will merely be familiar with just one kind of tactical radio, the Clansman. Our scalies were the Rick Wakemans of the radio world, capable of playing with twenty different types of radio at a single sitting. The two who confronted me now had the pallid, drawn complexion I'd come to associate with the species over the years – which, I guess, is how they got their moniker to begin with.

'Hi,' I said to the first scaly to remove his headphones, 'I'm

Cammy, down with some of the boys from Split. Where are the guys from D Squadron?'

Without saying a word, he pointed to another sectioned-off area deeper into the room. When we got there, we could see that this was the Regiment's main space. There were forty-odd bunk beds arranged in four rows in one half of the section, with the rest given over to work duties. The latter was stuffed with tables, foldaway chairs and racks for maps and 'int sums' – intelligence summaries. There was also a TV and a video, complete with a somewhat baffling selection of the latest rental releases – stuff I don't think had even made it into Blockbuster yet – from an electrical shop in Split, and the obligatory water-heater for our brews.

Unlike the curtained-off ops room, this area was bathed in what I suspected was permanent yellow light generated by a set of low-hanging bulbs. To escape from this, a number of bunks had been rigged with blankets hanging from the top bed. It was from behind one of these that a familiar face appeared.

Glen was a D Squadron troop sergeant I'd met a couple of times back in Hereford and always had a lot of time for. He'd been tasked as our welcoming party and had decided to get some kip pending our arrival. When we'd finished exchanging insults, he told us the rest of the lads were out and about on deployment. We were due to receive a briefing from an officer in his troop – a lieutenant called Nick – at 1900 hours. Since we still had an hour to go before this, he suggested we should get our kit, grab our bunks and then go get some scoff.

Half an hour later, the four of us were sitting in the canteen, staring at our food staring back at us. Though the place was busy, we'd been left alone by the other diners – green army kids, most of whom were still in their teens.

So much for our covert assignment. We'd joined the food queue and were standing in line, minding our own business, plates in hand, when the jostling youths in front of us began whispering and pointing – at us. The clowning promptly stopped and silence fell on the queue. I felt less like a member of Her Majesty's special forces and more like a school prefect. At least, though, we had no trouble getting our own table. I just wished it worked in restaurants.

We were shooting the shit about what we'd seen so far, and were in the middle of deciding that we weren't much impressed with the whole place, when an alarm sounded. In the Army, alarms go off regularly for all kinds of reasons, ranging from the anodyne to the terrifying, so it came as no particular surprise when the freckle-faced kids at the next-door table got to their feet and ran for one of the exits. Suddenly we were alone. And all the while, that bloody alarm was ringing – a constant, piercing din that went right through my head, ruining an already dodgy meal.

'I don't think it's an exercise,' Keith yelled, twisting round to help himself to a handful of chips off one of the abandoned plates behind him, 'they've left their diggers behind.' 'Digger' is Army slang for any eating implement. To leave your personal cutlery in the military is insane as it'll be nicked the instant your back's turned and you end up having to shell out hard cash for another set. The bigger surprise was that Keith felt inclined to help himself to seconds, but then, being a skinny bugger, every now and again he needed to take more than the average amount of fuel on board.

Paul got to his feet to ask the cooks what all the fuss was about, but a quick glance behind the hotplate told him that they, too, had abandoned their post. The place was now like the *Mary Celeste*, with a Black Sabbath bells-from-hell soundtrack as the backdrop.

'Shite,' Dougie said, between shovelled mouthfuls. 'Personally I didn't think the food was that bad.'

Among my appreciation of the banter, some sixth sense told me that this set-up wasn't as amusing as the guys were making out. 'Maybe we ought to go to the ops room to find out what all this is about,' I said, nudging Dougie in the ribs.

We were all struggling to our feet, when the double doors into the room burst open and a ruddy-faced officer appeared. There was a sheen of sweat on his brow and he was panting like a pervert. But from the look on his face it was also clear that he was pissed, mad as hell, and with us.

His eyes latched on to us like laser designators and then he was yelling at us, 'Fuck's sake, there you are! I've been looking for you all over the bloody camp. The HVO are mortaring the town and the rounds are falling this way. Everybody's in the shelter except you. So, let's move it!'

The next minute was a whistle-stop version of our earlier tour around the camp as we followed our escort at the double, down dark, narrow corridors and past dingy work areas recessed behind hessian curtains. We manoeuvred left and right with dizzying regularity, making it impossible in the end to know where we were in this dismal, unfamiliar place.

As we ran after him, the officer introduced himself. He was Nick, the D Squadron rupert who'd been due to brief us at seven. He told us that the alarm had been raised by a sentry in one of the corner towers even as the rounds were leaving their tubes, exploding seconds later in the middle of the town. Since then, two more rounds had come in, each a little closer than the last. It wasn't that the HVO were deliberately targeting the UN, he explained, but from past experience it was impossible to know where the next round might land. Only last week a stray shell had landed on the edge of the compound and blown in a long stretch of corrugated iron.

We barrelled past a wall made of sandbags and found ourselves in a large holding area. Somewhere along our mad dash from the cookhouse, the alarm had stopped, but instead of silence we were now greeted with a different sound – the hubbub from the sea of humanity that had gathered, many layers deep, in the improvised shelter where we had now come to rest. From the look of it you could probably get the entire camp in this section – about a thousand men – although today there was around half that number; the result, we were told, of so many personnel being out on patrol. Sandbags four or five deep and the height of a man surrounded the partitioned area. The only breaks in the fortification were the entrance-way we'd just come through and a large set of opaque plastic double doors directly opposite. Above us, was nothing more substantial than the tin roof that covered the rest of the compound.

'Smith? Smith!' a voice bellowed in my left ear. I turned and saw a burly sergeant-major with a bushy moustache that I thought had disappeared from fashion about a century and a half earlier. He was holding a clipboard and sweeping a group of squaddies with the same intensity as an eagle scanning for prey. The squaddies, who were dressed in mixed garb – those who'd been sleeping when the alarm went off were wearing PT kit or tracksuit bottoms, those on duty were wearing full combats – withered under his gaze. Behind them, the cooks, their tunics white against the drabness, were chatting among themselves as they waited to be ticked off by somebody else. These clusters, arranged according to troops or comparable units, were duplicated throughout the holding area. The air was filled with a baffling assortment of names as each man in the camp was checked off against a register.

'Smith! I know you're fucking here 'cos I saw you just a moment ago,' the sergeant-major boomed. 'Hands up, you vile little worm!'

Smith, his face contorting with fear and embarrassment, appeared from behind the cooks. He stammered out some excuse about not hearing his name and promptly endured a staccato burst of abuse.

I was still smiling at this Crimean War cameo when I suddenly heard my own name called across the throng. I looked up and saw Clive, the D Squadron sar'n't-major, whom I knew from Hereford, across the other side. He cupped his hands over his mouth and yelled again, 'All your guys here, mate?'

I gave him the thumbs-up and then shepherded the boys over to where he was standing. There, we found a bunch of other D Squadron lads and the scalies. As we settled down cross-legged on the floor, I felt the vaguest vibration in the earth below my arse. Moments later, the ground shook again.

I looked up and caught Dougie's expression. His hand was pressed against the concrete, fingers splayed wide. 'What do you reckon?' I asked.

'Ground-burst,' he replied, distantly, adjusting his fingers to tune into the vibration, 'definitely impact detonation, not prox fuse.'

A proximity fuse would trigger an air-burst three hundred metres or so above the ground, raining shrapnel on anybody below. This is standard practice against heavy concentrations of troops. Impact detonation, on the other hand, is what's dialled into the fuse when sheer bloody destruction is required. If these shells were coming down in the city, the Croats were unquestionably hell-bent on the latter course of action.

I smiled now at Doug's Apache scout impression, but the reading was bang-on.

Suddenly, the air was split by a double detonation – *brr-ooomf!* – as a shell exploded much closer to the camp. The shockwave blew open the plastic double doors, sending a cold blast of air into the compound. After my ears recovered from the pressure onslaught, I heard the gentle fall of earth and shell fragments on the roof.

' 'Bout a hundred metres away, that one,' Doug said, matter-of-factly.

'Christ,' a fresh-faced squaddie said behind him, 'that close!'

I studied the youngster's face, recognizing him now as one of the lads who'd been pissing about in the canteen a little earlier. He didn't look quite so Jack-the-lad any more.

'That's not close, laddie,' Doug replied reassuringly. 'Twenty metres is close.'

'What would happen if they put an air-burst over us?' the kid asked tremulously. 'Would the roof hold? Would we be all right?'

Boo-boom! Another explosion rattled the walls on the opposite side of the base from the point where the previous shell had landed. The problem with random mortar fire like this is not the shell that's just landed, but the ones in the air immediately behind it. A bit like the infamous German doodlebug of the Second World War, which used to crash and explode only when its engine cut out, the silence in between rounds going off was deafening. Against my better judgement, I felt the hackles on the back of my neck rise in anticipation of a much closer shell blast.

'Piece of piss,' Doug replied, giving the youth a horrible smile. 'Just pray that it doesn't catch the POL. Then we're all fucking toast.'

The kid's smile turned sour. There was POL – petrol, oil and lubricants – all over the camp, not to mention a small army of Calor gas containers for heating and cooking as well. A vehicle compound, it was criss-crossed with fuel lines. A piece of white-hot shrapnel in the wrong place and the whole camp would become a sea of flame in a matter of seconds.

'Probably be over in half an hour or so,' Clive said, tucking his roster under his arm. 'Usually happens about once a week.'

'We'll be all right as long as they're crap-hats on the other end of those tubes,' Keith said, picking some grit out of his hair.

'Last time I was on the receiving end of a mortar, they were Pira crap-hats,' I said.

It had been 1979 and my second tour of Northern Ireland. I

was in a base much like this one at a place called Newton Hamilton when I first heard the crump of a mortar round in the air. The IRA had recently taken to banging gas cylinders full of explosives out of home-made mortar tubes. They looked pretty hokey, but were serious enough if they landed on target. This particular round had crashed through the roof of the building I was in and exploded in a room two prefab walls away from where I was watching TV. By rights, a lot of people should have died that day. The Pira scored three direct hits on the camp. When I emerged from under the rubble and got outside it looked like some joyrider had been practising J-turns on the place with a bulldozer. We were lucky. Nobody died, although a guy sustained severe injuries.

'Pira's nothing, mate, compared to the fucking Argies,' Clive said, between thoughtful chews on the end of his pencil. 'We were getting barrages of 200-round salvos coming down on us on Tumbledown. If you didn't get dug down to your neck in the first twenty minutes, you weren't going nowhere, sucker.'

So, we were all agreed that this wasn't a problem. For the record, we told anyone who was mad enough to be listening in that the worst that could happen to us was a bit of masonry in our tea.

At that moment, there was the most God-almighty explosion just beyond the perimeter of the base, the biggest yet. Everything shook violently.

At this, the scaly I'd spoken to in the ops room tapped my shoulder. He removed his glasses and started wiping them clean of dust.

'Excuse me,' he said softly, 'but have you bloody idiots ever heard of the expression "tempting fucking fate"?'

For the next twenty minutes, feeling somewhat chastened, we kept our traps zipped. The tactic seemed to work because, like receding thunder, the booms of exploding mortar shells drifted lazily into the distance until they died away altogether, leaving only the faintest ringing sound in my ears to remind me of our welcome to the Bosnian interior.

In the end, our briefing didn't come from Nick, but from a bloke called Russ, who was much as you'd expect an Intelligence Corps guy to be – tall and thin, with skin so pale you could almost see right through it. Int Corps officers assigned to the SAS spend about two years specializing in a given subject. The Slime attached to the special projects or CT team are probably the best in the world. There's little they don't know about the world's major terrorist organizations or the people who lead them. Russ was Mr Bosnia. OK, he might not spend a whole lot of time on a sunbed, but, as briefers go, he was the best – straight up, and next to no bullshit. The natural antipathy between us and the Int Corps isn't all one way. Just as we complain about some of their dodgy intelligence calls, some of them see us as rude and disrespectful.

We got on with Russ because he often bent over backwards to meet our impossible demands. If we wanted a 3-D printout of the terrain around some covert observation post, he'd come up with it in double-quick time. In turn, we gave him our full attention and put up with his professorial quirks and eccentricities. But there's always this simmering tension in the Army between soldier and back-room intellectual that won't go away, no matter how much both parties try to keep it below the surface. For some reason, the tension was palpable today.

'Just tell us what we're meant to be doing,' I begged him. 'We're tired of moving around. We want to get stuck in.'

'Patience, Cameron, my boy. As it happens, we do have a little job for you.'

I sat up and cast a fleeting glance at the boys.

Russ responded like an amateur dramatist to my enthusiasm. His chest swelled and his voice dropped to a whisper. 'What do you know about Maglaj?'

I scratched my head, desperately trying to think back to what we'd learned during our briefing sessions in Split. 'Not a whole lot. A Muslim town about seventy klicks north of here. Been besieged by the Bosnian Serbs for nine months now. The presumption is it's bad inside, but no one really knows. There's no real information drifting out. The Serbs have got it sewn up that tight.'

Russ rubbed his hands. 'Right, except for one minor detail. A small stretch of turf around the pocket, between Maglaj and Zepce, is held by the HVO. It's one of those bizarre situations where the Croats and the Serbs have decided to link together to dispose of the common enemy, in this case the poor old Muslims again. As soon as they achieve their aims, of course, they'll turn on each other, as they have in dozens of other places.'

He plucked his glasses off his nose and started to polish them. 'But I digress somewhat. You're right. The essential point is, Maglaj is encircled. Food convoys haven't been able to get in for almost a year. People are almost certainly dying in droves. What we need is proof. Then there's a good chance we can break the siege.'

Now my ears started to prick up. 'Where do we come in?'

Russ slipped his glasses back on and looked at me. 'General Rose wants the UKLO to go in and take a look. Covert insertion, naturally. Given their experience, D Squadron will take the lead into the pocket with you guys playing combat support.'

I nodded appreciatively. This was more like it. Combat support wasn't the plum job – D Squadron had that for themselves. But this was only fair and proper. They knew the lie of the land and were best placed for making the on-the-spot assessment General Rose needed. We wouldn't be doing badly. Combat support meant backing up the guys throughout the mission, watching their backs. If anything went wrong, we'd be tasked with going in there and getting them out. As jobs went, it was a pretty good way of getting our hands dirty.

'General Rose's hope is that the Regiment will be able to detail the severity of the situation from the inside. If all goes to plan, the Serbs and the Croats will be faced with overwhelming proof of what's been happening in there and — following an international outcry, no doubt — be forced into lifting the siege.'

'So how do we get in?'

'Ah. The sixty-four-thousand-dollar question. For the past few months we've been working on the Croats. Somebody around here had the idea we might be able to bribe our way through their lines. As you've probably noticed, it's pretty anarchic out there so we figured we wouldn't lack for candidates. And we were right. We identified a number of local Croat platoon commanders who'd be up for it. Taking a "bung" is the expression, I believe. The going rate turned out to be a couple of thousand dollars.'

'But . . .' I prompted. I was getting the distinct impression that this conversation was going nowhere fast.

'We decided against it at the last minute. Too risky, I'm afraid. We were working on the assumption we'd be able to slip a couple of the guys into the pocket this way. The trouble is, of course, the plan doesn't cater for what happens after they've negotiated the HVO lines. To all intents and purposes, a bloke sneaking through from HVO positions is a Croat — at least, that's how the Muslims would look at it. Our chaps could end up getting shot by the very people they're going in to help.'

'Or by a bent HVO platoon commander, who's just pocketed our dosh,' I added.

Russ let out a sigh. 'Yes, that thought crossed our minds, too.'

'So, why don't you simply fly them in by chopper?' Keith asked.

Russ unfolded a map and spread it across the table. Dotted right the way across former Yugoslavia were circles in different colours and sizes. These were threat rings showing the range and type of the various SAM systems in theatre. They were relatively concentrated throughout the region, but positively overlapping in Bosnia, especially around Vitez, Zenica and Maglaj.

'These are simply the fixed and semi-mobile SAMs known to be deployed by the factions,' Russ said. The mere whiff of threat technology seemed to lift his spirits appreciably. 'Most of the kit is Soviet-supplied, of course – our old friend the SA-2 Guideline that shot down Gary Powers in his U-2 at twenty thousand metres over Russia in 1960 to the medium altitude SA-3 and SA-6, right down to the shorter range SA-13, SA-9 and SA-8 systems.'

'Say no more,' Keith said. 'I get the picture.'

'Ah,' Russ replied. 'But I don't think you do. Even this doesn't tell the whole story. There's so many bloody hand-held SAMs knocking about the place that we can't even begin to track them. There's the first generation SA-7 obviously, which you just plop on your shoulder, point and shoot. But we're pretty sure that some SA-16s have got into the hands of the HVO from their friends across the border in Croatia. The SA-16's a pretty deadly weapon. It looks just like an SA-7, but features an improved passive infrared seeker and greater range, plus a bigger blast-fragmentation warhead. It's comparable to the Stinger, which, of course, you guys know all about. One of those things finds its target and you're toast.'

'Tell me if I'm wrong here,' Dougie said. 'You're saying a helicopter ride is a bad idea, right?'

'That is the general prognosis,' Russ said, folding his maps away again.

'So how *do* we get in?' I asked.

'We're still working on that,' Russ said, doing his best to sound upbeat. 'We want you to support the insertion from a place called Tuzla, which is forty klicks or so west of Maglaj. From there you'll be much better placed to react to the situation and deploy rapidly if we get a window of opportunity opening up at short notice. We're going to continue working on the options here and will keep you fully in the loop. When we've decided how we're going to do this job, you'll be free to fine-tune the details of your side of the mission.'

'What happens in Tuzla?' Paul asked.

'It's the headquarters of NORBAT, the Norwegian UN deployment out here. You'll be their guests for a while.'

'The Norwegians?' Keith said, a little too hastily, remembering the fun that had preceded our Bosnian deployment.

Russ looked at each of us in turn. He had suddenly become the irritable schoolmaster who has just detected evidence of a jape in the making among his unruly pupils. Finally his gaze rested on me. 'Is that some kind of a problem?'

'No,' I replied, shooting a quick glance at Keith. 'We get on with the Norwegians just fine, don't we, mate?'

'Yeah,' Keith said, struggling hard. 'No problem. Lovely guys.'

'Good,' Russ said, getting to his feet, 'because in four nights' time we'll be at the darkest point in the lunar cycle. That's when we want you in place, ready to go.'

The following morning we started to sort ourselves out. We swapped the Land Rover we'd been given in Split for two hard-top models from the motor-pool. Doug immediately set to work adapting the vehicles to our demanding communications specification. The principal fit in each was the 319 long-range radio. This had to be mounted securely on brackets to allow us to communicate between the vehicles and with headquarters, if necessary, while we were on the move.

By the time Charlie and the rest of his patrol touched down in their Sea King from Split, Dougie had ensured that both radios were installed in the vehicles and plumbed into the electrics. The actual integration work was performed by one of the 264 Signallers. The rest of the day, Doug and the scaly spent making sure that we'd achieved full link-up with Hereford. This isn't as easy as it sounds, as transmission over such long distances depends on things like antenna length, time of day and shifting atmospheric conditions. The surrounding mountains don't do much for reception either.

In the evening, we sat down for more int briefs from Russ and James, who'd also journeyed up from Split on the chopper. By now, we'd established the final composition of the two patrols and fully agreed who was doing what. I was to lead the combat support mission into Maglaj, taking Doug, Keith, Paul and Kevin with me to Tuzla. Kevin was deemed essential because of his medical know-how. If things turned to rat-shit in Maglaj, he would be needed big-time with his trauma packs and battle-field surgical skills.

Charlie, in the meantime, had been assigned another mission. The Regiment had been warned that a VIP visit was planned for GV some time during the next week or so. Rumour control had it that it was going to be Princess Diana.

Though Charlie and the rest of his boys were disappointed not to be on the Maglaj job, the prospect of looking after Princess Di was fair compensation. And, seeing he was a posh sort of bastard, there was always the chance Charlie wouldn't disgrace himself by wiping his nose on his sleeve or by squashing peas on his fork with his knife. I wish I could have said the same about Ray, Fergie, Dave and Toby.

Most of the next day was spent recalibrating our GPS sets and our weapons. The latter was a relatively simple process and entailed a bit of time spent down at a pipe range 'checking zero' again on our various weapons.

Fine-tuning our GPS sets is always a little more convoluted. The hand-held systems we carry have to be realigned every time we deploy to a new area.

The global positioning system consists of a small constellation of satellites – twenty-eight at the time of writing – that orbits the earth, beaming highly precise positional data to anyone with a GPS decoder. Civilian systems give you accuracy to within a few dozen metres, but our sets, with their special in-built military interrogators, give super-accuracy to within a metre or so.

To log on to the network, you key in to within five hundred kilometres of where you are on the planet and the set automatically latches on to the nearest available satellite. Next, you have to feed in the datum. Every map has a datum on it, complete with a set of numbers that are unique to the particular country you're in at the time. Once that's inputted, the system goes through a software-based ritual of anything up to two hours' duration in which it extracts the information it needs from the nearest orbiting tin-can, roughly twelve thousand kilometres above your head. All you have to decide is the form in which you want your co-ordinates. On this occasion, we decided to work in latitude and longitude. The system does all the rest for you.

On day three, we topped up all our rations, made sure the Land Rovers had full tanks and loaded everything that needed to go with us into the back.

Then we set about working on our maps. Making up a map is a personal thing and each member of the Regiment is taught to spend time and care doing this. We normally carry two sets of maps. The first and most important is the 'operational working map', which is a detailed chart of the area we're expected to work in. Each bloke customizes his map with details he feels are relevant to him. In this case, I wanted to mark safe routes in and out of the area, which areas were in the possession of the Bosnian-Serb Army (BSA) – and hence closed to us – and the latest known positions of the three factions. Russ, the intelligence officer, played a vital role in helping us build a comprehensive picture of what was happening out there. When we were satisfied with what we had, we laminated the maps to make them more durable and to allow us to scribble updated data on them in chinagraph.

To complete the picture, we prepare what's called a 'theatre map', which takes in pretty much the whole region, just in case we need to look a little further afield. On a number of occasions, blokes have been caught out by having to deploy unexpectedly beyond the reaches of the working map. I didn't want that to happen to us in the Balkans.

At the end of the day, we made sure our Bergens were packed with everything we'd need to keep us going during our deployment. We were conscious of the need to travel light so, unlike the Gulf where we crammed everything we possibly could into our backpacks, the watchword was restraint. A small stove, some extra clothes, a flask, some spare mapping and a bottle of rum – primarily for bartering – pretty much did it. For me the list wasn't complete until I'd nipped down to Stores and bought a couple of cartons of Silk Cut.

By the evening, everything was ready and we were all set to move. Cracking Maglaj had presented me, Kev and Dougie with our biggest operational challenge since we'd crossed the border into Iraq in January 1991. Paul and Keith knew, too, that there was no substitute for operational experience and were raring to go.

By seven o'clock we'd received word that we were to move out to Tuzla at first light.

FOUR

As the sun started to slip below the peaks in the early evening, Tuzla hove into view. The NORBAT base was about ten minutes' drive out of town. We picked up a kind of ring road and set course on the final stage of our journey. As with just about every major town in Bosnia, there was evidence of fighting all around us, but from what we could see of it, Tuzla wasn't half as battered as GV.

We found the camp without a problem, booked in at the gates and showed our ID cards. There were no awkward questions and the guards all seemed affable enough. We asked how we might find the base commander and were pointed towards a prim set of brick buildings in the midst of a sea of canvas.

The NORBAT base was a small, tented city. But, far from being squalid, everything was neat, tidy and organized. The contrast with what we'd found at BRITBAT couldn't have been more pronounced. The white Daf UN trucks really were white and were set out in neat rows in the vehicle compound. In place of the duckboards at GV, the Norgies had built proper concrete thoroughfares between the buildings and the tents. I even detected the whiff of something that smelt half-edible drifting our way from the cookhouse.

'I'm not surprised,' Dougie said, as he switched off the ignition and yanked on the handbrake.

'Not surprised at what?' I asked. Doug had his I-know-something-you-don't voice on, which always instills in me a determination to sound as nonchalant as I can.

'At the state of the place, man.'

'What do you mean?' I probed.

'Well, it's like their campsites. You know how fuckin' organized they are.'

'I didn't know you, Edie and the kids had ever gone camping in Norway,' I said.

Doug coughed. 'Well, we haven't been camping in Norway, exactly,' the Great Scots Git conceded. 'But we did go to Germany once.'

'Doug,' I said, 'we're talking two very different places here, mate.'

'Ah, bollocks, Cammy. You know what I mean.'

I decided to leave it at that for the time being. But as I clambered out of the vehicle I made a mental note to get Kev to pass on one salient little detail to Doug during a quiet moment. The Norwegians had spent half the 1940s under German occupation. I wasn't sure I wanted his views on European harmony to crop up during some late-night drinking session with our hosts.

The five of us met between the two vehicles for a quick confab. It was agreed that Doug and I would go and seek out the base commander while the rest hung around the vehicles.

Inside the headquarters, it was light and airy. Instead of the malodorous base-camp atmosphere that lingered everywhere we went at GV, this place was no sweatier than your average office in Civvyland.

Doug and I reached the adjutant's office. I knocked and went in.

I found myself confronted by a bloke in his early thirties sitting behind a large, tidy desk. He was tall and thin, with the obligatory shock of short blond hair. There was a moment in which he gave Doug and me a rather disapproving look, then some flash of recognition passed behind his eyes. In an instant, he was coming round the desk to greet us, a big smile on his face.

'Hi,' I said. 'I'm Cammy Spence and this is Doug Ayres. We've just come down from GV. We're part of the UKLO team.'

The Norwegian shook my hand, then Doug's. 'Thorvald Svahn,' he said. 'We've been expecting you.' The grip was warm and solid. 'You guys want a drink? That drive from GV can be thirsty work.' Like so many Scandinavians his English was flawless, with scarcely a trace of an accent. In fact, had it come to a spelling contest between Svahn and us, I was fairly sure who'd come out on top.

I thanked him, but declined. I wanted to see his boss, clear things at the highest level for our presence on base. Being the only Brits at the garrison, we'd stand out like sore thumbs without some form of official alibi. I asked Svahn if it would be possible to have a few minutes with the commander. A couple of minutes later, we were ushered into the adjoining office.

The NORBAT commander was a big bloke. The name on the door said, Colonel Olof Bergstrom. Like the adjutant, Bergstrom was fair-skinned and blond, with just the merest hint of grey around the temples. I figured he was in his late thirties and that he liked a beer or two – he had that kind of a face. He smiled warmly when we entered and held out his hand ramrod straight. I held his gaze as we shook. Behind it, I sensed deep reservoirs of wisdom and experience. It looked like we'd come to the right place.

I started by telling him who we were and what the UKLO was about; how we'd come to Tuzla to have a crack at getting into Maglaj. He nodded sagely, listening, but saying nothing. He wore a look on his face that at first glance suggested a kind of bored resignation. For a moment, it threw me and I damned near said something about it. I'm glad I didn't, because, like so much else in Bosnia, I'd read it wrong.

I was treating our situation just like I'd treated any other tactical problem. Maglaj was a challenge and it had to be cracked. To be honest, I wasn't thinking a whole lot about the people inside – they were incidental. D Squadron had to get into the pocket and open it up. We had to support D Squadron. That was the brief. Once we'd achieved that objective, others would ensure that the aid convoys rolled in and people got the treatment they needed.

When I saw a column of white-painted trucks snaking its way into the town I'd be happy. Until then, I'd work at getting the problem sorted. If I'd learned one thing in the Regiment, it was that you couldn't afford to let people or situations get under your skin. It spoiled your concentration and stood in danger of fucking things up big-time.

Bergstrom must have seen dozens of new arrivals like me come by his office and give the same spiel. Bosnia, all the old hands said, wasn't just some tactical challenge, it was Bosnia. Like it or not, the place always managed to get under your skin.

Well, I told myself, we'd see about that.

The meeting lasted fifteen minutes. We concluded the thing affably. I knew that Bergstrom knew exactly who we were. Maglaj was in deep shit. Anyone who was considering trying to get into the place was either mad or special forces – or both.

As soon as we were done we got to our feet and shook hands again.

'Any help you need, just ask,' the commander said. 'You are our guests here. Treat it as your home for as long as you need us.'

I knew that we had a good ally in the NORBAT commander and I thanked him warmly.

Last thing before we turned in, after we'd rigged up the satcom equipment, I dispatched my situation report, or sitrep, to James at GV. The boys were out front, sitting with their coffees on top of the sanger, a big sandbag installation designed to stop blast and shrapnel in the event of an artillery or mortar attack. The evening was surprisingly warm. Their banter and laughter drifted in on the breeze. After the inactivity of Split and the squalor of GV, the patrol's spirits were well up. I recalled Dougie's observations when we arrived and smiled to myself. Maybe we were in a continental campsite after all.

James soon brought me down to earth. The Maglaj insertion was on, provided the D Squadron lads and ourselves could find a way into the pocket. That, he said, would be the object of our maximum effort over the days ahead.

The next morning we got to work. Word had come down from GV that the hopes that had been placed on bribing the Croats to allow us to do a 'walk through' had come to nothing. Instead, RHQ had come up with another plan. Whatever my initial impressions about it, I kept schtum. We wanted D Squadron to get into Maglaj every bit as much as they did. We had an interest in making sure that the mission happened and that it worked. For this reason I agreed with the rest of the boys that we'd say yes and worry about the logistics later.

We liaised with the D Squadron blokes closely, talking the thing through on secure channels via the satcom. How many guys did we need to get into the pocket? Ideally, five or six, they said, and we agreed.

Our job was to protect them. To do that, we'd have to get back again.

Five or six insurgents would require considerable logistical back-up. They'd need to take their satcom kit with them to fulfil their brief: getting word out to General Rose about conditions inside the pocket. On top of that, they'd need supplies – maybe a couple of weeks' worth, particularly if it took a while for Rose to persuade the Serbs and the Croats, once confronted with the evidence of D Squadron's eye-witness reports, to allow the convoys in.

But there was still the problem of how to make the insertion. For a while, we'd even seriously discussed making it by canoe, until the latest intelligence from James suggested the river was mined.

We were just going round in circles. Short of tunnelling into Maglaj, it didn't look like we were going anywhere near the bloody place.

At this point, Dougie had an idea. Why not head down to the helicopter pad and chat to the Norgie chopper pilots? If anyone knew the quirks and characteristics of the countryside around here, they would, right? The two of us set out to make contact.

We soon found that the hub of Royal Norwegian Air Force operations at Tuzla was a little bar and rest area set aside from the chopper pad. Doug and I walked in, feeling a little sheepish. The place was a kind of Portakabin, with all the amenities we'd come to expect from the Norwegians. It was brightly lit, tidy and warm. There were a number of pilots standing around and chatting – we'd seen their helos, a Bell and a Sea King, as we'd walked across from the main base area.

I made the introductions and asked if they could help. There was no point in being secretive: if we were asking about Maglaj, it was pretty obvious that we were looking for a way in.

The pilots were a great bunch of guys and we got on instantly. They produced all their photographs and maps of the area and spread them over the table. Coffees in hand, Doug, three or four pilots and I all hovered above them. Some of the pilots had overflown the area – before, I took it, intelligence had said that the Serbs had positioned mobile SAMs around the place. We asked them questions and they responded. Little by little, we began to get a feel for what we were up against.

*

I didn't sleep much that night. Try as I might, I couldn't get images of maps out of my head. General Rose, James had told me, was losing patience. If we couldn't come up with something by tomorrow the mission was likely to be cancelled. My mind teemed with madcap schemes. It was like trying to negotiate a maze. You think you've overlooked something blindingly obvious so you follow up the lead to see where it takes you. Everything's looking dandy when you run into a dead end again – your sleep-starved brain has forgotten that you'd examined that option just an hour or so earlier. It hadn't worked then, and it isn't looking any better now. You know that you should try to get to sleep because your last traces of common sense are telling you your brain is fucked, that you're better off leaving any kind of deduction or calculation well alone. But sleep won't come, because every time you close your eyes you see the map again. And so it goes. These were the demons that came for me in the small hours of that particular March morning.

The following day, having notched up a couple of hours' sleep, I headed down to the pilots' Portakabin to take one last look at the canoeing option. I didn't hold out a whole lot of hope, but doing something was better than nothing and, in any case, the pilots were good company – their banter, so different from ours, stopped me from turning in on myself.

I told them about the latest intel from GV, how the river was probably mined. At this, one of the pilots, a guy called Sven who hadn't been with us the day before, stubbed out his cigarette and started nodding thoughtfully. 'You heard that, too?' I asked. I hadn't figured on the Norwegians having particularly hot intelligence in Bosnia but, then again, you never know.

'You can't be certain from the altitude we fly at, but not long ago another pilot said he saw the Serbs stringing what looked like a load of mines across the water a few klicks downstream from Maglaj.'

'But this was a long time ago, right?'

'No,' he said quietly, but with conviction. 'Five days ago. Six, maybe.'

I put my coffee down on the table. 'He overflew the river Bosna a few days ago?'

'Some of us have to from time to time,' he said. 'You get a call to do a Casevac, a UN soldier down or a kid with a foot blown off by a mine and you don't have time to worry about the SAMs. In any case, our helos carry threat warners. We know when we're being illuminated by a radar-guided SAM battery. I read a lot about the BSA air defences, but they're not perfect. There are holes. Some of them around Maglaj.'

I pulled a packet of Silk Cut from my jacket and offered him one. He took it and waited for my next question.

I lit his fag, then mine. I inhaled as deeply as you can on a low-tar tab, then went for the big one. 'Do you think it's possible to fly a chopper into Maglaj?'

'Theoretically, yes. The spooks all say it can't be done. But,' and then he grinned, 'not many spooks fly choppers for a living.'

I looked at the rest of them in turn. They were all youthful guys. None seemed any older than thirty. They stared back at me impassively.

'What do the rest of you think?' I asked. 'Could a helicopter get through?'

It took a moment or two for the first guy to nod. Then the rest caught on. Pretty soon, they were all doing it to a quiet chorus of 'sure, sure' and 'why not?' If I hadn't felt quite such a rush of excitement, I might have thought I'd tumbled into the guest slot on *The Muppet Show* – a special devoted to clones of the Swedish Chef.

I found myself with a big stupid grin on my face. 'But, guys,' I said, 'we've been through the whole thing from top to toe. How come you didn't mention any of this yesterday?'

'Because you never asked us if you could get a chopper into Maglaj,' one of the pilots replied earnestly. 'We thought you were only interested in getting your canoes into the place.'

I nodded, struck by the inescapable logic I was hearing. 'So how come the Brits don't know about this?' I asked.

'It's very much a local thing,' Sven told me. 'We know the area and they don't. The same goes the other way around. We don't know the situation too well around GV. We pass as much intel along as we can, but I guess it all takes time to filter through the system.'

I flattened out a big pilot's map and gestured for them to gather round. Their exam was a theory paper: if they were a Royal Navy Sea King driver, I asked, how would they plot a route into Maglaj? Then I sat back and watched them get to work.

Over the next hour, they thrashed out a plan. The whole thing was worked out anecdotally. Old so-and-so had been flying from A to B the other day and noticed the Serbs moving an SA-6 launcher out of the area. That might suggest a gap in the defences. Or Lars Hoojamaflip had been trundling down the river at a hundred metres when he caught a blip on his threat warner. So, he moved a little to the north until the light on his ESM system winked out. Therein lay another gap. And so it went until, little by little, the Norwegian Air Force had plotted me a workable flight plan to give to James.

As soon as I could, I got on the horn to GV and ran it past him. As I took him through it bit by bit, his excitement grew. When he was satisfied it was workable, he signed off to go and run it past the Royal Navy chopper community, who were based at GV. He told me he'd get back to me as soon as he had any news.

A couple of hours later I was having a smoke outside the tent when Paul summoned me to the satcom. It was James. The rest of them gathered round as I sat down to take the call.

'Good news and bad,' James began. 'The RN has agreed to do it. In theory, they're on any time from tomorrow night.'

And therein, I thought, lay the bad news. 'In theory . . . ?'

'Yes, well, the problem is they're short of one Sea King.'

'What do you mean "short of a Sea King"?'

'The chopper force at G V is desperately overstretched,' James said, almost apologetically, even though he knew I knew it wasn't his fault. 'They've got a helo that can take the D Squadron boys in, but there's nothing available for the support mission – you and your guys – and nor is there likely to be for at least a week.'

I swore under my breath. Fuck, I thought. There we were, the poor bloody men of Europe.

'So where does that leave us?' I asked.

'I don't know,' James said. 'I was hoping you might tell me.'

Something in his voice made me stop for a moment. 'What are you getting at, James?' I asked at length.

'Well, you're at NORBAT, aren't you? Their chopper pilots were the ones who told you about this route in. Why don't you ask them if they'll fly your support mission for you?'

'James, this isn't their operation. I can't bloody ask them to do that and you know it.'

'Bosnia is everyone's fucking operation, Cammy. Give it a try, mate.' And with that, he signed off.

I replaced the handset and turned to the boys. The look on their faces said they had caught the gist of it. It was Kevin who broke the silence. 'Listen, Cammy. It's not much, but it might just be worth a shot. I've been hanging around with that feller Svahn, the adjutant, quite a bit over the past couple of days. I persuaded him to let me work on one of their medical teams. It turned out they were grateful for the support. All in all, I've managed to build up quite a rapport with the guy. I could always ask him, mate. It's got to be worth a try.'

And so we agreed to give it a shot.

*

By late afternoon we had got our interview with Svahn. Kev and I had briefed him on the mission and outlined the nature of our request. Svahn listened sympathetically, but said he had no direct influence in the matter. Only the NORBAT commander could make the call. As luck would have it, he told us, Bergstrom was with the pilots down at the helipad. He urged me to talk to him straight away.

When I got down to the Portakabin, I found the colonel leaning against the table in the middle of the room, coffee in hand, shooting the shit with the guys and having a bit of a laugh. The pilots gave me a cheery wave as I entered, but something in my expression must have given me away. As the laughter died, I lost no time in asking Bergstrom if I could talk to him alone for a moment.

We strolled outside. Bergstrom sniffed appreciatively at the clean air and spent a moment surveying the mountains that surrounded the camp. I guess he already knew pretty much what this was about. As he turned to me, his jaw was set firm.

I gave him the pitch. What General Rose needed was incontrovertible, independent proof of the situation in Maglaj, which was where the UKLO came in. It was Rose's plan to use our assessment as a stick with which to beat Karadzic, the Bosnian-Serb leader. Faced with the atrocities we all knew were being committed there, Karadzic would lift the siege. That, anyway, was the plan.

The big Norwegian looked at me for a long time. Then he asked, 'So what do you want from me, Sergeant?'

'I need to borrow a helicopter and crew off you, Colonel. I'm embarrassed to say that the Brits are all out of Sea Kings at GV. I'm asking if we might rely on your guys to fly the support mission instead.' Well, that's it, I thought. At least, it's out there.

There was another long silence. Bergstrom stared at his feet, then turned towards the windows of the Portakabin. Inside, the pilots were standing around the table, talking quietly.

'You know,' he said, at long last, 'that I cannot and will not order anyone to do this.' He waited another beat, then said, 'But I can *ask* them, Sergeant. Please, wait here.'

He walked back into the room. Through the window I was able to watch as he called his men around him. I don't speak Norwegian, but to understand what followed you didn't really need to.

Bergstrom gave a short introductory talk. When he was done, he reached up and removed his oak-leaf epaulettes and placed them on the table. Then he started talking again.

I studied the faces of his air-crew as they watched him and I wondered if I wasn't exceeding my authority here. These guys weren't special forces pilots, they were regular Air Force – Christ, maybe even conscripts for all I knew.

The next thing I knew, six hands were in the air. Each and every one of them had volunteered to go.

Bergstrom began talking again. When he was done, Sven and two others, a little older than the rest, had stepped forward. It looked like we had us a flight crew.

When Bergstrom joined me outside again, he told me in that flat, emotionless voice that Scandinavians seem to assume even at the best and worst of times that the Norwegian Air Force was offering its services for our mission to Maglaj. They were ready to go whenever we were.

I offered my sincere thanks, but Bergstrom was modest to a fault. He held his hands up and said it was the least he could do.

I was turning to go, when something in that remark stopped me. 'Least you could do?' I asked. I told him I didn't remember doing the Norwegian armed forces any favours.

The NORBAT commander paused a moment. A trace of a smile – or something approximating a smile – played over his lips. He started to tell me how he'd read of an incident in the Norwegian press a couple of weeks earlier. A Norwegian Army officer, some hotshot major, had got himself quoted in an article about how he was going to show the British SAS a thing or two about operations and tactics in an upcoming exercise somewhere in the Arctic Circle. I did my best to look him square in the face. But behind my blank expression, my mind was already scrolling back to a meeting we'd had with the officer in question.

We called him Mainwaring – I never did clock his real name – after the irritable character in the *Dad's Army* TV show. Unlike dear old Arthur Lowe, however, there was nothing remotely endearing or redeeming about this bastard. He was the boss of a company of Norwegian Army alpine troops who'd been assigned the task of guarding our target, a big coal-mining complex, for the duration of the exercise.

The deal was simple. We were the 'red team' – for the sake of argument, a Russian Spetsnaz sabotage group – hell-bent on incapacitating the target. Because the exercise was set to run over a limited time-period, we'd travelled down the day before from our HQ, a hotel in the nearest town, to discuss the ground rules. The meeting had taken place in Mainwaring's office, which had temporarily been established in the heart of the mine complex. We'd gone in – me, a major from B Squadron and his sar'n't-major, thinking the chat would be friendly enough, but it turned into a right ding-dong from the word go.

Mainwaring was tall and blond, your regular Nordic type. Mostly, we got on with the Norwegians just fine, but this bloke was different. He started by telling us, a big smirk on his face, that we'd need the whole of B Squadron and my group, A Squadron's Mountain Troop, to stand any chance of taking the mine down. Anything less, he added, and we might as well not bother turning up.

The major from B Squadron explained, with some patience and humility, I thought, that this wasn't the Special Air Service's style. In short, the OC said, we'd be using a single patrol to attack the mine; just four men. The truth was, we couldn't have spared B Squadron: they were off in another part of the country doing something else. But Mainwaring didn't need to know that.

The tall Norwegian stared at us and laughed. He didn't care if we were the SAS or a troupe of transvestite clowns from a three-ring circus. No mere patrol was going to get past the pick of his mountain troops, Norway's best. We'd have to do better than that.

I thought the British Army had some prize twits for ruperts, but this took the bloody biscuit. Before I knew it, I was addressing the Norwegian, outlining the plan. The OC and the sar'n't-major looked on, faintly bemused expressions on their faces. When I caught up with what my mouth was saying, I realized why.

We'd take the mine out, I'd promised, not by sticking a bomb in the kharsi, or some other draughty little place on the periphery of the complex, but by getting into the very nerve centre of the thing. We'd blow it so bad, I said – managing to keep it light and breezy, even though inside I was seething – that should the bomb go off the mine would be closed down for ever.

I like to think I caught a muscle pulling at the corner of Mainwaring's left eye, but it was probably wishful thinking. Of course, there was no way the bomb would actually go off, even though the one and a half pounds of plastic high-explosive in it was real enough. But I let the words hang, all the same. Before Mainwaring had time to rally, I hit him with the deal. He could keep the lights on around the complex if he wished – these were big buggers, the kind you get at sports stadiums – and we'd still do it; only it'd take us three days. Or he could switch half of them off and we'd do the place in one. It was up to him.

Mainwaring gathered himself and pronounced he'd not even need twenty-four hours to round us up. And, he bragged, we'd never even get close to the mine. The guy was clearly off his rocker, because he'd managed to get himself quoted, repeating the boast for Norwegians to read in their national newspapers that morning. The bugger of it was, word of this had filtered back to Hereford. Our blowing up the mine had become a matter of professional pride for the whole Regiment.

Luckily for us, even though Mainwaring had gone back on his word and lit the place up like Blackpool's famous illuminations, our efforts had paid off.

As soon as Joe and Kiwi blew the incendiaries on the ridge-line, the guards started to run around like extras in the big death and destruction finale of a Bond movie. And then, as the flames subsided, silence descended once more. Within seconds, we were surrounded. Then the guards led us directly to Mainwaring.

Mainwaring didn't believe us, of course. He was seething, and I could see why. All around him, the floor was stockpiled with flares, chermoulies, smoke-grenades, flash-bangs and blank rounds. 'Blimey,' Keith had said, somehow managing not to crack a smile, 'did somebody around here say Alamo?'

We took them to the shaft and showed them where we'd placed the bomb. Even though you could see the bloody thing in the recess, Mainwaring refused to believe it was the device, so Keith had to go and get it for him. Having almost tumbled to the centre of the earth a little earlier, I figured it was his turn. To give Keith his due, without so much as a flinch, he stepped into the void, shuffled along the ledge and brought the bomb back. With immaculate poise, he placed it squarely in Mainwaring's outstretched hands, under the full gaze of his troops.

I don't know how much Bergstrom knew about us but, like I said, I'm pretty sure he knew a hell of a lot more than he was letting on. An awkward second or two of silence followed as I rapidly brought myself back to the present. I had this bad feeling that this was his way of telling me that the deal with the chopper pilots was about to be called off.

Precisely, and somewhat quaintly, he said, 'Sergeant, let me tell you that I know this man, this major, and he is a total and

complete arsehole, an embarrassment to all of us. Your SAS
did the Norwegian armed forces a favour when it showed him
up in the way that it did. As I say, my fellow countrymen are
happy to help you here in Bosnia. It is the least we can do. In
return, however, perhaps there is just one thing I could ask of
you.'

'Sure, sir. Anything.' I was still reeling from the surprise of it
all.

'Look after my men, Sergeant, because if the worst happens
you can be sure that they will be looking to you to get them home.'

'Of course,' I said, trying not to look as stunned as I felt. 'You
can count on it.'

After the satisfaction of the helicopter deal came the let-down.
We spent the following day running over the game-plan with
Sven and his crew. Though the flight was fraught with risks, the
Norwegians seemed as genuinely excited about going as we
were.

We left the details of the hook-up between the Norwegian
Bell 412 and the Royal Navy Sea King to the flight crews involved.
We were merely along as passengers. The plan called for us to
hover high above Maglaj as the Sea King went in and dropped
off the D Squadron patrol. If there was any hint of a problem,
as support group, our job was to get in there and sort it out.

As scheduled, I called James at 1800 hours to see if we were
'go for launch'. I could see no reason why not. The sky was at
its darkest point of the monthly cycle and the weather was OK.
There was thick cloud cover, but most of it seemed to be above
the altitude we'd be flying at: around three thousand metres.

The moment I heard James's voice I could tell there was a
problem. 'What is it?' I asked.

'We've just heard. There's a no-fly activity directive been
posted for tonight,' he said. 'No Nato or UN aircraft are allowed
to fly over Bosnia for at least the next twelve hours. And in

answer to your next question, mate, no, I haven't a fucking clue what's going down.'

'So, when's it back on for? The mission, I mean.'

'I don't know. We should have some more news tomorrow. Until then, keep smiling.'

Later, I went and checked with the pilots. I found Sven, his gunner and his loader all mulling over the no-fly order. It had just reached their ears, too. They told me it wasn't the first time that this had happened but, as yet, nobody had figured out what it was all about. Because they were now more personally involved than ever, they speculated that the order might have been imposed because of a change in the threat picture. The most likely explanation was that the Serbs or the Croats had moved a new SAM system into the area. We chucked this scenario around over a beer or two, wondering how it might affect our mission, before turning in to our respective tents. We all wished for better luck tomorrow.

First thing the next day, I checked with James. There was still no news about the no-fly directive. We'd just have to wait and see what happened that evening.

To stop me counting down the minutes, Kev came bouncing up to me with a proposition. He told me that he and Doug had been hanging around with this doctor, a really good bloke, who answered to the curiously un-Nordic name of Tommy. Tommy was so impressed with Kev's and Doug's knowledge of medicine, the story went, that he'd invited them to attend – nay, participate in – some of his operations. I'm not entirely sure I'd feel comforted by the sight of either of these two administering my anaesthetic before going down for the count but, be that as it may, that's what they had become: Tommy's anaesthetists.

'Tommy wanted to know if you'd like to join us on his rounds today?' Kev asked me. 'We're about to head down to Tuzla General to check the place out. How about it?'

This wasn't normally how I'd choose to spend my spare time,

but anything that took me out and about had to be better than hanging around camp, waiting for news about the mission. 'All right,' I said, 'you're on.'

Kev had come across Tommy in the infirmary. As the patrol's senior medic, he had been on the scrounge for some extra drugs to top up our trauma packs for the Maglaj mission. Tommy had been impressed with Kev's knowledge of the kit that was lying around the place. They got chatting about some new clamp or other that did the business on some particularly horrific battle wound and that was it – the rest is history.

Within the Regiment, everyone acquires some special skill outside the regular remit of his troop. Mine, in an odd kind of juxtaposition, was demolition and languages, specifically, Arabic. Those who become medics learn a heck of a lot more than a bit of first aid. Once you've been on a course all about stabilizing battlefield wounds, which is serious enough, you go on to do a ten-week medical course, which, they say, is the equivalent of two years at medical school. After this, you go off on a month-long practical that can see you seconded to a casualty department at any hospital across the country. The only person who knows that the 'new arrival' is a member of the Regiment is the consultant. Everyone else presumes him to be a student looking for a bit of practical experience. As a result, the pressure to perform is horrendous. But that's the whole point. If you can hack working round the clock in a major casualty department, then chances are you're not going to crack with the fur flying all around you someplace like Maglaj.

We were hanging around the door of the infirmary when this bloke caught my attention. He was as bald as a coot on top, but had wispy bits round the back of the head and ears, giving him a faintly comical look, a touch of the Coco the Clown. I nudged Kev, who's getting a bit thin on top himself, and said, 'Bloody hell, mate, give it another three years and that's what you're going to look like.'

'Keep your voice down,' Kev shot back. 'That's Tommy.'

Well, Tommy and I got on like a house on fire. He was in his late forties, I suppose, talked superb English and had a great sense of humour. He also liked his beer and fags, which endeared him to me even more. 'Everything in moderation, Cammy,' he'd say to me, three Marlboro extra hards dangling from one hand and a couple of beers in the other.

Kev and Doug did the introductions. Then we set off. In ten minutes, we were inside the hospital. It was horrific. What little light there was was the result of an ancient generator we could hear chugging out back. A musty smell of decay pervaded the place. There were beds and bodies scattered everywhere. In the gloom, you could end up tripping over some unfortunate soul who was waiting for treatment, so you had to watch your step.

Soon after we walked in, Tommy dived into a room off the main corridor and emerged clutching three white coats and a corresponding number of stethoscopes. 'Here,' he said, handing them around, 'put these on. That way they won't ask questions.'

I found myself struggling into the coat before I'd even had time to think through the consequences. It was all I could do to keep up with Tommy, Doug and Kev, who had set off at a fearsome lick on Tommy's rounds. I could see from the looks on the faces of my two colleagues that they were able to lose themselves in the details of their profession. In a sense, this was an extension of their training back home – the ultimate practical. For my part, I wish I could have found some reference point in which to have immersed myself. But without that vital medical training for background, I was left with no protection.

The injuries were unimaginable. There were kids with legs blown off and old women with rape wounds. There were babies blinded by phosphor, there were shrapnel lacerations the like of which I had never seen, and hideous burns. Every now and again, Tommy, Doug and Kev would pull up beside a bed and study the wounded person who lay on its bloodsoaked bare mattress. They would discuss between them the severity of the injury, then make an on-the-spot assessment of what needed to be done. Tommy was seeking to get the priority cases back to the base hospital, where at least he had the medicines and equipment to treat them. But it was a tough call. There were so many deserving cases. In this place, even minor wounds were life-threatening. It was the only hospital I'd ever visited where the bandages were washed and boiled ready to be used on the next patient. A voice at the back of my head kept saying over and over, 'And this is Europe.'

That night, I lay awake on my bed for a long time. I have two kids of my own, so it was only inevitable, I guess, that I ended up seeing their faces substituted for those of the Bosnian children in the amputee ward. I tried not to, but the imagery was too powerful. It wouldn't go away.

I wondered if this was what happened to other blokes who were approaching the end of their time in the SAS. Things had always seemed simpler. I was getting angry with myself and tried to fight off what felt like sentimentality. The only way around it, I told myself, was to do what Kev and Doug had done: to lose myself in work. Anything less was not merely unprofessional, it could wind up getting us killed.

If nothing else, I had come to understand the look that the Norwegian CO had given me when I first arrived at the camp, the look that said, 'Try as you might, Bosnia will work its way into your bloodstream and end up poisoning your mind.'

I gritted my teeth and rolled over. Not me, it wouldn't. Like Tommy, I too had work in which I could lose myself. His was medicine, mine was war. Lose sight of that, I told myself, and I might as well go home.

I was just drifting off to sleep when I heard it. At first, it was scarcely audible above the sound of the wind blowing around the tent. But as it pulsed on the gusts in and out of my hearing, it took on a ready familiarity. I nudged Kev in the next-door bunk. It turned out he was listening to it, too. The others were all asleep.

'Is that what I bloody well think it is?' I said. The sound of the aircraft, a big four-engined turboprop, droning somewhere above the base was now unmistakable.

'So much for the fucking no-fly order,' Kev whispered. 'I didn't know the Serbs or the Croats had transport planes.'

I shook my head. They didn't. 'That's a C-130, mate,' I said. I'd travelled on a bloody Lockheed Hercules enough times to know its sound signature by heart, even when one of the damned things was stooging around at an altitude of five thousand metres.

The noise steadied as the aircraft began to circle. Then, after two or three minutes, it began to fade. Eventually, it dwindled to nothing. If it hadn't been for Kev, I might have come to believe I'd imagined the whole thing.

'What the fuck's going on?' Kev said. 'If they can fly, why can't we?'

'I don't know,' I replied. But I resolved in the morning to find out.

FIVE

The official version was that Kev and I were off our rockers. I checked with GV and a bunch of other places, but the response was the same: nobody knew anything about any night flights, least of all one involving a C-130. As for the no-fly order, it was still firmly in place. All aircraft were grounded until further notice.

Bewildered, frustrated and bored, we retired to the pilots' bar and rest area, by now our second home, and passed the rest of the day shooting the shit about nothing in particular. We were beginning to lose all hope that we were ever going to do the Maglaj job.

If we were going to cool our heels anywhere, we felt more comfortable doing it in the company of professionals. By this stage, we made little pretence with the Norwegian air-crew about who we were. It would have been pointless, not to say ungrateful, to have attempted to pull the wool over the eyes of people who had volunteered to risk their lives for us. The alternative would have been to hang out with the green army kids at the base, many of whom were conscripts. It's difficult for any member of the Regiment to find common ground with people who are merely biding their time in an army.

The atmosphere in the pilots' bar and rest area varied from

soporific to hectic. When the guys had to drop everything for some shit or bust Medevac or shuttle mission, we made ourselves scarce. There's nothing worse than having people hanging around who aren't part of your set-up when things are humming. These moments, however, were rare adrenaline rushes in an otherwise long, dull day.

By late afternoon, we were sitting around with our brews and comparing experiences. They wanted to know all about the Gulf. We, in turn, grilled them about some of their hairier missions.

At six, I put in my regular 'sced' call to James.

'Are we sitting comfortably?' he asked.

I wasn't much in the mood for banter. I grunted irritably, 'Don't tell me. The world and his wife are out flying the skies of Bosnia tonight but we're still grounded by a no-fucking-fly order.'

'No,' he said, keeping it tight, 'you're on. Headquarters has just confirmed the news. It's go for tonight.'

I could scarcely believe it and told him so.

'Get yourselves sorted, Cammy. The D Squadron chopper will be lifting off at approximately 2200 hours. We will give you guys a final go/no-go confirmation at around 2100, but barring the outbreak of the Third World War, this thing is going down. Your Norgie pilots will need to work out the last-minute logistics with the Sea King crew, but the big picture remains unchanged. You're to act as support and to engage only if they're engaged. Maglaj is on a hair-trigger, so the damned thing could go either way. But General Rose is adamant. Something has got to be done to break the impasse. Somebody has got to get word out of the enclave so we can lift the siege. There ain't a whole lot more to say. I'm sure you've got a lot of last-minute preparations you need to attend to, so I'll wish you good luck and bugger off.'

And that was it. No more talk. No more bullshit. No more no-fly orders. At long last we were on our way.

*

Last-minute preparations was about it. Having spent the best part of the week on tenterhooks, hot to trot at a moment's notice, we'd been ready to go for days.

The idea was to travel light. Our transport that night would be a twin-engined Bell 412, a close relative of the Huey that had been the US Army's aerial workhorse of the Vietnam war. For personal kit, we ditched our Bergens and loaded everything that we'd be taking with us into our much smaller 'day-sacks'. Into these, we each loaded our small escape and evasion (E and E) survival kits and our individual first-aid packs. My E and E kit consisted of a baccy tin that had come with me on pretty much every operational deployment I'd ever undertaken. What went in it largely depended on the mission and my theatre of operations at the time. On a good day, I'd be able to pack around forty items into this tiny space. These included hacksaw blades, tweezers, needles, a scalpel, razor-blades, an animal snare, plastic bags, Oxo cubes, water sterilizers, anti-shit tablets, a candle stub and pieces of chocolate. If we went down behind enemy lines and had to go on the run, these oddball items could easily end up spelling the difference between death and survival. I checked each item carefully and resealed the tin.

Then I donned my 349 personal radio, which was the same throat-mike and earpiece system we'd used in Norway. We did a test among us to check that our comms were all in working order. For longer-range communication, between us and GV or even Hereford, Keith carried the large 319 backpack radio set. Kev, meanwhile, ensured that he had a fully equipped trauma pack, just in case the shit really hit the fan. Except for odd moments when we cross-checked each other for various key items, everybody worked in silence. It was a job that required little brain-power but a lot of concentration. Like packing a parachute, your life – and everybody else's – could depend upon the merest thing left in or out.

Since we didn't need to pretend that we were anything other

than what we really were, we binned our SA-80s and readopted our good old M16s. All that was left to do was to charge our magazines. I've always found something curiously settling in the moment when I finally sit down to check those bullets into the springloaded workings of a mag. This time I was carrying eight spares, which meant a lot of bullets to be checked in.

The key to tonight's operation was ensuring that I loaded the right ratio of tracer-tipped to ordinary rounds. At night, the optimum loading is one in four: for every four rounds that feed into the chamber, in other words, one is going to be phosphor-tipped. This is handy when you're firing in darkness without the benefit of night optics. With tracer one-in-four you can literally walk your fire on to the target. At the end of the mag it's a good idea to load three or four tracer rounds back to back. That way you know when you're about to have to change mags.

As I clicked each bullet into place, I thought about the task that lay ahead and why we were doing it. Around me I could see the rest of the guys working to the same methodical rhythm; each man lost in thought. It's that last period of calm before you're swept along by events you're powerless to stop. If there's a prospect of action ahead, it's customary for a soldier to tie down those loose items in the mind that might otherwise rattle around and distract him when the fur starts to fly. Charging a mag – the click, click, click of each bullet sliding into place – always helped me to focus on what might be required of me in the hours to come. By the end, I'd be totally psyched up and ready, if necessary, to confront the jaws of hell.

This was just as well. At precisely nine o'clock the call came through from James at GV. We had our final confirmation to proceed.

We set off from our tent, crossing the base in silence until we reached the helicopter pad. There, in the middle of the concrete landing area, was our 412. There was no one in it so we took a look around. It seemed a little cramped at the back, but I'd seen tighter spots. Keith, Paul, Dougie, Kevin and I then stood in the darkness, waiting for the rest of the flight crew to show.

I glanced up at the sky. There was intermittent cloud cover and a thin slice of moon. Thanks to the no-fly order we'd lost the darkest nights of the month. A little bit of moon would give us something to see by. However, I conceded ruefully, it would undoubtedly help the Serbs too.

Beyond the base compound, Tuzla was eerily silent except for the occasional bark of a dog way off in the outer suburbs.

Presently, the rest of the flight crew appeared. The loadie and the gunner were lugging what I thought at first were sacks of coal. Before I knew it, one of these things was thrust into my arms.

The loadie must have sensed my hesitation because he said, 'Please, there is no shame. You see, we all wear them.' He did a 360-degree twirl and now I noticed the parachute strapped to his back.

'Thanks,' I mumbled. I looked at Keith and caught his expression in the dim red glow of the Bell's port navigation light.

'Christ,' he said, as the Norwegians left us alone to struggle into our chutes, 'I've never seen one like this before.'

'Must be some bonkers Norgie design,' Paul said.

I studied the unfamiliar straps and harnesses. 'Shit, how the hell does this thing work?'

'Haven't a clue, mate,' Paul replied. 'Let's ask one of them.'

'We can't,' I told him. I remembered the promise I'd made to Bergstrom, the Norwegian CO. 'These guys probably think we do this sort of thing every fucking day.'

'But we're Mountain Troop,' said Dougie, who was holding his chute at arm's length, like it might bite him or something.

'Listen,' I whispered, 'if they think we can't even put on a parachute, what's that going to do for their confidence? We're just going to have to bluff it.'

At that moment, the gunner appeared from around the front of the helo. 'Is there a problem?' he asked.

There was a chorus of rustling and clicking as we all stepped into our straps and did up the harnesses any old how.

'No, mate,' I said. 'No problem at all. We're all raring to go.' I trusted that in the darkness the Norwegians wouldn't be able to see our faces and conclude otherwise.

'Then, let's go kick bad-guy asses,' the gunner said, betraying only the merest lapse in English as he walked past, holding one hand up in a clenched-fist salute and clapping the other on my shoulder.

As I hopped aboard, I noticed an unusual bunch of black boxes on the forward part of the tail-boom. I asked the gunner what they were.

'Radar warning receiver and chaff dispensers,' he said, giving the set a hard but affectionate swipe as he clambered in behind me. I caught the flash of his teeth as he grinned in the darkness. 'For the SA-6s, you understand.'

I nodded. The SA-6 was radar-guided, hence the need for the RWR, which was designed to provide warning of any track and lock by the guidance system of this or similar SAM systems.

I asked the gunner what protection the helicopter offered against shoulder-launched infrared guided missiles like the SA-16, systems that the Serbs and the Croats were known to possess.

The gunner shrugged, a gesture I took to mean, 'Not a whole fucking lot.'

He paused for a moment, then added, 'At least with an SA-16 you wouldn't know anything about it until it blows you apart. On this bird, there's no warning systems against IR-guided missiles.' His teeth flashed again. 'We prefer it that way.'

'Me, too,' I replied, trying not to let the side down. I took my seat in the darkness and concentrated on stowing my kit.

I guess he was right. Sometimes, in this business, you really can know more than is good for you.

The loadie handed out headsets. No sooner had I put mine on than there was a crackle in my ears.

'Good evening, gentlemen,' Sven said, 'I'd like to thank you for choosing UN-Air for your journey to Maglaj this evening. I think we can promise you an exciting and interesting trip.'

Now I really did wonder what we were in for. There was definitely more than a whiff of madness in the air.

Kevin nudged me in the ribs and prised the right-hand bin off my ear. ''Ere, Cammy, did he mention excitement?'

'I think he was kidding, Kev.' I fucking hoped he was.

In the mute glow of the cockpit lighting, I watched Sven's hands dance over the instruments. He continued to talk while he tapped gauges and threw switches, making sure that everything in the 412 was as it should be before he finally cranked up the engine.

'We'll be going in high, about three thousand metres,' he said. 'Any lower and we're vulnerable to small-arms fire. Helicopters are good sport around here for just about anyone with a rifle. Any higher, of course, and we all start running out of oxygen.'

To my right, luckily unnoticed by the gunner and the loadie, Paul tapped the side of his head. I think he was trying to tell me that oxygen starvation had probably accounted for most of the crew's sanity already.

'How will we see the other helicopter?' I asked Sven. The D Squadron mob would be flying in at low level. From three thousand metres and in darkness I was concerned the RN Sea King would be difficult to spot.

'I spoke with the pilot,' Sven said. 'He'll be flying in with his identification lights on. We should be able to pick up the strobes from quite a distance.'

'What about the Serbs?' Dougie asked. 'Surely they'll pick them up, too.'

'Your colleagues will be terrain-following all the way in, under the radar curtain,' Sven replied. 'With any luck they'll be long gone before anybody can point an AK at them.'

I didn't know who had it worse, the Sea King or us.

'OK,' Sven said, with disarming nonchalance, 'let's go, shall we?'

He reached up and threw some switches. There was a whine from the roof as the left-hand turboshaft lit up, then a judder through the airframe as the revs rose and the engines strained.

Suddenly we lifted off. The gunner pushed the sliding door back on its rails and swung his big, heavy .50 machine-gun into the slipstream.

As the helicopter banked in the direction of Maglaj, now no more than twenty minutes' flight time away, we got a king-size view of the blacked-out terrain below us. Sven turned and gave me a thumbs-up. I half expected him to plug in an eight-track and start belting out the 'Ride of the Valkyries'.

We thundered through the night, climbing steadily. Within five minutes, Sven had established radio contact with the pilot of the Sea King. We were plugged into a comms circuit that allowed us to listen to the flight deck and chat among ourselves.

After about twelve minutes, Sven spoke directly to us. 'OK, we're approaching the pocket. Stand by to pick up the other helo.'

We all crowded by the open doorways to lend the gunner and the loadie a few extra pairs of eyes.

At first, it wasn't possible to see anything. Then, through the darkness, I became aware of a dim glow towards the horizon. 'What's that?' I asked, nudging the gunner and pointing.

'That's Maglaj,' he replied. 'They haven't had proper electricity for months. What you're seeing there are small fires and odd lights from generators.'

It was a strange sight. I raised my binos and took another look. As my eyes became used to the light, I could pick out details: windows framing naked lights, a white-painted mosque, the odd headlight picking its way through the streets . . .

And then something in the corner of my eye grabbed my attention. I swung the binos round and focused them on a set of winking lights moving fast left to right, heading straight for the enclave.

There was a clipped exchange in Norwegian up on the flight deck. Then Sven put in a call to the Sea King. Two seconds later, the lights on the Sea King went out. The R N pilot had just put them into stealth mode.

'O K,' Sven said, 'he's going in and we're descending. I'm taking her down to a thousand metres. From there, we should get a good view of the landing.'

'Maybe also our rotor noise will drown the sound of the Sea King on approach,' the gunner said hopefully.

That, I thought, would definitely be a bonus. If the Serbs thought anyone was landing in Maglaj tonight they'd probably have a crack at them.

We dropped down sharply and held at a thousand metres. Below, I could still make out the white body of the Sea King as it hugged the rooftops of the town. Then it started to slow. I took a quick scan around the black shadowlands beyond the city walls to see if I could detect any activity by the Serbs. I saw nothing, but that didn't mean anything.

Sven's voice was calm and authoritative in my headset. 'O K, he's flaring now.' A momentary pause, then, 'Yup, he's down.'

I shifted the binos and found the Sea King in a patch of clear ground close to the centre of the town.

I counted down the seconds. All being well, it'd be heading back for G V in less than half a minute. We, on the other hand, had to hang around, hovering here for nigh on a quarter of an hour to mask the noise footprint of the Sea King as it exited the area – and to act as backstop in case the D Squadron boys ran into any problems. I knew that every one of those fifteen minutes was going to seem like an eternity.

Just then, there was a flurry of dust and grit as the Sea King rose into the sky. Around the doors, we settled down and got comfortable. Each of us was lying prone, scanning our heads off with our binos and night optics for anything that denoted trouble. For background, we had Sven's commentary on the progress of the Sea King as its pilot legged it, hell for leather, back towards G V.

We must have been there for only four minutes, max, when suddenly there was a screeching sound in my ear – like an electronic car alarm, only worse.

Then I heard Sven. He was swearing his head off.

Cool as a cucumber, the loadie reached over and slammed the door shut. On the other side, the gunner did the same. With hindsight, that was the moment in which we were hanging there at the top of the ride, a second before our rollercoaster plunged into the abyss.

It was the moment, too, in which the crew of that helicopter saved our lives.

'Brace yourselves,' Sven said. Beside him, on the instrument panel, I caught a glimpse of a flashing red warning light. I knew then without a shadow of a doubt that we'd been locked-up by a surface-to-air missile.

Fortunately, I didn't have time to dwell on it, because in the next second the helicopter twisted to port in a vicious, spiralling turn. There was a chorus of profanities – a curious babble of English and Norwegian – as seven bodies in the back of the chopper hit the walls and the roof. If those doors had been open still, half of us would have tumbled into space.

I fell back on to the floor as the helo turned the other way and just had time to grab one of the seats. I held on for grim life. Someone's foot hit me in the face, but I felt no pain, only a dull thud between the eyes. My brain was tuning in to the sounds that enveloped me: the roar of the engines, the pounding wok-wok of main rotor blades clawing for air, the unremitting noise of the R W R as it hammered out its urgent warning to the flight crew . . .

Christ, I thought, is this how it's all going to end?

Among the chaos, I was conscious of my eyes tracking a range of snow-capped peaks as they whipped in and out of the window frame beside me. The mountains reappeared every one and a half seconds as we continued to spiral and descend. I found myself half mesmerized by the sight of them. It anaesthetized me from the surefire knowledge that a missile was on its way towards us; a missile half the height of a house whose seeker would not stop signalling its control systems until it had blown us out of the sky . . .

Suddenly the Gs came on. I felt my body pressed hard against the floor as the pressure built. The noise of the blades grew to a crescendo. At the back of my brain a voice was telling me there was only so much strain that a helicopter could take – 2 Gs, 3 Gs max – before the blades would sheer at the hub and we'd be flying ballistically. Straight down.

And then, as quickly as it had all started, we were straight and level again. The Gs had dropped off and the engines weren't screaming any more.

I looked around me. There were bodies all over the place. Equipment was everywhere. One of my first conscious images was of Dougie patting his torso in a desperate search for his ripcord handle. He glanced up and caught me staring at him, then gave me a sick grin.

'Fuck,' he said, expelling the words slowly. 'Who'd be in soddin' Air Troop?'

Twenty minutes later, we landed back at Tuzla. As we replayed the event in the bar, we learned that a Serbian SA-6 system had achieved full track and lock on us, but, for whatever reason, its crew had not initiated a launch.

I took a Croatian special brew back to the tent and set up watch next to the radio. I knew that the next twelve hours of the D Squadron operation in Maglaj would be critical – the hours between an insertion and contact always are. If things started popping, we were on a moment's notice to go in and support them. As each member of the team drifted back from the pilots' bar, we organized rotas for manning the radio. For those not on duty, there was one clear and overriding priority.

We slept the sleep of the dead.

The next morning, we found out the identity of the VIP whom Charlie and Fergie and the BGs from D Squadron had been assigned to protect. Not Princess Di but as important, if a lot less pretty. Prime Minister John Major and his defence secretary Malcolm Rifkind flew into Sarajevo by C-130 and proceeded on a tour of Bosnia that took in some of the principal locations where British forces were stationed. These included GV and Vitez, as well as UNPROFOR's forward headquarters in Sarajevo. Major spent the whole day tearing around the place, pressing the flesh of Coldstream Guardsmen and locals alike. He concluded, according to Charlie and Fergie, with a hair-raising city-tour of Sarajevo, which also took in meetings with General Rose and the Bosnian president, Mr Izetbegovic. Despite the omnipresent threat of sniper attack, the BGs did well and the whole thing passed without incident.

Meanwhile, we commuted between our tent, where we had the 319 permanently set up to receive e-mail-type data on the Maglaj situation, and the pilots' Portakabin, where we had a line established with GV for voice traffic. With every hour that passed quietly, the likelihood of our being called to any contingency in Maglaj diminished. Even so, I put in repeated check calls with James just to make sure we weren't missing anything.

After their drop-off by the Sea King, the four D Squadron lads infiltrated the Muslim positions and eventually made contact with local commanders. As luck would have it, a separate attempt to get into Maglaj, by two blokes from D and G Squadrons, also worked. This was a last-minute resurrection of the walk-through that had been drawn up at the outset. Whether they had resorted to serious bribery of the local militia, I never did find out, but they managed to sneak through the Croatian lines without encountering any opposition and soon hooked up with their four Regimental colleagues in the town.

What they found was shocking, a hellish time-warp. Theirs was a window on a world that the international community had not seen for almost a year. Though deprived of food, the population had survived through regular, if paltry, air-drops into the enclave. Thanks to a well-organized internal structure, the Muslims had ensured that such food as landed within the town's confines was distributed fairly.

The starvation issue aside, however, the covert Regimental insertion witnessed the extent to which the population was being terrorized. Up to seven hundred rounds of Serb shell-fire were landing in the town daily. Locals swore that the rate had not dropped below five hundred rounds for the past several months. The town, like GV and so many other front-line flashpoints, had been pummelled into ash and rubble. Somehow, the Serbs' shell and sniper fire had failed to break the will of the twenty thousand inhabitants.

Maglaj was one of the last major active war-zones within central Bosnia. It was probably for this reason, the insertion team concluded, that defender and aggressor alike had so single-mindedly and grittily held out against each other.

Armed with the insertion team's report, James told me,

General Rose and the diplomats were now actively seeking to put an end to the madness.

When I heard about the food drops, I thought that this might have explained the no-fly order. I asked Sven and his mates if the UN might have elected to do night-time supply flights over the enclave. The Norwegians sucked their teeth. It would, they agreed, have been highly irregular and quite unnecessary. Why fly at night, they asked, when there was no need for secrecy? Only a covert objective would have required flights under the cover of darkness, not a relief operation.

Still the conundrum niggled. I did a bit of lateral thinking. AC-130 is a common aircraft platform worldwide, but it is not a strategic aircraft. Any flights over Bosnia would have been mounted locally, intra-theatre – by which I mean from within, not outside, Europe – and, as far as the Bosnian operation and the UN were concerned, that implicated just a handful of key players: the UK, Germany, France, Italy, the Netherlands and Belgium. In an idle moment, I decided to do a bit of amateur sleuthing. After a few check calls, I discovered that the Regiment had a liaison officer at one of the big US Air Force bases in Germany. I knew these locations well: we'd used places like Ramstein and Rhein-Main as staging posts for many an exercise. During our passage to the Gulf in December 1990, just before the outbreak of hostilities with Iraq, we'd staged through Ramstein *en route* to Saudi. I figured, therefore, that if anyone knew about unusual night-time movements of C-130s over the past week, a guy at a USAF base in Germany – especially as he was one of ours – might have a few answers.

After several tries, I eventually managed to track down the LO. He was a bloke I knew pretty well and we soon got chatting. Eventually, I popped the subject of the flights.

There was a deathly pause on the other end of the line. 'How the fuck do you know about that?' he asked.

'Know about what?' I replied.

'Those bloody flights.'

'Because I was underneath the damned things for two or three nights. I could hear them in my sleep.'

'That's real fucking heavy-duty,' the LO said, his voice dropping to a whisper. 'You know damned well the Yanks aren't meant to be involved in this . . .'

Well, of course, that explained everything. Bosnia was a UN operation and the US wasn't yet directly involved. The whole of Bosnia was under an arms embargo, which nominally meant that no weapons were being shipped in to any of the warring factions. In the case of the HVO and the Bosnian-Serb Army, this didn't much matter since they were pretty well armed to the teeth by their mentors in Croatia and Serbia. However, the poor old Muslims had lost out big-time. Apart from a few meagre tanks, armoured personnel carriers and hand-held stuff they'd appropriated from the Yugoslav Army at the outbreak of hostilities, they had little with which to fight off the aggressor. They'd begged the international community to relax the arms embargo so that they could procure weapons with which to defend their towns and villages. But the UN had resolutely refused to lift it and the Muslims had had to rely on whatever they could scrounge, manufacture or procure from middle-men.

Not any more, it seemed. I could only guess at the deal that had been hatched in some dark, smoke-filled room in Washington or Riyadh, but I imagined it involved a lot of money from some benevolent Arab state and a Central Intelligence Agency that was only too happy to put it to good use. And so it was that C-130s – crewed, no doubt, by the CIA – were being regularly loaded with crates of weapons bound for the Muslim enclaves of Bosnia.

I'd heard of these mysterious weapons drops, many of which had drifted off-course and ended up in either HVO or BSA hands, but I'd never put much store in the reports until I'd heard about it from someone I could trust 100 per cent. The LO had seen the damned planes being loaded on the far side of the airfield amid much security. Not uniformed security, but in the form of guys with shades and earpieces wearing T-shirts and jeans – always a bit of a giveaway where the CIA is concerned.

I put down the phone and sat back, satisfied. I hate to see loose ends left undone.

The best news came two days later with the announcement that the Croats and Serbs had agreed to lift the siege of Maglaj and allow into the town a big UNHCR food convoy escorted by British Army light tanks. Faced with the overwhelming evidence presented by General Rose of the suffering to which they were subjecting its citizens, they'd had no choice but to back down. Within hours, a company of Coldstream Guards and their Warrior armoured fighting vehicles (AFVs) were ensconced in the middle of the town and mounting regular patrols. There were reports of sporadic sniping still but the shelling had stopped. It was, I thought, a stunning vindication of what could be achieved by a handful of guys operating under the aegis of a tough and resourceful UN commander familiar with the ways of special forces.

'We're all done here,' I said, during my regular sced to James that night. 'Where next?'

'You're ready to freewheel,' he said, which is military parlance for make your own speed home. I told him we'd see him back in GV the next day. I could tell from the tone of his voice that he was pleased with the way things had gone. This was hardly surprising. With peace – albeit a tenuous one – between the Croats and the Muslims, and with UN access to Maglaj, there were relatively few pockets of conflict left. All we had to do now was crack open the last remaining siege towns one by one. Maglaj had shown us it could be done.

I remembered the old firefighting analogy. The trouble with Bosnia was that no sooner had you put out one brush-fire than a spark would set off another somewhere else. But now we were on the verge of something significant – a moment in which we had it within our grasp to put out all the fires at once. And then, perhaps, we could stabilize the situation for good. It sounded lofty, but I found myself believing that Bosnia might just be set for peace.

That night, we had a few jars with the pilots at their bar. Colonel Bergstrom sent down a crate of champagne with his compliments, and later came over and shared a couple of glasses with us. By the small hours, the Norgies were all honorary members of the Regiment and we were told we could have as many complimentary air miles with the Norwegian Air Force as we liked.

As we wove precariously back to our tent, I clapped an arm over Keith's shoulder and reminded him of where we had been less than a month earlier – shivering our arses off as we prepared to blow up Captain Mainwaring's mine, somewhere north of the Arctic Circle.

'Well, old son,' he said, turning to me, 'I reckon we buried the hatchet and buried it good.'

We sang a-ha songs all the way home.

SIX

'Ah, home, sweet home,' Doug announced, as we pulled into the BRITBAT fortress at GV. A warm front was sweeping up from the south-west, banishing the last traces of snow from the lower reaches of the mountains. But the weather system also brought rain – lots of it. This was just what GV didn't need. As our Land Rovers manoeuvred into the parking compound, I noticed that some of the duckboards had floated away.

The contrast between what the Brits had built for themselves and the set-up the Norwegians had couldn't have been more acute. We entered the low-lit, medieval atmosphere of the accommodation area, with its hessian partitions and diverse odours, and set about looking for the rest of the patrol. We eventually caught up with James in the ops area. We tried not to brag about our luxury lifestyle courtesy of the Norwegians, but it was hard not to. In between times, we caught up with what the rest of the patrol had been doing while we'd been away.

Ray, Dave and Toby had been dispatched to a local Muslim-Croat flashpoint a few miles down the road. After the success of their bodyguard stint with Major and Rifkind, Charlie and Fergie had joined them. This particular pocket was under MAL-BAT control. The Malaysians had been having difficulty gaining access to a number of villages in the pocket. When they eventually got in there, abetted by the other half of our troop, they found out why. The place had been ethically cleansed on both sides. In one village, all the Muslims had either been killed or driven out, while in the next it was the same thing, only this time it was the ethnic Croats who'd been on the receiving end. An eye for an eye ... Decades, perhaps hundreds of years of bitter resentment, exorcized in a few days of insane butchery. This, we were rapidly finding out, was the way the world turned in Bosnia.

I was expecting James to dispatch us to this place as well, but he had other ideas. We were to oversee the next round of food and medical supplies into Maglaj. After the initial relief convoys, the UNHCR had arranged for several more to enter the place, but it was still very much bandit country and the convoys were in need of an escort. That was where we'd come in. With three, perhaps four, big convoys due to make the journey, the job was likely to take several days.

'Where do we make for?' I asked. 'Is there an SF base anyplace nearby?'

James shook his head. 'No such luxury,' he smiled, gesturing with not a little irony to our surroundings. 'You're to make for a small settlement nearby called Zepce. It's part of the Croat-held pocket on the edge of Maglaj. You'll just have to find yourselves a *basha* when you get there. I'm afraid there's no shortage of bombed-out properties in that neck of the woods. Check with the D Squadron lads. Some of them know the place well. They'll point you in the right direction.'

We agreed to be in Zepce by the following afternoon. From there, apparently, it was just a short eight-klick drive into Maglaj. The idea was to rendezvous with the convoys in Zepce itself, then head down together into Maglaj, with us smoothing the way and offering protection where it was needed.

The next day, having checked with a couple of the D Squadron blokes as to where we ought to be making for, we set off. The drive was uneventful, and after several hours we soon entered the confines of the town. Zepce had seen conflict, but not on the same scale as GV, Tuzla or Maglaj.

Our house was just off the main drag. We could tell we'd found the right place by the picture-perfect digs that nestled either side: neat little Bosnian houses with their sloping terracotta roofs, Hansel and Gretel shutters and immaculately trimmed front gardens. On the surface, our house was no different. However, when you looked a little closer, you noticed the odd smashed window and grass that had grown a little too long. Things were missing, too: there was no light from within and washing was absent from the line. Some time in the past few months the family who had lived here, part of the Muslim minority, had been driven out – probably by the neighbours, in whose company they'd lived, quite happily I'm sure, for years.

When we entered the place, it was clear, too, that they had gone in a hurry. The basic furniture had been left intact – chairs, settees, tables and beds were all pretty much in their places. More poignant were the smaller items that lay scattered all around: ornaments, china, photographs, letters, toys, a Koran and other religious artefacts. There was a lot of rubbish, too. It had obviously been used as a doss-house while it had lain vacant.

I found Paul upstairs. He was staring at the twisted body of an Action Man on the floor beneath the window. I imagined that the kid whose room this was had posted the toy on the window-sill in the forlorn hope that it might protect him and his family from the community that had risen up so suddenly against them. I could see from the look on Paul's face – he had a young family, too – that he was having trouble coming to terms with the things that he saw around him. 'Fucking bonkers,' he said, stooping to pick up the toy.

'Come on, mate,' I said. 'Let's go get ourselves sorted.'

He nodded and we both headed downstairs. Before Paul left, he put the figure back on the window-sill.

The first convoy arrived mid-afternoon the following day. It consisted of five trucks laden with grain, rice and medical supplies. Once we'd checked that everything was all right, we placed a Land Rover at either end of the column and set off for Maglaj. Exactly eight kilometres later, we reached the river Bosna and the bridge that took the road into the town, which was a complete mess, the savagery of the shelling made all the more stark by the sight of so many ancient buildings reduced to rubble.

We manoeuvred our way past checkpoints under the watchful gaze of a Warrior AFV parked on the Croat side of the bridge. Its gun turret swept the surrounding hills restlessly. I nodded to the Coldstream Guardsmen as we swept past.

James had told us to be wary of the media, which, following the lifting of the siege, had trickled into Maglaj. Now I reminded the blokes. After our reversion to type at Tuzla, we were doubly careful to conform to the rules of the green army again. Apart from the fact that we were carrying sidearms, there was little to distinguish us from any other British Army NCOs in theatre.

However, the fact that we were meeting the convoys and escorting them into the town was reason enough for reporters to be suspicious. If confronted about our identity, we would tell them the truth: that we were UKLO under the direct command of General Rose. It didn't take a rocket scientist, of course, to conclude that the UKLO was not a regular unit. If pressed about who we were – particularly whether we were Regiment – I reminded everybody that we should give them the name of our parent regiment, thus technically telling the truth, and no more.

Across the bridge we were met by a couple of burly Muslims in combat fatigues with Viva Zapata moustaches, a portly bloke in a beat-up suit and two other guys whom I recognized. I clambered out of the Land Rover and walked over to greet them. Glen, the D Squadron troop sergeant who had been our reception committee at GV, gave me a big grin and a firm handshake.

Next to him was Nick, his boss, the bloke who had pulled us out of the canteen when the base came under mortar fire.

'Well, if it isn't the seventh cavalry,' Glen said. 'How are you doing, mate?'

'Good,' I said. 'How about you?'

'Fair to bloody,' he replied, but the smile told me he was happy to be in the thick of it. 'Gather you had a bit of trouble over Maglaj the other night. Something about some Serb SAM crew giving you a bit of a scare.'

I could tell from the looks on their faces that they'd enjoyed the description of our experience that night. No doubt, too, it had grown some in the telling.

'I'll send D Squadron the fucking laundry bill,' I said.

I liked Glen. He was a Scouser with a strong accent and a great sense of humour. He was about my height and build and approximately the same age – that is late thirties. He was one heck of an operator, too, having amassed a great deal of experience in the Regiment. He reminded me very much of a guy called Tony who'd been our mobility king in the Gulf during the Iraqi shindig: brave as a lion, unflappable and modest.

Glen did the introductions. The civvy was the mayor of the town and the swarthy types in combats were his escort.

We spent the next half-hour handing over the logistics of the supply column to the mayor and his team, then we retired to the main square where the bulk of the unloading operation took place. Here we pulled in beside the two D Squadron Land Rovers and shot serious shit over a couple of brews with Glen and Nick and the rest of their crew. It transpired that the Maglaj insertion had gone relatively smoothly. Glen hadn't been on the Sea King flight, but had arrived in the pocket soon after it had been opened up.

When the trucks were emptied, we took the column back to Zepce. From there, it was safe for them to make the return journey to Split unescorted. We rested up at our digs in Zepce that night and took one more convoy into Maglaj the following day. It passed without incident.

Since it looked as if the operation was up and running successfully, it was agreed that we should hand the whole thing over to the Coldstream Guards. There was nothing more for us to do. By the third day, we were back in GV.

At the base, we waited impatiently for our next mission. The place was such a doss-hole that the last thing any of us wanted was to hang around if we could possibly help it. I think James sensed this. On our second day there was still no word from Rose's headquarters. Though many pockets were still under siege in Central Bosnia, none was deemed critical enough to merit Regimental infiltration in the same way as Maglaj.

After three days of cooling our heels, James finally came up with a scheme that would get us out of his hair. 'You're all heading down to Split,' he told me. There was a visible look of relief on his face.

'Split?' I said. 'What the hell for?' Split was about as far as you could be from the front line in the Balkan theatre of ops. It was also home to that dismal bloody barracks where we'd spent our first few days upon our arrival from the UK.

'Language training,' he replied, drily. 'Charlie and his half of the troop are making their way there already. I've spoken to the int people and it's their assessment that it's going to be quiet for a while. An ideal time, therefore, to get you lot into the classroom, maybe for three or four days. It'll be hard work, but worth it, particularly as it looks like your next job will be a deployment to the front lines on mapping duties.'

I nodded reluctantly. With the Maglaj flap I'd almost forgotten about that part of our brief. The Muslim–Bosnian-Croat front had to be mapped and new positions agreed by 12 April. Today, somewhat worryingly, was April Fool's Day.

From what James was saying, the whole process was progressing smoothly enough, but with so much riding on the outcome, none of us could take it as read that this situation would last. If we were to deploy in a few days' time to help speed the process along, a bit of Serbo-Croat under our belts might come in handy. Besides, it would be good to hook up with the other half of the troop and find out how they'd been getting along.

The next day, we took the two Land Rovers back to Split. To our immense relief, we were directed not to the main barracks where we had spent our first few nights in the Balkans, but to a warm, spacious double-decker Portakabin on the periphery of the compound. We found Charlie, Fergie, Toby and Dave already settled in. It was the first time we'd been together as a troop since parting company in G V a fortnight earlier.

All of us agreed that it felt a lot longer.

The following morning, it was straight into the classroom, the place within the main barracks where we'd had our initial int briefs before deploying into the field. It was here that we met our teacher, a conservative, somewhat matronly Croatian in her late thirties called Crusha.

Her name sounded like something out of a tag-wrestling bill in Wigan. Then she pointed out that the U in her name was pronounced long. 'Croosha' sounded a lot better than 'crusher'. Any lingering doubts we might have had about her were dispelled when she talked to us a little of her life. Crusha, we soon discovered, was a passionate and intelligent woman with a heart of gold.

In a country torn apart by hatred and prejudice, this former school teacher's views were refreshing. She was honest enough to admit that everyone – ethnic Serbs, Croatians and Muslims alike – shared responsibility for what had happened in the former Yugoslavia. She reserved some venom for the Serbs and I didn't like to ask why. It was always possible that marauding bands of Cetniks, Serb partisans, had wiped out members of her family or her friends. This animosity was the only shadow on a character that, it seemed to me, was little short of saintly.

We started our language lessons in the usual way, learning some basic grammar and syntax, but concentrating mostly on set phrases and vocab. Most of it was not the sort of stuff you would find in your average schoolbook – definitely not *la plume de ma tante*.

Ja sam Britanac.

I am British.

Stoj.

Stop.

Nemate pravo na vrsenje pretresa vozila UN.

You have no right to search a UN vehicle.

Mi smo sa UN.

We are UN personnel.

Ima snajpera tamo.

There are snipers there.

Razumem.

I understand.

And then back to the beginning again.

Ja sam Britanac.

I am British.

Ja sam britanski vojnik.

I am a British soldier.

And so on.

We tried to study, but our minds weren't really on it. On day two, we spent most of the time grilling Crusha about life in Croatia and Bosnia before the war. To no one's great surprise the picture she painted was of an ordered and peaceful society. Not drab and grey as it had been under Soviet Communism, just uncomplicated. A place where tolerance was a way of life and things worked. 'We never thought it would come to this, never,' she said. 'If it can happen here, it can happen in a dozen other places across Europe.'

'What do you think about the UN?' I asked, remembering the reception we'd received at the hands of Croatian Immigration and Customs.

She sighed and sat on the edge of the table at the front of the classroom. It was a while before she answered. 'Cammy, I think what the UN is trying to do here is good. I just don't believe it will work. I don't think anyone here really does.'

'Then what is the answer?' I asked.

'I'm not sure there is one,' she said. 'Tito was strong. He held us together. While everything functioned, we hung on to the belief that the federation was right, that Yugoslavia was good. But we were just fooling ourselves. What is the point of order, if the people who exist beneath it are living a lie?'

'What do you mean?' Charlie asked.

'Throughout my life, Charlie, I have counted many Serbians and Muslims as my friends. I am no different now from what I was three years ago, when Croatia was still within the federation. Now that we are independent, many of those same people, people I used to play with as a child, would not hesitate to kill me if they were given the chance. Yet how can that be? I have not changed since childhood. I am still the same person. Now I ask myself, did they always feel that way about me?'

She plucked rhythmically at the rings on her fingers, looking at each of us in turn. 'I do not know the answers to these questions. All I do know is that when you pack up and leave here, the problems will not go away. Today it is Bosnia, but tomorrow it will be Macedonia and the day after that it will be Kosovo and maybe then Albania. And then one day it will start all over again.'

Ima snajpera tamo.

There are snipers there.

Naprijed je opasno zbog pucanja.

It is dangerous ahead because of the firing.

I thought back to the elation I'd felt a few days earlier after the success of the Maglaj operation. It had all seemed so cut and dried. We had sorted one problem, swept up the pieces and bagged them. But if what she was saying was right, no amount of UN troops and no amount of special forces intervention was going to help this place.

I'd voiced it before and now I said it again. 'Then what on earth are we doing here?'

'Because somebody has to try,' Paul said. He had been even quieter than usual since our couple of nights in the house at Zepce. 'Otherwise, we all might as well pack up and go home.'

I remembered the look on his face as he'd put the Action Man back on the window-sill in the child's bedroom. 'We can't afford to get too close to this one,' I said. 'If we get involved, we lose our objectivity. That goes and so does your judgement. You've got to keep a clear head on your shoulders. You can't do that if you get caught up in the issues. It's that simple.'

'I don't know,' Fergie said, shaking his head. 'I think the times are changing, mate. Five years ago, the world was simple. It was Nato against the Warsaw Pact, us against Spetsnaz. We knew where we stood. Well, nothing is simple any more. They want to use us as peacekeepers? In my book that's no bad thing. All of us have to adapt to survive, Cammy.'

Fergie was a bloke whose opinion I respected enormously. Though he wasn't in my troop – he was a Freefaller – we'd known each other a long time. He'd been attached to the unit to bring up the numbers. Whenever Fergie spoke, I listened. I was desperately trying to get my head around what was being said.

In the Regiment we thrived on impossible missions. They were our lifeblood. Our job was to make the impossible possible. If the objectives were strictly military, we could crack the nut, however tough it was. When it came to soldiering, nothing was impossible if you put your mind to it. But drop us into a situation where the problems were socio-political, not military, and I began to wonder whether using the SAS was ever going to be the answer.

'Fergie and Paul are right,' Charlie said. 'If we give up, then the bloody UN might as well pack up and piss off home.' He looked at Crusha and gave her a wavering smile. 'So to speak, you understand.'

Charlie, the perfect gentleman, seemed momentarily flustered at his own lapse in language.

Crusha smiled back. 'No offence taken, Charlie.'

I nodded. Of course we had to try. Onward Christian soldiers and all that. It was what was happening inside the soldier that concerned me. 'Just make sure you hang on to your objectivity, mate. That's all I'm saying here.'

Charlie clapped a friendly arm on my shoulder. 'I know what you're saying, Cammy, and you're right. But look at us. We're not machines. And we're not kids. I'm not going to drop my guard. But I do feel that the answer to policing this place is more about involvement than objectivity – and I'm also convinced that that's no bad thing.'

Away in the old part of the city, a bell started to toll. I realized in a sudden moment of clarity that I wasn't trying to convince them: these guys, many of them so much younger than me, already had their shit together. All along, with this talk of involvement and detachment, I had merely been trying to convince myself. The issue was tugging at me and I hadn't resolved it – and that, more than anything else, left me feeling unsettled.

I looked up and found Crusha's eyes. The look she gave me said she knew exactly what was going through my mind.

That night, a bunch of us decided to go out and get some beers. I had some things to square away but promised I'd catch up with Keith and Paul at a certain bar that had been recommended to us. I got a lift downtown with a bloke from D Squadron who knew his way around. The four of us met up and we had a good enough evening, crawling in and out of one or two dodgy dives and taking in the general ambience. Split had escaped the rigours of war, so much so that I almost forgot we were only a few dozen klicks from the front line.

At close to midnight, we drained our glasses and headed back to the base. Keith and Paul swore they'd left the Land Rover in one of the little cobbled streets nearby, but the harder they searched, the more I became convinced that the UN was going to have to kiss one of its vehicles goodbye. Like Naples, Split had a reputation as a Mecca for black-marketeers. I was pretty positive that our Land Rover was either a different colour by now, with its serial numbers switched, or that it had been broken down into its constituent components and flogged as so many spare parts.

It was as we were trawling the darkened streets that I got spooked. There was nothing overtly threatening about our sur-roundings, but the sight of three blokes wandering, seemingly aimlessly, through the back-streets was an invitation to any disaffected Croat to bounce us. Like our Land Rover, it wouldn't take much for our body parts to disappear either. Though we were dressed in civvies, you didn't have to be a brain surgeon to realize we were a bunch of Brits out on the piss.

If it hadn't been for the uneasy feeling that came over me, I probably wouldn't have paid any heed to the bloke who was maintaining a steady pace about 150 metres behind us. We changed directions a couple of times, descending ever deeper into the criss-cross network of streets that made up the old town.

I stopped to light a fag, glancing briefly over my cupped hand as I shielded my lighter from the wind. He was still there, head bowed against the chill, feet scuffing the cobbles as he trudged up the street behind us. A big bloke, seemingly nonchalant – but then, maybe that was the intention.

I turned and caught up with the others, electing to keep quiet about our friend for the time being. There's nothing worse than crying wolf when you're in the company of people who are trained in the same surveillance and counter-surveillance skills as you. But as Keith and Paul crossed the road to head down another alleyway, I noticed our shadow cross too.

I decided to say something. 'Don't look now, guys,' I called softly, 'but we might have company. Some bloke's been tailing us for the last five minutes and he's still there.'

It was all I needed to say. We carried on looking for the Land Rover, but every now and again Keith or Paul would turn and say something to me or crack a joke. Whenever they did so, they weren't looking at me, but scanning over my shoulder.

A couple of minutes later, everyone was agreed. Like it or not, the guy was still there.

I knew what it was like to do surveillance in built-up areas, but I'd never been a target before. Not as far as I knew.

Every so often, we're called upon to take part in what is known as an 'operator's exercise'. This is a lukewarm name for some of the most realistic and brutal training anyone can receive prior to heading 'over the water' – to Northern Ireland. The emphasis is on picking up then following a subject, plotting his or her every move, without compromising yourself.

The student intake comes from a broad section of the military and intelligence communities. Guys from the Regiment attend, too, but where we really come into our own is in our portrayal of the 'enemy'. Because we have to undergo what many consider to be a harrowing selection process to join the SAS, we know what it is like to be on the receiving end of violence. We know how to dish it out, too.

We make a pretty convincing enemy.

On this night, in an old, unfamiliar city with next to no street-lighting, with a guy apparently tracking our every move – and God only knew who else lying in wait for us – one operator's exercise in particular came to mind.

Six of us were playing 'red team' against a student who had been told to tail a bloke who was acting out the role of a 'known IRA terrorist' on the British mainland. The student knew nothing of our involvement. All he knew was that he was close to the end of his course and that this 'practical' might well determine whether he passed or failed.

To up the ante a bit, the people who run the course tell the students that henceforth they are all potential targets of the Provisional IRA, so they should be careful in everything they do: watch out for suspicious packages, check under their cars, etc., etc. This, of course, is sensible advice, but it is also calculated. For it instills in them the idea that they are all in some way marked out. Like it or not, everyone on that course can't help developing just a twinge of paranoia, an urge to stop every so often and cast a quick glance back over the shoulder. This is the key to a major piece of skulduggery that is about to be perpetrated upon them.

On this particular day we are tasked with intercepting our student in Bristol. The student is told that his target is holding a rendezvous in the city and that the meeting is to take place at 1230. Once he has identified the subject, the student is to keep him under surveillance until further notice.

The student knows nothing about us, but we know everything about him. We are also told about his movements well in advance, which allows us time to set up watch before the meeting. In other words, our man will be watching over the Pira and we'll be watching over him – like some mindless Jeremy Beadle jape, only a fuck of a sight less jolly.

Two hours before the meeting, we pull up in a car-park close to the RV. We've brought with us a Transit-type van and an unmarked saloon car. Our dress-code is CI5 casual – the jeans and bomber jackets that are a dead giveaway on Bodie and Doyle but a little less obvious on us.

We carry out a detailed recce of the RV area. Since we're in constant contact with the student's controllers, we know that the subject will be parking his car at the other end of the shopping centre and walking up the precinct towards our car-park, where the Pira R V is due to take place. After a thorough casing of the street, we determine where we'll grab him and how to make the extraction with the minimum of fuss. The local police are told that we're working on their beat, but the news is restricted to a fairly senior level. It's always possible that our subject has friends in the force who could tip him off. Security has to be the watchword in even the smallest of details.

Everything is going to plan, everyone is in place. We have guys in shops with views over the street, we have blokes pretending to browse in shop windows.

Shortly before the allotted hour, our surveillance begins in earnest, everyone is straining for that first glimpse of the guy as he wanders up from the car-park on the far side of the precinct. The beauty of it is that our target can't be late, because the timing of the Pira R V sets the schedule.

But at 1210, when we really should have caught sight of our man, we're getting nothing from our picket at the top end of the street. Another couple of minutes inch by and still nothing. I'm pretending to stare wistfully at a range of dodgy-looking togs behind a big plate-glass window in Top Man. Set back in the entrance-way, I have a perfect view down the street. Across the way, I can see another member of the team, a guy called Fritz. He, like me, is craning for that initial eyes-on, but still, somehow, managing to look casual.

It's at that second that I catch something out of the corner of my eye; an image of someone I know, because photographs that I've spent hours studying have burned an image of him on distant parts of my brain. I turn and see him. Instead of walking up the street as he's promised his controllers, he's hit it half-way down via a side-alley. He's walking briskly, almost running, and his cheeks are flushed.

And then I get it. The fucker's late, so he's taken a short-cut.

At that same instant, Fritz must have caught the look on my face, because instinctively he turns, following it, and finds himself gazing straight into the eyes of our subject. There can only be about five yards between them. And they're staring each other out.

In what passes as excruciating slow-time, I watch the stand-off: Fritz and the target mesmerized as each tries to make out the other.

To Fritz, the encounter has happened so quickly, and so utterly differently from how he imagined it, that he finds it impossible to conceal his reaction. There is a look that we all give when we see someone we recognize, even if it is some almost imperceptible movement behind our eyes. And the harder we try to cover it up, the more obvious our reactions become.

Our subject saw that flash of recognition in Fritz's eyes and he hit the precinct running.

Cue a moment in which mayhem erupts. Fritz breaks free of his paralysis and starts to pound after the target. I yell into my radio then leg it in the same direction. Luckily, the target makes a big mistake and turns up an almost deserted side-street, so that next to no one else notices the ruckus.

It takes a couple of seconds for Fritz to catch up with him, a few more for him to grab him and pull him down. A moment later, I'm there and within a quarter of a minute so are two other guys. By this time, the back-markers have called in the vehicle support. Everyone's pulling together to atone for the fuck-up.

Some people will undoubtedly find this gratuitous, but I can assure them it's necessary. Each and every student who goes on an operator's exercise is training for war. If they fuck up over the water, the Pira will (literally) nail them to the floor. If a guy's going to crack, therefore, it's better to find out on this side of the Irish Sea than on the other.

I can't even say I had any of this in mind as I hit the subject, but as Fritz pulled his head off the ground I whacked him hard across the face and then again in the ribs. Suddenly everybody's giving him a pasting. None of us says a word, we're just all over the poor sod like a rash.

It's while all this is going down that a copper walks bold as brass into the alleyway.

Faced with what he undoubtedly thinks is a mugging, the policeman yells for us to stop. He may even have asked us, I don't know; but that's the way it seemed. The sound of his voice, cracking with fear, rings out across the cobbles.

We drop the almost unconscious subject and turn to face the law. The bloke looks like he's just passed out of the academy – all loose-fitting uniform, ungainly shoes and facial bum-fluff that's just started to turn a shade darker.

On cue, Fritz steps away from the mêlée. He's a stocky bloke who looks like he crawled out of a gene-pool filled to the brim by Oliver Reed and Mad Frankie Fraser.

In a fluid rush, before the cop can open his mouth again, Fritz pulls out a Browning 9mm. The piece is as big as a chainsaw and it's in the policeman's face.

In a low snarl, Fritz says, 'You! Fuck off!'

The copper stares at Fritz, his mouth gaping for air, the blood draining from his face. The shock is so absolute, he's so convinced that this is the moment in which he'll meet his Maker, that all he can do is pitch forward and spew his guts out. The surprise of it, even to him, is enough to kick in his instincts for survival – he turns and runs.

A second or two later, there's a screech of tyres as our van reverses up the alleyway. The doors fly open and one of the blokes jumps out the back and ushers us inside. The next thing I know, we're haring through the city streets, trying to get a sack over the subject's face as we're banging from one wall of the Transit to the other.

Then, as soon as it had all started, we're back to a sensible speed and negotiating the roundabouts on the edge of the city. The subject is quiet, almost comatose. We've looked him over and know he's basically all right. His wrists are tied and he's gagged good and tight. Throughout the whole thing, apart from Fritz's exchange with the copper, none of us has said a thing.

Presently, we pull up and throw open the doors. On this beautiful day I'm confronted by the sight of bluebells, an endless sea of them, nestling beneath a fresh spring canopy of old oaks. I recognize it as the scene of the endgame; a place that we'd found and recced earlier. It is a patch of forest on top of a hill suitably cut off from the rest of the world. From somewhere a cuckoo calls. It can call as loud as it bloody well likes, but the only people who can possibly hear it are us. It's that remote.

The subject is taken to the edge of the bluebell field and made to kneel. The sandbag is removed from his head. There's a large bruise on his face and defiance in his eyes. I long to know what is going through his mind. If he's on the point of cracking, he doesn't show it.

One of the team, a bloke who looks not unlike Gabriel Byrne, grabs a shovel out of the back of the van and, in a quiet voice laden with Irish menace, orders the subject to start digging.

Now I see panic in the subject's eyes. He looks at the guy who's doing the talking, he looks at Fritz, he looks at me. None of us bats an eyelid. Fritz's 9mm makes the point again: start fucking digging.

As the guy scrapes at the earth around his knees, Mr 'Byrne' fires his questions. He manages to maintain the accent. To me, it sounds good. The subject, I imagine, is in no fit state to tell whether it's genuine Fermanagh or a put-on job. It's gone way beyond that now.

'What unit are you from?' Byrne asks quietly. 'We know you're security forces. What unit are you from? Come on, tell us. Tell us and we can stop this and let you go. Just give us your unit and tell us your mission. We don't want to hurt you any more than we already have.'

The guy grits his teeth and shakes his head. I can see tears behind his eyes. So can Mr Byrne. He nods to Fritz.

Fritz kicks him in the chest and orders him to dig faster. Classic 'good cop, bad cop' stuff. Presently, there's a hole in the earth that's just about big enough for a man. The drama is almost played out, but not quite. There's a little more left to come.

The subject is shaking. Quietly convulsing with fear. Mr Byrne continues to ask his questions, but I'm no longer sure they're registering. I'm almost wishing the guy to crack so we can tell him it was all a bit of play-acting. But unfortunately, especially in these last few seconds, there's everything still to play for. And so, it goes on.

Mr Byrne snaps his fingers and the sound of Fritz cocking his 9mm cracks back in reply. Fritz moves round behind the subject and grinds the muzzle into the nape of his neck. When Mr Byrne speaks, there is no more civility in his voice. He takes hold of the subject's hair and pulls his head back so that they're staring at each other, eye to eye.

'This is your last fucking chance, you piece of shit,' he shouts. 'What unit are you from?'

Tears and grit combine in a hideous kind of facial scrub on the subject's cheeks. His eyes stare back from grey holes of despair. Something crosses his face, a look that is so intensely personal that it is difficult to read, and then he opens his mouth and he screams, '*Go on, fucking do it! Kill me, you bastards! Fucking do it. Do it! Just do it!*'

But even now, it isn't over.

In a sudden and cruel twist, one of the team shouts from the van that there's cops coming down the trail.

The subject is bundled into the van, the sack replaced over his head. The plan now is to drive him to our secure training area close to Hereford, where he'll be taken directly to Bunker 31. This is a specially constructed facility that, from the inside, will look like some walled-up farm outhouse. At Bunker 31 the interrogation will begin again, but with none of its previous pace and violence. Now, in fact, the guy has to be brought down to a state where he can cope with the news that all of this has been an exercise and that he has just passed the test with distinction.

I came back to the real world to find Keith glancing over my shoulder again, urging me with a whisper and with a forced smile to drop our pace to see how our tail responded. We kept walking, only now Keith fell back beside me, leaving Paul a few feet in front, and we slowed everything down. If we were bounced, Paul, stocky but built like a brick shit-house, would be shielded long enough from the initial assault to be in there like Flynn with his fists flailing. Our hands were out of our pockets now and we were listening intently. We picked up the footsteps when our man was about twenty metres behind us. The last few feet were the killer, because I could feel each individual hair standing up on the back of my neck like a tiny receptor. The urge to spin round was overwhelming, but training dictated otherwise.

I turned to confront the man who'd been following us for the past ten minutes, echoes of Bristol still running through my head. A quick trawl of his features from the feet upwards, a momentary glimpse of a hard, dark face, stubbled cheeks and chin, then I found his eyes and held them. The eyes give you a moment's warning of a person's true intentions and I scanned them hard. The darkness didn't help, but I thought I saw a second of indecision, a ghost of a moment in which this big man had been sizing up some kind of a play against me.

But the lack of a weapon in his hand, the absence of a balled fist, forced me to let it go. 'All right, mate?' I enquired, as casually as I could.

He gave me an awkward smile, then accelerated past us. A moment later he disappeared down an alleyway to be swallowed up by the shadows.

I found myself wondering whether I would be able to find the courage of our subject in the operator's exercise, this rookie intelligence operative, if Croat extremists really were out there and plotting to take us down. Fortunately it never became an issue because Keith suddenly gave a shout of recognition. He and Paul had parked the Land Rover much further away than they had thought, but here it was, jacked up with a tyre missing and the spare gone. But at least we had found it. Something in the back of my mind said it hadn't been a moment too soon.

We got on the radio. With a bit of support from base we managed to get the vehicle back to the barracks half an hour later. For once it felt good to return to its confines. R and R in the Bosnian theatre of operations didn't feel right. With so much left to be done, this wasn't the time or the place to be out downing beers.

Like the guy in the bluebell wood, I just felt a burning need to get on with it.

I got my wish the next morning. We were just about to go back into the classroom when I was called to the radio to talk to James.

'Got a job for you,' he said. 'More like two jobs, in fact.'

I reached for a pen and started to jot notes. There was a developing problem in a place called Mostar, a city of around a hundred thousand Muslims and Croats situated in a large patch of Croat-held territory in the south of Bosnia-Herzegovina, around seventy kilometres inland from the coast.

The eastern half of the city, the Muslim half, had received a relentless pounding from HVO artillery for several years, which had reduced the place to rubble. As with Maglaj and GV and a string of other towns, the Muslims had brazened it out – I suppose they had had little choice – and now, at least, they were seeing some semblance of peace. The shelling had all but stopped, although sniping was still a regular hazard, not to mention disease, the cold and malnutrition.

The real problem, as far as the Regiment was concerned, was that Mostar was falling behind in the race to conclude the peace deal that would cement the Muslim-Croat federation in Bosnia. That old deadline of 12 April was now rocketing towards us. But in Mostar things were moving way too slowly. Unless new borders could be plotted here, James told me, there'd be a glaring hole in the agreement in a little over a week's time and that, in turn, could jeopardize the entire peace process. To compound matters, the D Squadron mob that had worked the sector for the past month or so was being withdrawn to other duties. We were taking over, James said, and we'd have to hit the ground running.

The other job was in the town of Gorazde in the eastern part of the country, close to the border with Serbia. Gorazde was a Muslim enclave and supposed 'safe haven' that had received the full Serbian siege treatment for several years. Over the past few days, the Serbs had started to shell the place again after months of comparative quiet. A couple of beleaguered UNMOs (UN Military Observers) were sending back daily reports of the damage to General Rose's forward HQ in Sarajevo, but the time had come for detailed information. The General had decided, therefore, that he would go to Gorazde to see for himself what was happening and that a detachment of SAS should be dispatched into the town at the same time, under the guise of ordinary UN soldiers. That detachment would be made up of D Squadron guys and topped up by a handful of blokes from our troop. It was up to us to sort out who went where, James said, but it was his belief that Charlie should lead the patrol into Gorazde and I should head up the group that went to Mostar. He outlined his reasoning. Gorazde was a pocket and there was always something special about a pocket, especially one that was a designated 'safe haven'. As the boss, it was only right that Charlie went there, the more so since he had plenty of back-up in the form of the D Squadron contingent.

'In any case,' James told me, adopting a semi-conspiratorial tone, 'Gorazde isn't going to be that hairy a deal. The view around here is that the place is a statistical blip. It's not going to blow. There's a little aggravation that we need to dampen down, but that's it. Mostar's different, though. If that one isn't sorted, mate, the whole fucking sector could go up in smoke. I'd say on balance, Cammy, you've got the better job.'

'When do we move?' I asked.

'Think of this as a rough warning order. Get yourselves sorted and then head back to GV at first light. When you're here, we'll fine-tune the plan and get you dispatched to your allotted destinations.'

I signed off and went and told the boys.

When we returned to the classroom, it was even more difficult than usual to focus on the Serbo-Croat lesson. Since Crusha was security cleared, we started to ask her about our two destinations. When she heard that Charlie was headed for Gorazde, she turned to me and asked if I was joking. If it hadn't been for the look on her face, I might have thought that this was her idea of a wind-up. She was visibly shocked. I told her I wasn't kidding, then asked what the big deal was.

'If you go to Gorazde,' she said, looking at Charlie and barely keeping her emotions in check, 'you will die.'

I laughed nervously. 'Come on, Crusha. I know there's some shelling going on there, but a lot of places have seen much worse. In any case, the UN says it's fine, just isolated stuff. It'll probably all blow over in a couple of days.'

'Besides,' Charlie said, putting his arm around her, 'it's a safe haven. The Serbs know that. If they attack, then Nato will attack them. They wouldn't risk it, Crusha. We'll be fine, I promise.'

She started to cry. We got to our feet and drew a little closer. As a group of individuals, we're not known for showing the more sensitive side of our natures. Kevin, however, offered her a handkerchief. She took it, looked at him and smiled self-consciously. 'I'm sorry,' she said, 'but I know what I am saying. Gorazde is a bad place. Ask anyone. The Serbs are building for something there. There will be much killing.'

She was so resolute that nothing we could say would dissuade her. Continuing the lesson was hopeless, so we kicked it into touch.

Crusha wiped away her tears. We were all moved by her concern, but embarrassed, too. We were grown men, part of Britain's special forces élite, supposedly, and quite capable of looking after ourselves. Yet this softly spoken woman, whom we'd all come to like in the short time we'd known her, was adamant that if we went to Gorazde, we wouldn't be coming back.

We said our goodbyes and wandered back to the Portakabin. A long discussion ensued. We double-checked with GV. An hour later, after we'd shot a lot of shit and talked to various members of Green Slime, we satisfied ourselves that a bit of light shelling was nothing to be unduly concerned about. The place was in no more danger of exploding than anywhere else, or so the Slime said.

The next day, bright and early, we drove back as a troop to GV. At the checkpoint on the approaches to Diamond Route, the big MSR leading into central Bosnia, we were told that there had been some breakdowns on the road and that we'd be held up by at least two to three hours. Instead of going through on our own, the MPs told us, we'd have to 'scab' on to a big Ukrainian battalion that was due through later in the day. When they eventually showed up, it was quite a sight. I've never seen so many BMP and BTR armoured fighting vehicles (AFV) in my life. Five years earlier and we might have been staring at them through the cross-hairs of a Milan missile launcher. Now they were our friends.

We wandered over and took a look. After we'd dispensed a few packets of cigarettes, the Ukrainians invited us to take a look around. Their AFVs were a pretty sorry sight, with their loose-hanging wires, ripped seat covers and flaking paint. No matter which vehicle we went into there was a pervasive smell of boiled cabbage and cheap cigarettes. That Nato had ever been scared of these characters was hard to believe now, but in their day, I had to remind myself, when the Red Army had been properly funded, these troops would have poured through the Fulda Gap on day one of the Third World War.

When we got into GV, it was straight into the ops room to get our tasking orders. The following morning, James told us, Charlie, Fergie, Ray, Toby and Dave were to head down to Sarajevo where they would be briefed by General Rose about the Gorazde situation. Rose himself wanted to go into the pocket and see the shelling at first hand, but so far the Serbs had refused his request. The negotiations continued. Everyone was hopeful that by the time Charlie's lot arrived permission to enter the city would have been granted.

As for us, it was a case of make all due haste for Mostar. Keith, Paul, and I were delighted. It seemed like a plum job. The Spanish battalion, or SPANBAT, the UN detachment charged with the security of the place, had been informed of our impending arrival. We were to check in with the commander as soon as we got there. Our immediate Regimental contact was to be a D Squadron sergeant called Reggie, from whom we would eventually be taking over the mapping operation. We were given instructions on how to find him.

The composition of my team was to change radically over the next few days. Dougie had to return to the UK soon after we got to Mostar to attend a medical course. It was something that couldn't be put off any longer and he was gutted. I would be sorry to see him depart as he had been a stalwart of the mission from the word go.

Kevin, meanwhile, was to remain in GV as squadron operations sergeant. He had mixed feelings about this: as ops sergeant, he would be based in the ops room, becoming the link-man between the patrols in the field and the Regiment's senior hierarchy in Bosnia. It was the right move for him, as ops sergeant is often the first step towards some fast-track promotion within the Regiment. He was sorry about leaving us, as it was a step back from the hard-core operational work that the rest of us would be carrying on with.

Unhappy as I was to see Kev go, I knew that having him in place in GV would be a bonus for us. The ops sergeant knows everything that is going on at RHQ level; he gets to look through a window on to a privileged world.

I looked out of our window and saw black rainclouds approaching. Angry tendrils of vapour reached down from their lower levels towards the mountains.

Another storm was rolling in off the Adriatic. The weather patterns were becoming familiar; the meteorological situation easier to predict. GV, the last place that needed it, was about to get another soaking.

Deep in the hinterland of Bosnia, another storm was brewing; an almighty one. Only this time, the swirling, roiling tensions that characterized its development had passed almost unchecked by those whose business it was to monitor these things.

Not that any of us knew it then, but over the coming days, we, the guys on the ground, would need all the friends at RHQ we could get.

Early the next morning, in the darkness of the pre-dawn, Charlie's half of the troop lined up to see us off. The air was clear and cold in the aftermath of the storm that had tracked inland during the night. A thin sliver of light was just visible above the mountains to the east. Our feet sloshed in the Passchendaele mud. Not a religious man by nature, I uttered a quiet prayer. *Please, God, let there be solid foundations beneath us in Mostar.*

We had no real idea how long the journey would take. The city was only seventy or so kilometres due south of GV as the crow flies, but getting to it along route E73 was a waste of space. On the map, the road wove alongside the river Neretva all the way to Mostar and several times crossed over it. The trouble was, a number of main bridges had been blown up, making the E73 impassable. So we'd be taking the ferry at Jablanica instead.

Charlie and I shook hands and promised to stay in touch via satcom. 'It'll do your career good,' I said, 'brown-nosing to General Rose.'

He laughed. 'Are you sure you don't want to swap places? From some of the things I've heard these past few days, Cammy, yours could probably do with a bit of a lift.'

Around me, the rest of the guys traded similar insults. As we drove away, I caught a glimpse of Fergie in the rear-view mirror, his tall frame silhouetted against the reddening skyline. 'Oi, Fergie,' Keith yelled after him, 'tell General Rose to come down here and sort out that fucking cookhouse, mate.'

Fergie's reply was lost in the grinding noise of the gears as the Land Rover churned its way out of the compound on to the open road.

We sped through Prozer, the garrison town where we had witnessed on our first trip to GV the bizarre cross-section of humanity that characterized the anarchic world of the HVO. Fortunately, it was too early for the *Mad Max* villains to be up roaming the streets. We were still within the safety limits of Prozer's hang-over zone. The only problem was, you had to peer hard through the windscreen to avoid the dead slivovitz bottles.

After a couple of hours, we started to pick up directions to the ferry crossing. At a bend in the road, we saw a beat-up wooden sign that pointed us down a dirt-track. I did a quick check on the map and the global positioning system, ever mindful that the local citizenry could be up to its old tricks. It seemed, however, that we were headed in the right direction. The sign was genuine.

Within minutes, we found ourselves joining a queue of clapped-out cars and trucks. We were the only military vehicle and certainly the only party that had anything to do with the UN. The cars and trucks were filled with paltry produce that, no doubt, was being traded at outposts up and down the river. We saw weeping jerry-cans, moth-eaten sacks of potatoes, the odd scrawny live chicken, firewood and used building materials – one commodity that Bosnia had in abundance.

As I strolled along the line of vehicles, a group of children played football in patches of roadway between the bumpers. I noticed they were careful not to kick their ball off the track. Walking off any recognized pathway was an invitation to die. The children, I guess, knew instinctively about mines.

Music floated softly from the vehicles, filling the air with local songs. I felt I had stepped back in time to join a refugee column fleeing the Nazis.

I had counted ten cars and trucks when the river opened up in front of me.

Through the mist that still clung to the slow-moving surface of the water I could just see the steep-sided banks on the other side. On this side, just in front of the lead car in the queue, the ground sloped gently into the river. There was no sign of the ferry, so I had no way of knowing how many vehicles it could take at a time. Nor was there a timetable. I looked around for someone who might be able to tell me and spotted a crusty old bloke smoking a fag down at the river's edge.

He turned out to be one of the ferry operators and within minutes we'd done the deal. For the price of a couple of cartons of cigarettes and a bottle of duty-free rum, we managed to get ourselves on the next ride. I didn't like jumping the queue so obviously, but if we'd let nature take its course, we wouldn't have made the trip until the following morning. The ferry could take only four vehicles at a time and it didn't operate at night. Our mission to Mostar couldn't wait till the next day.

Just as we manoeuvred the two Land Rovers to the front, the ferry hove into view. It looked like a cross between the *African Queen* and some hideous Thames dredger. It was, in fact, two barges lashed together and overlaid with thick wooden sleepers. It was about sixty metres long and thirty wide. It had edges that were raised a few centimetres above the level of the gunwales to stop the vehicles sliding into the water. Considering how oil-stained everything was, this was no bad thing. I could smell the ferry when she was still a hundred metres from the shore. I extinguished my fag in a hurry.

As soon as its rag-tag collection of vehicles had been driven off, we were ushered on board. Within half an hour or so, after the vehicles had been secured, we were off. There was a belch of oil-smoke and an angry growl from somewhere deep below the water-line as we pulled away from the bank, then a steadying of the revs as we headed with the flow towards Muslim-held territory. After a minute, the put-put sound of the engine was scarcely audible. In everything they drove, Bosnians had mastered the art of throttling right back to the point of stall to preserve precious fuel.

Keith, Paul, Dougie and I got out of the Land Rovers. We vowed not to get back inside until we'd docked. If this nautical monstrosity hit any kind of obstacle, we figured she'd go over in a second, leaving nothing to remember us by but a shimmering film of oil on the dark surface of the Neretva. Outside, we might stand a chance. Looking around us, nobody else seemed that bothered. They stayed in their vehicles to ward off the early-morning cold.

The journey was scheduled to take about three-quarters of an hour, so we settled down and admired the view. Within a few minutes the river opened up and the mist lifted to expose a vista that was both stunning and sinister. Ahead of us lay a good clear stretch of river. Either side, the mountains dropped straight down into the water as sheer-sided granite cliffs. Above, the cloudbase, heavy and oppressive, hung like a grey drape between the mountain-tops. Apart from us, there was no sign of habitation. We could have been explorers of some vast lost world, navigators on the edge of oblivion.

A bridge loomed out of the mist. It was the sort of thing that Isambard Kingdom Brunel would have been proud of – a great Gothic span of steel and stone, built to link the two sets of cliffs hundreds of feet above our heads.

Keith, not normally given to sentiment, said, 'Jesus, would you look at that?'

I sucked hard on a Silk Cut and nodded. 'I know, mate,' I said sombrely. 'Whoever did it certainly knew what they were doing.'

The bridge was down now – rigged with charges and blown clean across the centre span – and from what we could see, it had been expertly done. We watched as it arced by and finally slid back into the low-lying clouds.

Suddenly, Keith said, 'Christ, you don't think this bloody river is mined, do you?'

For some reason, none of us had even thought of it before. Within an instant, however, my mind had replayed one of the conversations I'd had with the Norwegian pilots in Tuzla. One of their company thought he'd witnessed a string of mines being laid across the river Bosna during a low-level sortie. If it had been done there, there was no reason why somebody couldn't do the same here. I told Keith that it had to be unlikely, though. You don't run a regular ferry-service knowing there's a real risk you're going to be blown out of the water.

Do you?

Keith saw the hesitation in my eyes and insisted on checking with the crew.

Presently, Dougie, Paul and I watched him emerge from the wheelhouse, a dilapidated wooden structure on the rear of the starboard barge with windows running round the top of it.

'Well?' I asked.

'There's good news and bad news,' Keith said. He looked a little shell-shocked.

'Give us the fucking bad, mate.'

'The river *is* mined.'

Paul, Dougie and I responded in unison. '*What?*'

I wondered how there could possibly be any good news in this development.

'But,' Keith continued, 'at this time of year, apparently, with the river full and all, they tend to float into the banks and stay there.'

I chucked my fag into the water. 'Bollocks to that,' I said, 'we're going on lookout. What do they look like?'

'Like those Second World War jobs, the crew said – you know, big ball thingies with spikes sticking out of them.'

So that was how we passed the rest of the journey, two of us up front and two at the back scouting for mines. We felt a bit stupid since the crew obviously couldn't have given a toss. Apart from the helmsman, they all remained heads-down in the wheelhouse, playing cards.

It was in this atmosphere, tense and strangely surreal, that we finally chugged into the Muslim-held territory outside Mostar.

SEVEN

The outskirts of the town were a straight eight klicks from the ferry drop-off point, but longer after we'd wiggled and wound our way through the mountains. As we dropped down towards the city, we saw the first houses, then clusters of them. These were Muslim hamlets on the edge of East Mostar. They looked normal from afar, but the nearer we got the more the damage pulled into focus. Close-up, we could see they were wrecks; mere shells with no more than a few centimetres between bullet holes. I don't know how most of them managed to keep standing.

To our left there were fields; to our right, a few hundred metres away, the river. As the sun rose and burned off the last of the mist, we could see the high-rises of Mostar proper off to the right. Stretching away between us and the city were fields lined with trenches and barricades, the odd farmhouse interspersed between them. By our maps, the front lines were still several kilometres away. These were reserve positions; places you could fall back to and hold in the event of an overwhelming attack. They were also holding positions for the front lines; fodder farms for Croatian cannons.

As we ground past the farm buildings, we could see groups of soldiers gathered inside and out. They were old for fighting men; not one we saw was under sixty. A group playing cards at a table watched us with suspicion as we chuntered past. They were sitting on seats that had been ripped from knackered old cars, their weapons propped nearby. Some had A K s, others had shotguns. All wore the dark, olive green uniform of the BiH army.

'Where are the young blokes?' Keith asked. 'Or is that a stupid question?'

'I don't know,' I replied. The choices, however, were limited: they were either deployed closer to the front or dead. I suspected the latter.

I gave an old geezer a nod as we filed past his farmhouse. His eyes held mine like a sniper's open sights, but they registered nothing.

The landscaping changed on the left-hand side. Instead of trenches, we now saw acres of flat land bordered with barbed wire that was hung with warning signs about the mines. After a few hundred metres, the wire and the signs ran out, but, pound to a penny, that didn't mean the mines had. They went on, no doubt, unmarked and uncharted.

A few yards further on, we saw a cluster of mines pulled over on to the side of the road. I asked Paul to stop and jumped down to take a look at them. I recognized them as Yugoslav copies of a German Second World War model – a great big fuck-off thing that must have weighed around twenty kilos. If a tank hit it in the right place, its tracks and wheels would probably end up in Romania. I dreaded to think what other uses the Muslims had put this monster to. Given the constraints of the arms embargo, they were known for adapting weapons to roles never dreamed of by the manufacturers.

We pressed on, following directions to the S F base. This was on the other side of Mostar in Croatian-held territory.

Suddenly we were in the town and, from nowhere, surrounded by people. We saw women, kids and old men, but, again, no males between the ages of sixteen and sixty. The kids were playing in the ruins, running in and out of charred buildings as if the whole thing was one big adventure playground. Their mothers and grandmothers, dressed in scarves and drab dresses, kept a discreet watch on them. If there was a common strand running through the dress-code it was that multiple layers were the in thing. At first I didn't get it, as it was quite warm under the midday sun. Then it dawned on me that if you had to flee in a hurry – as these people had many times, I'm sure – then all you had were the clothes you stood up in. In the meantime, you sweated.

'Why is everybody here?' I asked. 'It's not as if they're doing anything.'

'There's nowhere else,' Keith said. 'These people aren't city folks, see? Look at their clothes. They're peasants from the outlying countryside. They're here because they feel safety in numbers. But there ain't nowhere for them to fucking live, poor bastards.'

Our two Land Rovers slowed to walking pace to get through one particularly congested area. Somewhere the water mains had burst because half the street was ankle-high in water. The air was heavy with the stink of raw sewage, which lapped around the bricks that spilled from the bomb-sites into the street.

Before we could pick up speed again, the kids were on us. There was no begging as such, just lots of jostling and laughter and shouts of 'mister, mister'. Fortunately we always kept lots of sweets in our pockets, and these we dispensed through the open windows.

I spotted one scrawny little kid at the back, who, try as he might, was always elbowed out of the way by his mates before he could even get close to a liquorice allsort. I asked Paul to stop the car. The children parted as I clambered out. For some reason, the little kid never moved. I dipped my hand in my pocket, came up with a fistful of bonbons and handed them over. His eyes swelled to the size of hub-caps, then, quick as a flash, he grabbed them and ran off, squealing with delight as he was pursued by the others into the ruins.

'Not getting soft on us, are you, mate?' Keith asked, as I climbed back into the Land Rover.

'Nah,' I said. 'Just took pity on the poor little runt, that's all.'

We drove off again. Moments later, we pulled up at a Muslim checkpoint. Either side of it, running through the city like a poor man's version of the Berlin Wall, was a barbed-wire barricade. There were lots of mines in the dead zone either side of the fence. A soldier stepped out of a sandbag position close to the barrier and asked for our papers. We told him we were UKLO, not that he seemed to care, and that we were trying to get to SPANBAT HQ. When he was satisfied, he dragged away some mines that had been positioned on the road in front of us and waved us through. We had to go through the same rigmarole at the Croat checkpoint fifty metres away. Finally, after several minutes of negotiation, we were off and in the clear.

We rounded a corner and blinked. Stretching away in front of us was the continuation of the same street we'd just trundled down. Where there'd been filth and rubble on the Muslim side, here we saw bright shop windows and cafés and pavements. The buildings were hardly scratched.

'What the fuck . . . ?' Keith said. 'Did we just breeze into an episode of *Time Tunnel* or something?'

I knew what he meant. Not only did it seem like a different era, it felt like we'd been plonked down in a different city. I hadn't seen so many neon lights and posers with shopping bags since the Via del Corso in Rome.

This, I realized, was a bottled version of the Muslim–Croat divide across the whole of Bosnia. While the Muslims suffered, the ethnic Croats just got on with it, their needs met by their big brothers across the border in Croatia proper. You couldn't help but wonder how the Muslims had held out for so long.

SPANBAT HQ was ten miles outside the city, well into Croatian-held territory. We followed a road leading out of Mostar, navigating by the map. Shortly before we got to the base we passed a big motel by the side of the road. I noticed the car-park was bumper to bumper with UN vehicles. This was not a good sign. At that time of day, early afternoon, I couldn't see any earthly reason for their being there.

Moments later, the SPANBAT garrison swung into view. Reggie and the three other D Squadron lads in his charge were living in a house in the shadow of the SF base. We parked up and walked in through the front door. The place was much like the *basha* we'd stayed in at Zepce, though a lot sprucer. It belonged to a Croat woman who rented it out to the UN.

Reggie was there to greet us. I hadn't worked with him before, but I knew him. He was stocky with dark hair and game for a laugh most of the time. He was also a highly professional member of the Regiment who thrived under pressure. Not surprisingly, he was having the time of his life in Bosnia.

'Chuck your kit down, we're starting right away,' he said, as soon as I'd done the introductions. 'The sooner I get you lot briefed, the sooner I can bugger off home.'

Given the importance of the mapping task, which was the prerequisite to the handing back of land between Muslims and Croats, it seemed madness on the face of it to recall the D Squadron contingent now. Reggie and the rest of his patrol had been in Mostar for the best part of two weeks; they knew the score. The handover was scheduled to take place in a week's time and there was a lot to be done.

But Hereford operated to its own unique timetable and it wasn't always possible to yield to international events. The rotation system – when one of the action-ready standby squadrons swaps places with the counter-terrorist squadron or its training oppo – was an immutable facet of Regimental lore. Reggie was going home and we were taking over and that was

(*From left*) Keith, Paul, Jack (who was just about to leave for home), Toby and the author at the British base in Gornji Vakuf. The UN vehicles were painted white so as not to to be mistaken for combatants' vehicles. It also made them easy targets. You might also just be able to make out the 'also available in white'-style graffiti behind the back wheel, which reads 'knob'. At this stage, spirits were still pretty high.

A factory next to the British base in Gornji Vakuf. This was once used as a makeshift hospital by the Muslims and had suffered repeated artillery attacks from the Croat forces. In the foreground is a Warrior armoured personnel carrier on guard duty.

A Warrior APC at the British Base in Gornji Vakuf. The damage to the building was caused by Croat mortar and artillery fire; the same stuff we enjoyed on our first night in GV.

Kevin with the Norwegian Bell 412 on the helipad at Tuzla. It was this helo that flew us in when we covered the breaking of the Maglaj pocket and had to try to evade a SAM lock-on. One hell of a ride.

A UN armoured convoy taking a break on the way to Zepce. Whenever you stopped in or near built-up areas, the kids were never far away. We all kept bags of sweets in the vehicles to hand out. Somehow they managed to keep smiles on their faces.

The author having a brew and a smoke in Zepce. Now a ghost town, domestic and personal items were left untouched in the houses in the rush to escape the most brutal extremes of ethnic cleansing. The pet dog got left behind.

Nearly all the bridges of the Neretva which ran through Mostar had been sabotaged. This had been done with a high degree of precision and expertise and, like the destruction of the city's buildings, without the use of air power.

Soviet-designed D30 artillery gun, now owned and controlled by the Muslims. Although this one was located at one of the UN checkpoints, it was positioned and bedded in, ready to cover likely Croat troop movements in the event of an emergency.

Toby, in front of what would once have been a quiet residential scene. The flooding was a result of the water mains having been blown; an effective way of closing areas down and forcing people out. Those who lived in these pockets had long ago got used to having to drink water direct from the river.

The dividing line. The author on the dead ground between the two factions. Although unseen in the photo, you knew that many sets of eyes were following your actions – and that any of them could belong to snipers. The buildings, although beyond repair, were often the only protection from the elements that the locals had.

A home-made Muslim tank covering the approaches into Mostar. An excellent example of the ingenuity shown by the Muslims in the face of far better equipped opposition. The armour plating is simply made up of sheets of metal welded to the sides. Unlike a proper tank, this contraption's only real armament was a medium machine-gun welded to the top.

No man's land in Mostar, an area normally covered by snipers from both factions and troops occupying concealed positions. The tents were in preparation for the area's use as a checkpoint for families' day. The devastation is the sort normally only seen as the result of intensive aerial bombing.

The author (*right*) and Keith, on the Croat side of Mostar the day before the big fall-back. The tape barriers were to protect the unwary against landmines and booby traps, which still riddled the remains of the buildings on the front line.

An armed UN convoy on the route through the mountains between Split and GV. Although it was kept open by the Royal Engineers, the sheer drops on either side, the sharp U-turns and the wet slushy surface made for a less than relaxing driving experience.

A Royal Navy Sea Harrier FRS 1 of the kind shot down by a Serb SAM over Gorazde. This picture was taken over Split in Croatia. The yellow band that can be seen at the front of the 1,000lb bomb, visible underneath the jet, indicates it's live and armed, should it be necessary to use it. (© Neil Mercer)

Fergie. The last picture I got of him, taken on training in the Middle East before our deployment to Bosnia.

that. Besides, we're trained to jump into another man's shoes at the drop of a hat. It's an attitude thing. There's no debate about it. You just make it happen.

I leaped into his Land Rover and we headed back towards the city. We drove along the front line, sticking to the Croat side. I tried to follow the course of the demarcation line, but it was not especially clear. This, Reggie explained, was because in the town itself the front zigzagged in and out of neighbouring houses with baffling complexity. In certain cases, there might be Muslims in the loft and Croats in the basement across the street. Mapping these positions, Reggie said, was difficult.

Over the course of the next two hours, Reggie gave me the full Cook's tour. He showed me where the bridges were, the positions of the weapon-inspection points we had to monitor and a long stretch of road where they'd had a lot of trouble over the past ten days from a lone Croat sniper. Every time a UN vehicle passed down the road, this guy had a pot at it. It was Reggie's belief that he wasn't deliberately trying to hit these vehicles but that he was probably bored out of his skull and just having a bit of fun. But each time, he maintained, the bullet strikes would get a little closer. On the face of it, this suggested that the sniper had great ability, backed by supreme confidence. But sniping was a highly precise art, dependent on a range of factors, many of which were unpredictable. A perfect shot over a distance as great as this was the result of a number of things coming together in a way that the marksman had to understand intuitively. A minor mistake in computing the bullet's ballistic arc or a failure to account for wind-drift could make all the difference between a bit of fun and a guy receiving a high-velocity slug through his guts.

'Why don't you take him out?' I asked.

'Because the UN would never agree to it. Even if they did, by the time we'd be close to getting the green light this guy would be long gone. He's a wily bastard, Cammy. He knows what he's doing. It'd take a concerted effort just to find him. We don't have the time and he knows that. Besides, the Spanish are pretty pathetic. They're out of this place in a couple of weeks and won't do anything that smacks remotely of risk.'

We pulled up at the beginning of a straight stretch of road. Reggie slipped the Land Rover into neutral and produced a pair of binoculars. He pointed to a large block of bombed-out flats five hundred metres away. That, he said, was where the sniper's position was. I did a quick scan with the binos, but could see nothing. There were perhaps a hundred shattered windows from which the Croat could conduct his work. I saw what Reggie meant.

'The problem is,' he continued, 'this is an essential route between the SF base and the front lines. If you don't use it, the detour takes a lot longer. For the Spanish, it's a foregone conclusion. They take the detour. But then, like I said, they don't really give a toss what happens here. Which really puts the ball pretty firmly in our court.'

He slipped the Land Rover into gear and we headed out on to Sniper Highway. Reggie maintained a steady pace, holding the speed at about 30 m.p.h. If the guy was going to shoot, there was no sense making things difficult for him.

Fifty metres passed, then another fifty. Half-way across and still nothing happened. Finally, we were in the clear and out of range. I breathed a sigh of relief. Reggie relaxed his grip on the wheel.

I glanced at him, saying nothing.

He stared back sheepishly. 'Straight up. I swear, Cammy. The guy is out there. Take my word for it.'

If it hadn't been for the expression on his face, I could have sworn that this was one of Reggie's wind-ups.

We drove back in silence for some early scoff. Our duties proper would start at first light the following morning. First thing, we had to meet the faction commanders, check out a weapon-inspection point, then go introduce ourselves to the Spaniards.

Things were popping at last.

I would have liked to attend both of the daily meetings between the UKLO and the commanders of the two warring factions, but it rapidly became clear that this was impossible. The river Neretva split Mostar pretty much down the middle. There were two bridges linking east and west, but these were so dilapidated that taking a vehicle over them was not an option. Walking between the two factions' HQs every morning was also out of the question – the distance was too far – as was staggering the meeting times. That left one last alternative: we'd have to split the patrol down the middle, one half dealing with the Muslims, the other with the Croats. It was agreed that Keith and Doug would take the Croats and Paul and I the BiH.

And so it was that on our first full day in Mostar, I found myself with Reggie a short walk from the Muslim HQ in the eastern part of the city. We parked up in a bomb-site. Loose bricks, pieces of pipe and bits of rusty corrugated iron were scattered all around the place. A group of kids were kicking an old tin-can nearby as we set off in the direction of the HQ. As I looked back, I could see markings on the ground around the Land Rover. To my surprise, I realized this *had* been a car-park before the war. Ours was the only vehicle there. Looking at the kids, I wondered if it'd be there when we got back. Reggie reassured me that no child would be stupid enough to nick a car from under the nose of the BiH corps commander for the Mostar region. I forced myself to relax.

The meeting ahead was critical. The BiH commander had established a good relationship with Reggie over the previous two weeks and it was important that I got on with him, too. I felt like I was coming to pay my respects to some local Mafia *capo*. Keith was on a parallel mission on the other side of the divide with one of Reggie's muckers as escort. Dougie and Paul were back at the *basha* rigging up the comms and generally sorting out our shit.

We dived into a back-street, with Reggie setting a brisk pace. After fifty metres, he took a right, then almost as quickly a left. We passed by dark doorways and under clothes-lines dripping with grey, wet washing. I tried to mark the route by noting little details. I spotted a burst water-main, logged it in my mind as a suitable way-point, then, almost as quickly, discarded it. By tomorrow, the damned thing could have been repaired. I needed to pick my landmarks more carefully. I made a mental note to ask Reggie to walk the route again to cement it in my mind. The place was a maze and I wouldn't be happy until I knew it like the back of my hand. Right now, I couldn't see when that would ever be.

After ten minutes of ducking and diving, we stood in front of a shell of a building, nothing atypical by Mostar's standards. The only indication that it might have some kind of military significance was the two sentries who stood just inside the open doorway. Look a little closer and you saw sandbags shoring up the inside. I wondered about that, then concluded that putting them on the outside was an open invitation to having them nicked. I was catching on to the crazed logic of Bosnia's looking-glass world.

One of the soldiers stopped me and asked for my ID; they waved Reggie straight through. Once they were satisfied that I was who my papers said I was, Reggie and I climbed a set of rickety stairs and found ourselves in what I imagine a dentist's waiting room might have looked like in England during the war. Dim light spilled from a bare low-watt bulb in the centre of the peeling ceiling. There was chicken wire on the inside of the window to catch the bigger shards of glass in case the place got mortared. Inside a main military headquarters you expect to see files, phones, maps and noticeboards. The only concession to officialdom, however, was a manual typewriter on a table by a door that led into the commander's office. From outside, I could hear the put-put sound of an overworked generator.

The door opened and the commander's aide walked in. 'General Kislic will see you in a minute,' he said, looking at Reggie.

Then, the staff officer turned to me. 'You must be Spence. Welcome to East Mostar, Sergeant.'

We shook hands curtly. The Muslim never offered his name, though the pips on his shoulder denoted him as a colonel. He looked like a hard son-of-a-bitch, probably no more than thirty and likely to be the veteran of a dozen hand-to-hand battles. I knew Reggie had booked this appointment the day before and warned them about me. It was supposed to give both sides a chance to get to know each other.

The aide gave me the once-over. I was wearing a light blue UN baseball cap, but was otherwise dressed pretty much as I had throughout Bosnia – normal fatigues covered by a long green Arctic parka. Without warning, the aide reached out and slapped my chest with the flat of his hand.

'No body armour, Sergeant? Perhaps you are visiting Mostar as a tourist.'

I looked at Reggie. He wasn't wearing body armour either. None of us in the UKLO did. This was in stark contrast to regular UN soldiers for whom Kevlar plates about the upper body were standard. We took the decision that body armour would send the wrong message as we went about our work. If the locals couldn't afford it, or had chosen to reject it, then we wouldn't wear it either.

I smiled. 'I knew I'd forgotten something when I left for work this morning.'

A momentary flash of doubt passed behind his eyes, then I think he realized I was kidding. He didn't seem amused by my stab at levity. I couldn't say I blamed him – as jokes went, it was pretty piss-poor.

'Then, tell me, Sergeant, did you forget to bring your pistol also?'

I wasn't sure where this was heading. This time, I gave him a dead straight answer. 'No. That goes with me everywhere.'

'Then I'm afraid I must ask you to remove it before you enter General Kislic's office. Of course you can pick it up again on the way out.' He turned to Reggie. 'As your colleague will tell you, this is the custom in Bosnia. When you are ready, please enter the general's office.' And then he about-faced, closing the door behind him.

'What the fuck was all that about?' I asked Reggie, who was already removing his gun-belt. 'Do they think we're going to slot the guy or something?'

'Bah, take no notice, mate. It's just psych-games. I went through the same ritual when I first arrived.'

'Don't these bastards realize they'd be dead without the UN? From everything I've seen so far, they need us a fuck of a sight more than we need them.'

'Forget it, Cammy. It's a macho thing, mate, a sign of respect. That's all.'

I did as he said and removed my gun, placing it on the table beside the typewriter. The issue riled me more than I should have let it. If this was the way of things in Bosnia, then I could see we'd have a problem here. I was beginning to understand how these people worked. It wasn't just the Muslims, it was the whole bang lot of them. Today it was a pistol, tomorrow it'd be a weapon-inspection point or a vital section of the front lines we were supposed to map.

There was a subtle game afoot here of master and servant, a game in which respect was all. If we lost that respect, we were in trouble. Like a new teacher before a class full of unruly fourteen-year-olds, we were being probed for our weaknesses. Blink, and we'd lose it. Things had to change here. If they didn't, there was a good chance we were all headed for an almighty showdown. Mostar was already on a knife-edge. None of us could afford to let it slide an inch either way.

We knocked and entered. The general's office was much like his anteroom. The only piece of furniture was his desk across the room from us. On this was an in-tray with a few bits of paper in it and an old telephone.

The general was sitting at his chair, attending to some paperwork. He did not look up as we entered. Though his head was bowed, I could see from his hands that he was young, probably in his late thirties. He was much slighter than I'd imagined, with sloping shoulders and a marked stoop in his neck. It seemed as if the weight of responsibility for the defence of Mostar had physically borne down on his appearance and half crushed him. His aide hovered just behind his right shoulder, his eyes darting between Reggie and me. He looked like the general's hunting bird, watching, listening, waiting.

When the general lifted his head at last, I could see that he wore a pair of schoolmasterly horn-rimmed spectacles. The image was not what I had expected. In the British Army, at the height of the Cold War, a corps commander in Germany might have had fifty thousand troops under his authority. This bloke probably had fewer than eight thousand, most of them old men.

The general got to his feet and we shook hands. He was softly spoken and courteous to a fault. His English was impeccable.

We spoke about what I'd been doing since I'd arrived in theatre (I told him the truth, but fudged over the Maglaj operation) and what I hoped to achieve in Mostar. I got the feeling that the gun issue was not of his making, but something that had been engineered by his minions. This guy had much deeper things on his mind. He looked like he'd lived his life already and was now just seeing to the loose ends. He was the saddest bloke I'd ever seen.

I told him that we'd need to continue the mapping operation

with all due haste if we were to meet the deadline for the signing and the subsequent handback of land. It was now 6 April. The signing was due on the twelfth, the land-swap the following day. It was tight, and with Reggie going, I knew I couldn't afford to have my authority tested.

'Any help you need, Sergeant . . . Please, my door is always open.' He rose to shake hands. Behind him, his aide continued to watch me.

Reggie and I picked up our sidearms and kept walking.

As we twisted and turned through the side-alleys back to our Land Rover, I knew that the general was someone with whom I could do business. What worried me was the world of lawlessness that existed between him and the front line. In the back of my mind, a small voice told me that this was where the Mostar mapping operation would stand or fall.

In the afternoon, Reggie took me to a weapon-inspection point, one of two we had to monitor in East Mostar.

The inspection process was more complicated and barmy than I'd first realized. Part of the agreement between the Bosnian Croats and the Muslims covered the removal of heavy weapons from the battlefield. Both sides refused to allow the weapons to be placed under UN control, but conceded that they could be taken out of the front line and positioned in recognized areas. These could then be inspected daily by UN monitoring teams. The weapons, which on the Muslim side were mostly big mortars, were literally primed and ready to go. In some cases, they even had a round up the spout. All were angled deliberately towards the nearest Croat position.

It was our job not just to make sure that the requisite number of weapons were there but to check off serial numbers, too. It would have been all too easy for the Muslims to have maintained the quota of weapons at the inspection points, but to have swapped some of the more modern ones there for knackered systems kept back covertly in the field. It was a tedious job, but an essential component of the fragile peace process.

By late afternoon, there was only one thing left to do, Reggie told me, and that was for me to go press the flesh of the SPANBAT commander. Reggie had already told me that the Spanish were next to useless, but it was still vital that we maintained good co-operative links. They didn't quite know what to make of us because we were Rose's men, his eyes and ears, yet none of us carried more senior rank than sergeant. Given half a chance, their officers wouldn't even have acknowledged our presence, but they knew, too, that it didn't pay to piss off the UNPROFOR commander. As a result, both camps maintained an uneasy co-existence, not helped by the fact that the Spaniards were de-mob happy. This explained the rows of UN vehicles I'd seen outside the motel, the only watering-hole for miles. In two weeks' time, this lot were due to be relieved by some other Spanish regiment. In their minds, they were already out of Mostar. None of them wanted to get taken out by some rogue sniper in their last days of active duty. They were going home and couldn't have given a monkey's about the place.

Reggie had arranged to meet the SPANBAT commander at eight. We turned up and reported to his adjutant, a thin, immaculately pressed individual, who fluttered around us with the nervous energy of a trapped songbird. We reminded him about the appointment and were greeted with a cluck of annoyance and a shrug of the shoulders, body language that signalled, in no uncertain terms, OK, but only if you insist.

Twenty minutes later there was still no sign of our being called in to see the commander. The adjutant breezed past us nervously again and this time we collared him. We were trying to be polite – I think I even saluted him when we first met – but it was hard, really hard. I got the feeling he hadn't even told the commander we were there.

Faced with two pissed-off looking individuals, however, he

gave a shrug of resignation and said, 'Oh, he'll see you. But he's really very busy. You'll only have two or three minutes with him, I'm afraid. You must understand that there are many demands upon the colonel's time . . .'

Reggie and I followed him in. The commander was sitting at his desk, spooning something that looked like risotto into his mouth off an immaculate bone-china plate. It was like standing in front of an overly comfortable hippopotamus. Like everything else about this man, his desk was big. There were three phones on it. People were running in and out like bit-part players in a French farce.

The commander raised his dark, leaden eyes, clocked us, then went back to his plate. He mopped up the remaining juices with a piece of bread, dabbed at the corners of his mouth with a napkin, then barked something loud and guttural into the ether. Two privates burst into the room and jostled for position. Each wanted to be the first to remove his plate. This guy shouted, 'Jump!' and everyone wanted to know how high.

When we were alone, the commander pushed the interval for as long as he dared before addressing us. Reggie did the introductions and I, in turn, did my best to be civil. I told him I looked forward to working with him as my first full day in Mostar had told me there was a lot to do.

'Actually,' the hippopotamus replied, in a rich Spanish Hollywood accent, 'there's not a lot for you to do around here, Sergeant Spence. I think you will agree that we have it all very much under control. You can tell that to General Rose – personally, from me.'

Behind him, the nervy little adjutant beamed. I thought he was about to break out into spontaneous applause.

Reggie and I made our excuses soon afterwards and left.

'You can see why I'm not exactly gutted to be leaving this place,' he said, as we strolled back to our *basha*. 'All I can do is wish you all the best of British, mate.'

After a quick break for food, I got on the satcom to GV. As nightly sceds went, it was pretty routine. I told Kev about the weapon inspection, and the meeting with the Muslim commander. I mentioned that the Spanish might become problematical the closer we got to the wire. I told him, too, that Keith had established contact with the Croat side and that this meeting had gone well. The next day, we would familiarize ourselves with the front-line positions on both sides, ready to begin the mapping operation the day after.

Kev, in turn, had a couple of pieces of news for me. The Serbs had launched an attack on Gorazde's outermost defences and had breached them in several key areas. A number of villages had fallen and refugees were heading in from the country towards the town. This had accelerated General Rose's efforts to enter Gorazde. He was due to try to visit the enclave tomorrow, with Charlie's patrol as his escort. Negotiations with the Serbs were ongoing as they spoke. They were likely to go deep into the night.

I asked Kev if the Serb attack was an all-out assault or some kind of probing mission. He didn't know. Nobody knew. There was a long silence between us. An image of Crusha permeated my tired mind. I suspected Kev was wrestling with some similar vision. Neither of us, I knew, wanted to believe that the UN's colossal intelligence operation in Bosnia had just been outdone by a school-teacher from Split.

'Let me know if anything big develops,' I said. And then I hung up.

In the morning, I checked in with the Muslim corps commander and picked up my escort for my visit down to the front lines. He was a serious-looking bloke, an officer called Mohamed, who told me he'd been fighting the Serbs and Croats for as long as he could remember. That turned out to be the past two years, a period that seemed to qualify as a lifetime in Bosnia.

Mohamed's family were all dead. His grandparents, mother, father, young brother and baby sister had all been burned alive in the cellar of their house. Witnesses said the Croats knew what they were doing when they poured petrol down the coal chute and tossed a match after it. Mohamed had only been saved because he was studying late at school that day. He was nineteen, but looked thirty-five.

We drove to the centre of the city in silence, only speaking when we had to negotiate the various checkpoints. We got as close as we could, then parked up and walked. I rounded a street corner and thought I'd been transported back in time to Stalingrad.

The houses at the front had all been turned into bombed-out shells, but I was used to that. If you can imagine a street of terraced houses, then join those houses together by an intricate network of rat-runs, that was the essential framework on which everything was built. Every single position, be it the front room of a house, a loft or a basement, had a fall-back position. The gaps between houses were filled with long, deep fire-trenches. Where a hole had been blasted through by shell-fire, it had been plugged with firing ramparts, turning whole streets into the walls of some medieval fortress. Each position was linked at ground level, but more than likely it had other connecting points, too. A firing position on an upper floor would usually connect with another in the house next door via the rafters. The same was true of the cellars, most of which were linked by tunnels chiselled through the earth; they also made extensive use of the sewer network.

The British Army trains to fight this way using a method called FIBUA – Fighting In Built-up Areas. It is one of the hardest things a soldier can learn, especially if he is the attacker. A defender who fights from room to room and house to house always has the advantage.

The Muslims had elevated FIBUA to an art form. The entire

front line was a carefully crafted maze. Know your way through it and it'd save your life. Stumble into it and it was like trying to get out of the labyrinth with the fucking Minotaur breathing down your neck. The only way it might have been improved upon, I thought, donning my strategist's hat, was by blocking off certain routes to create funnels into which the enemy could be drawn then ambushed. Better still, if this technique could be supplemented with booby-traps. I asked Mohamed about this, but he shook his head. I got the impression they didn't have the raw materials to make them.

He warned me about mines and snipers, though. Where they couldn't plug a gap in the defences, they mined it instead. None of these would be marked – standard practice in a war-zone. For this reason, Mohamed told me to stay close. A wrong turn and it could be my last. I began to realize why it was that the Spanish never set foot down here.

The men occupying these positions lived in them all the time. Since they were never sure when an attack might come, they could not move. Several told me they'd been here for over a year. Many had lost entire families in the fighting; all of them had lost someone, Mohamed said.

It told in their eyes. It was a look not helped by their subterranean existence: I hadn't ever seen such white skin. White isn't descriptive enough: it's the colour of the belly of a lake fish that lives its entire life among the roots of rushes, away from the light.

Every so often along the front there'd be a bunker, a holding area for the troops while they weren't squinting down the sights of a rifle at the Croats in the house two doors away. Here, the old men would congregate and shoot the shit while oiling and re-oiling their weapons. At their time of life, they should have been sitting in front of a fire, dandling grandkids on their knees. As there were no mites left to dandle, cradling an AK was the only alternative in East Mostar.

As I walked through these positions, Mohamed leading the way with a candle, I could see that no two blokes were kitted out the same. It was much like the situation on the surface during our drive from the ferry, only here it was like being in the company of the undead. The stink of men who haven't changed their clothes for months, especially in the confines of an airless bunker, is something else. It's enough to bring tears to your eyes.

The key to the mapping operation wasn't so much the plotting of the trenches and the forward positions, it was sussing out where these holding positions were and how many men each contained. You knew a holding area when you came across one. They were basic, but unmistakable: there'd be an old sofa, a makeshift bed or two, an upturned crate for a table, several bottles of slivovitz on it and a couple of candles. Some of the more sophisticated ones had cooking and washing facilities.

I was especially vigilant for evidence of any heavy weapons on the front line, as this would be in direct contravention of the ceasefire. Either they were bloody good at hiding them, though, or they were all accounted for at the inspection points. The heaviest weapons I saw were rocket-propelled grenades.

I made a point of stopping in each holding area and, through Mohamed, chatting to the occupants. They told me that most of these positions had changed hands several times during the fighting. To fight so bitterly over a few yards of turf seemed every bit as senseless as any of the myriad insanities of the First World War, unless, of course, you lived here.

During these bonding sessions, both Keith and I got the distinct impression that these people desperately wanted peace. The problem was the mistrust that existed on both sides after the years of war. Each side questioned the other's commitment to honouring the ceasefire. They couldn't believe the old enemy was someone you could ever do business with.

In this, Keith and I knew that the day of the withdrawal

would be the day when it could all turn to rat-shit. The draft terms of the Muslim–Croat peace agreement said that each side had to withdraw its forces at least a hundred metres from present positions. As for the centre of Mostar, this was to be cleared of troops and weapons, becoming, in effect, a demilitarized zone. Civilians would then be permitted to return to their former homes. The remainder of the front line out in the country would be characterized by a 200-metre-wide buffer zone. In time, it was hoped, this military no man's land would permit tempers to cool sufficiently for the fronts themselves to be dismantled. Then everybody could go home.

The problem with this scenario was what might happen if trust broke down. It would be all too easy for one side simply to advance into the vacated positions of the other on the day of the withdrawal. The only way we would stop this was by maintaining the faith and spreading the gospel. If there was the merest smidgen of suspicion on either side about the other's intentions, then the entire sector would blow – I had little doubt of that. It was a concern that we all carried with us wherever we went. The trick was in somehow not letting it show. The holding areas were critical because they contained the biggest concentration of troops. If we could push these back, we could remove a great deal of latent mistrust.

At the same time, we had to convince the two parties that they had to reduce the numbers of men within each holding area. Because of the relative strategic values of these positions, both the Muslims and the Croats would do anything to stop us finding them. Whenever I asked about the nearest holding area to the point in the front line where I happened to be, they'd always try it on. A typical exchange went something like this.

'He says the next holding area is four houses away,' Mohamed would say, mimicking the sincerity on the face of the bloke for whom he was translating.

'Tell him,' I'd reply with a smile, 'that I'd like to see that for myself, if he wouldn't mind.'

Somewhere between our present position and that house four doors away I'd find twenty old men armed with AK-47s and shotguns hiding out in a cellar or a loft. I never got angry at this deception. There was something so predictable about it, that it almost became endearing, a naïve game.

Along the way, however, I wanted to send the strongest of signals that they weren't dealing with amateurs here. I don't think they knew who we were – if they did, they certainly didn't let on – but they must have wondered how it was that we were up to their tricks. What I wanted to say would have given the game away in an instant: 'After the Pira, my friends, finding your hides is really a piece of piss.'

When I'd seen enough for one day, Mohamed and I started back for the Land Rover. Over the course of the past few hours, I'd noticed that he'd been getting increasingly protective of me, if that's the right word. Given our training, this was not entirely necessary, but it was a welcome sign, since it was the only real measure by which I could see that we were starting to win these people over.

Mohamed was especially concerned about the Croat snipers, who, he said, were still active in this neighbourhood. Whenever we came to an exposed area, he would indicate the direction of threat, pause to check that the coast was clear, then usher me across the fire zone. As any sniper's attention was by now drawn to the scene, the bloke who followed was exposed to the most risk. But Mohamed insisted on going second. He wouldn't have it any other way.

And so it was that when we were on the return journey I threw caution to the wind and stepped out into a clear patch of ground between two houses. All my instincts, all my training, made me want to run to the safety of the nearest shattered wall

– all that was standing of the house across the way. But I stood my ground and stopped.

'My God, Cammy, what are you doing?' Mohamed choked.

I raised my eyes to the Croat positions on the other side of the street. 'I'm just trying to get a better look at their side of the fence, mate.'

'Cammy, please,' Mohamed said, a rising note to his voice, 'step into the safety of the next house. There are Croat snipers there. They will kill you.'

I turned to him and held my hands out in a gesture of reassurance. It was actually intended to show the Croats that I was unarmed and a member of the UN. If they hadn't clocked my blue baseball cap by now, then they had to be blind. And since I was sure they could see me, I hoped they'd get the message: we had a job to do here and nothing was going to stop us doing it.

'Cammy, please,' Mohamed begged. 'Your coat, it is exactly the same colour as mine. Look.'

I stopped in mid-twirl and stared at him. My Arctic parka was damn near identical to his jacket and of the same olive hue. It was a minor, and potentially fatal, detail that had eluded me until this precise moment.

Then I swore I heard the metallic chorus of a dozen Croat bullets sliding into rifle chambers from across the street. The temptation to jump to the sanctuary of the next house was overwhelming, but I fought it. Somehow, I managed to find some reserve of discipline and stepped slowly and deliberately into the safe zone.

When I turned I saw, to my horror, Mohamed breezing across the same stretch of open land, calm as you like.

'What did you do that for?' I asked him, as soon as he had made it.

'What is good for you, my friend, is good for me,' he said.

'*Allahu akbar, huwa al-azeem.*' God is great, he is Mighty. 'He will provide for me.'

'And me?' I queried.

'Ah, my friend, you have General Rose on your side. This is almost as good.'

For all his persuasive qualities as a soldier and leader, General Rose had been prevented from getting into Gorazde the previous day, following his protracted negotiations with the Serbs. He had turned back towards Sarajevo with instructions from Radovan Karadzic, the Bosnian-Serb leader, to try to arrange a meeting with the Bosnian Army commander, General Rasim Delic, to discuss a cessation of hostilities along the entire Muslim–Serb war front in Bosnia.

The official version expressed by Ratko Mladic, the chief of the Bosnian-Serb Army, was that the UNPROFOR commander would have to postpone his visit to the enclave for 'security reasons'. Quite what this meant was unclear at the time, although it rapidly became obvious over the course of the next few days.

By way of compensation, and pending the resolution of a ceasefire on the broader front, the Serbs told Rose that they would stop shelling the city, but reports from the handful of UNMOs *in situ* said that there were still rounds incoming. The Serbs maintained that most of these were *outgoing* rounds from Muslim weapons within the city. It was a confused picture.

The truth needed to be told, Rose told the Serbs. It was, he said, just as much in their interest as it was in the UN's that the real story of Gorazde got out.

Caught on the horns of this moral dilemma, the Serbs had no choice but to agree to Rose's suggestion that a small party of 'liaison officers' in the UNPROFOR commander's party, experienced UN soldiers who could tell the difference between an incoming and an outgoing artillery round, should be allowed into the enclave. Rose may have lost the public-relations battle to get into Gorazde, but he'd secured another key objective: at long last, the SAS was headed for the besieged pocket.

That was the theory, anyhow. That night, the night before my visit to the front-line positions in East Mostar, three UN Land Rovers stopped at a little guest-house in Serb-held territory just outside Gorazde. In command was Charlie, with six good men under his wing: Nick, the D Squadron rupert who'd first briefed us in GV, Glen, the highly competent D Squadron sergeant I'd met up with briefly in Maglaj, and then the rest of our A Squadron troop – Dave, Fergie, Toby and Ray. Also with them was a UNMO, a Canadian called Carl, who turned out to be a great guy – he could down half a pint of slivovitz and still hold it all together. In most people's eyes, this was something worthy of respect.

At the hotel, the Serbs started to play their favourite game: mind-fucking. While outwardly they played the genial hosts, dishing out slivovitz like there was no tomorrow, they had clearly decided to try to prevent Rose's liaison officers from entering the city. Maybe they thought that, without Rose around, the UN party would shrug its shoulders and bugger off. If this was so, they hadn't counted on Charlie, who argued convincingly and persuasively that there would be dire consequences for the BSA if it was to go back on its word. The Serbs seemed to get the point.

As a result, the following morning – this morning – Charlie and the lads took the scenic route into Gorazde. They drove down from the high ground to the north-east, manoeuvring their way through the Serb lines, under escort, towards the main bridge on the east side of the city. Along the way, the patrol paid a heavy price: half of their medical supplies were taken as 'payment' by the Serbs for the privilege of safe passage.

Every member of the Regiment goes into battle with a 'giving set' in his belt kit, which consists of a litre bag of saline fluid, a tube with a needle that punches into the bag, a valve for regulating the flow and a needle-cum-plastic-sheath arrangement that sticks into the vein. If a guy gets hit, is losing a lot of blood then goes into shock, you've got a problem, as any medico will tell you. The blood tends to 'pull' into the torso and the result is that it's damned hard to find a vein. Leave it long enough and the veins in his legs and arms will collapse altogether. Israeli special forces overcome this problem with a simple remedy: when they're headed for a serious combat zone, something like a hostage-rescue situation, they 'pre-drip' themselves with needles and tubes already taped to their bodies. It's a drastic solution but effective, since the moment they're hit, their colleagues don't have to faff around. They simply plug a saline bag into a connector and get squeezing. I once had to cut down into the thigh of a man to try to find a workable vein in a body racked with shock and ended up with the thing slithering around between my thumb and forefinger while another guy tried to stick a needle into it. Regrettably, we were too late. The guy was already dead.

The Serbs prized the 'giving sets'. For the patrol, their loss was a major pisser.

At the bridge, the final checkpoint, there was another hiatus. The Serbs turned over their identity papers, weaponry and equipment in one last bid to find a reason not to let them into the city. Just at the point when Charlie thought they were going to be turned back for the hell of it, their hosts of the previous evening tapped him on the shoulder and told him to go, just go. They had finally relented.

Charlie scrambled into the lead vehicle before the Serbs changed their minds again. Just as he was about to lead the convoy across the bridge, the senior officer of his Serb escort stopped him. 'You should know, Charlie, that Gorazde is not going to be a good place to be in the coming days.'

Charlie looked at him levelly. 'But the ceasefire . . .'

'Ah, yes,' the Serb said, studying the clear blue sky above their heads. 'The ceasefire . . .'

Charlie waited for an answer, but the Serb did not seem inclined to provide one. A hundred metres ahead, on the other side of the bridge, the Muslims, seeing the UN party lining up to advance, began to remove the mines from the roadway around their own checkpoint.

Charlie saw his chance and went for it. The three Land Rovers charged helter-skelter from Serbian-held territory into the confines of the city. They drove directly to a bank in the middle of Gorazde, which the three UNMOs already there had taken as their headquarters.

That night, as preparations continued to try to get the Serbs and the Muslims around the peace table, the UN in Sarajevo put out its own upbeat view on the situation.

'Our assessment,' a spokesman said, 'is that Gorazde is not in any danger of falling.'

EIGHT

April 8 started normally enough, and by nightfall, even, it still appeared normal – if you judged it, that is, by the standards of a place in which law and order, decency and honour have next to no meaning. But looking back, with all the benefit of hindsight and history, it was a day like no other in Central Bosnia.

In East Mostar everything was quiet. It was my last chance to pick Reggie's brains, as he and most of his party, plus Dougie, would be pulling out in the afternoon, ready to return to Hereford. One D Squadron bloke was to stay behind, a young rupert called Adrian, who would be on hand to assist Keith in his mapping operation on the Croat side of the lines.

As Reggie and I drove towards our daily morning meeting with the Muslim corps commander in the centre of the city, I tuned into my little short-wave radio and listened to the BBC World Service. Late the previous night, General Rose had secured a twenty-four-hour ceasefire between the Muslims and the Serbs and was now engaged in some desperate shuttle diplomacy between General Delic, the BiH commander, and General Mladic, his BSA counterpart, to make it last. Though there were reports of isolated shelling incidents in Bihac and Gorazde, for the most part it looked as if the truce was holding. Once again, Rose seemed to be working his magic.

But unknown to him or us, the cogs of the Serbian war-machine, having had a night's respite, were once more gearing up for action. Unnoticed by Nato reconnaissance, Serb tanks were rumbling into position on the steep ridge-lines to the north and east of Gorazde. BSA gun crews, having enjoyed a lull in their activities, now had a fearsome fresh stock of shells in place beside their weapons on the hills overlooking the city. BSA troops and Bosnian Serb irregulars, including much-feared Cetnik partisans, sat in their trenches checking and rechecking their weapons prior to the signal many knew they were about to receive.

Whatever was happening on the peace front in and around Sarajevo, someone somewhere in the Bosnian Serb stronghold of Pale had decided that this was the day that Gorazde would be taken in the name of the Serbian Republic of Bosnia-Herzegovina.

But fate had a surprise up its sleeve for these bastards.

By the end of the day, Serb guns would claim another casualty. As injuries went, it wasn't even that big a deal; and it certainly wasn't life-threatening. But it would be this casualty – out of all the tens of thousands that had occurred in the Balkans since the war had begun – that would change the course of things in Gorazde once and for all; and perhaps, even, the course of the wider conflict as well.

As Reggie and I went about our duties, our minds weren't focused on the big picture. With the countdown to the deadline for the withdrawal, things were hairy enough where we were, at ground-zero in East Mostar. Once more, we drove down the road that Reggie had identified earlier as the haunt of a persistent Croat sniper, and once more he looked a little sheepish when the pot-shot he'd been expecting never happened. We drove back to the *basha*, satisfied that everything was ready for the plotting operation to begin the next day, and sat down at the table together for the last time, for a final group feed.

'Well, mate, thanks to all the good work D Squadron's put in around here, looks like you bastards are going to clean up on all the glory,' Reggie said, between mouthfuls of stew. This was something Dougie had prepared from a delicate Glaswegian recipe handed down to him by his mother.

'Well, I'll make sure I send you some of my fucking medals,' Keith said.

'Mmm, Dougie,' Paul chimed in, 'you've been hiding your light under a bushel, mate.'

'How's that?' Doug asked suspiciously.

'This food, it's . . . very, very interesting.'

'If that's the best you can manage, you fuckin' heathen, then 'tis as well I'm heading for a place where my talents are appreciated,' the Great Scots Git said.

We would miss him.

We lined up to see them off at about three o'clock. No sooner had they gone than Paul and I headed back to the east side of town and Keith to the west. We wanted to drive around just to familiarize ourselves with the place – our first opportunity to do this on a solo basis – before the critical mapping job began the next day.

When I got back that night, I went over to see the Spanish at the SF base. I needed to be sure I could count on their full support for tomorrow's operation. On my way into the adjutant's office, I noticed a bunch of officers crowded round a TV set. I heard the CNN reporter mention Gorazde. 'What's happened?' I asked the adjutant.

'You haven't heard?' he said. He wore the slightly satisfied look of a man who knew something you didn't.

I fought to control my annoyance. 'Heard what?'

'It would seem that one of your men got hit today. In Gorazde. General Rose has sent some of you UKLO people there, I think, yes?'

I stared at the television, but the story had moved on. Instead,

I about-turned and legged it back to the *basha*. Within moments, I was on the horn to G V. I spoke to James. 'What's all this shit about one of the boys getting hurt in Gorazde?' I asked.

'It's true, mate – but listen, from what we can gather, it's not serious. It's Ray. He picked up some fragment from a shell that exploded close to where he was standing. It's not even a Casevac job. He's going to carry on.'

'Bloody hell, James. What happened to the ceasefire?'

'What ceasefire?' James asked laconically. 'It all went for a fucking ball of chalk, didn't it?'

'I thought the pocket was supposed to be reasonably calm,' I pressed. Calm by Bosnian standards, at least.

There was a long pause. For a moment, I thought we'd lost the sat-link.

'Let's just say it's getting interesting,' James replied.

I hung up. What I'd heard had just given me real cause for concern – not for Ray, it was pretty obvious that he was going to live. A small part of me, I think, was even a little bit jealous that things were hotting up for Charlie's patrol. This, after all, was what we had all passed Selection for, the chance for action.

What worried me was James's choice of words just before he'd signed off.

I wondered just what the hell was going on in Gorazde.

It turned out that things had been 'interesting' for Charlie and his patrol since they'd crossed into the city. It happened that their arrival coincided with one of the few lulls in the fighting since the Serb siege had begun. Soon afterwards, though, things got back to normal again. It was almost as if the city hadn't known how to handle the interlude because war was the devil it knew.

Having checked out the bank, the seven men set about unpacking their kit. As an HQ, it wasn't ideal, but it was workable. Besides, in a city that had been half razed to the ground, beggars couldn't be picky.

There were twelve floors. Nothing much happened at ground level as it was glass-fronted. The third floor had space for sleeping, a big meeting room for parlays and another room that would serve as an ops centre. This was where the patrol had set up shop.

The UNMOs and UNHCR representatives mostly hung out in the basement. Here, there were cooking facilities and bedrooms, as well as a shower. It was also shelter from just about anything except a direct hit.

Three UNMOs were already established at the bank. Two of them, a Kiwi and a Frenchman, looked reliable enough. The third, an Egyptian, seemed to be on the verge of a nervous breakdown. He had been in the pocket for seven months and looking for almost as long to get out.

At four o'clock, Charlie got everyone into the meeting room for a confab. Present were the three incumbent UNMOs, plus Carl, the Canadian UNMO who'd come in with them, and the local Muslim military commander, a bloke who drove around the town in a big flash Mercedes. How he got the petrol to run the thing, nobody was quite sure.

During the meeting, the commander told Charlie that he was free to roam the city without an escort. He provided them with a couple of English-speakers, one a civvy called Misha, the other a BiH Army officer they nicknamed Mucky, who'd do their interpreting for them.

Charlie went to some pains to tell the commander that the Muslims of Gorazde had not been forgotten by the world and that the presence of the seven-man UKLO team, Rose's own men, was the proof. But the commander seemed unimpressed. The prevailing view in the city, he explained, was that if the UN had cared, it would have shown up a fuck of a sight sooner.

Things were just wrapping up, when they heard somebody pounding up the stairs. A moment later, one of the Muslim's sidekicks burst in through the door. He was fighting for breath and ashen-faced. He held a short, sharp exchange with the commander. Then, without a further word, the Muslim contingent left, leaving a motley crew of UKLOs, UNMOS, UNHCRs and interpreters.

As the sound of tramping boots receded down the stairs, Charlie turned to Fergie, who was already on his feet. There was a faintly bemused expression on his face. 'What the fuck was all that about?' Charlie asked.

'Jesus,' Fergie said. 'If I picked up half of that right, the Serbs have just fired chemicals into the southern part of the city.' He looked at the interpreters for corroboration.

Misha, the civilian, nodded grimly. 'Gas shells,' he added simply. He looked as if he was about to chuck up on the spot.

At that moment, the sound of distant shell-fire shook the outer walls. To anyone not familiar with the noise of battle, it could have passed as the first rumblings of an approaching storm.

Glen, Dave and Toby volunteered to get as close to the scene of the action as they could. They asked one of the interpreters if he'd go with them. To Misha's great credit, he never even hesitated.

They jumped into a Land Rover, stopping every so often to plot the sound of the gunfire and the explosions on the ground. According to Misha, the shells were falling in a relatively depopulated part of the city, close to the point where a footbridge crossed the river.

By the time they reached the general area, the shelling had stopped. From a patch of high ground overlooking the scene they could see several still-smoking craters close to the banks of the river Drina.

Everyone looked for the tell-tale signs of a biochemical attack – dead women clutching dead children, asphyxiated soldiers, dying rats pouring from the sewers, birds fluttering on the ground . . .

Nothing. Nothing, that was, except for a small party of soldiers slowly approaching one of the craters, then leaning over the edge for a better look. It was too far to shout a warning. Using the binos, Dave could see wisps of vapour still emanating from the crater. If they're going to die, he told the rest of the group, it'll happen in the next few seconds.

The Muslim recce team had their hands over their faces, but otherwise seemed none the worse for wear. For Glen, the senior and most experienced member of the patrol, this was the only cue he needed. The four of them legged it towards the scene.

When they got there, they realized they had no detector paper. It had not been provided because nobody had thought that Bosnia was in any danger of going chemical. That the Serbs had fired some kind of chemical shell, however, was not in dispute. From the size of the holes in the ground, the calibre of the round appeared to be 105mm. The wisps of vapour coming from the craters were definitely not caused by a white-phosphor shell, which can, at a pinch, be mistaken for an NBC round. There was a heavy chemical odour in the air and several people complained of eye irritation.

The three-man UKLO team was baffled. They thought they were probably dealing with a salvo of shells that had contained a couple of CS-gas rounds. Why the Serbs should have done this was not clear. Maybe it had been intended as another psych-trick to rattle the defenders. If that was the case, it had worked.

That night, while Charlie was on the horn to GV to report in with his first sced, the Muslims got on their radios and did their best to convince anyone who was listening that the Serbs had now resorted to NBC warfare in their barbaric and determined efforts to take Gorazde. If anyone heard, they took little notice. Bosnia had already propelled the term 'ethnic cleansing' into the living rooms of the west. After nightly horrors on television, and in a war few understood, even the prospect of chemical warfare seemed to have little impact. This, however, would *not* have been so at Nato headquarters, where any attempt by the Serbs to escalate the conflict in such a radical way would have been viewed with grave concern.

Charlie's report, based on Glen's authoritative findings at the scene of the crime, helped to calm a lot of nerves. Within hours of its arrival the U K L O team in Gorazde was earning its money. Anyone less experienced could well have been responsible for tipping an already unpredictable conflict across the chemical divide. The consequences don't even bear thinking about.

The following morning everyone split into two-man teams. Nick and Fergie jumped into a Land Rover and headed out to an area called Salihoba-Raban, where they established an observation post (O P) at the top of a television tower that gave a grandstand view of the fighting in the hills to the north.

Ray and Dave took one of the interpreters and a second vehicle out to the north-east where, in the lee of the steep hills that all but surrounded Gorazde, they monitored Bosnian-Serb shelling of Muslim positions close to some outlying hamlets.

Glen and Toby took the third vehicle to a patch of heavy fighting to the south-east. At the last minute, Charlie decided to go with them. Mucky, the military interpreter, was roped in to go, too.

After three klicks the four-man party parked up and proceeded the rest of the way on foot. They headed for a heavily defended Muslim position that seemed to be receiving a lot of attention from a Serbian tank around four kilometres to the south.

The Muslim position turned out to be an eighteen-man semi-submerged bunker built out of wooden staves and earth. The U K L O team were welcomed inside just as a salvo started to get their range. The ground shook as twenty rounds straddled their position. The roar of explosions was deafening. The lulls weren't much better. They were filled with the sound of shrapnel falling on helmets, guns and other items of exposed metal in the outlying trenches.

At the same time, across the valley, the Serb guns had zeroed in on Ray and Dave's OP. Charlie, Glen and Toby heard their two colleagues' increasingly vocal account of the shelling over the small two-way radio they'd brought with them.

Charlie decided they'd seen enough and led the others out of the position back to the Land Rover. Just as Glen was preparing to follow them, a shell whistled in and exploded against the side of the bunker. There was a shower of earth and white-hot shell fragments, but miraculously no one was hurt. Glen picked up his SA-80 and set off after Charlie and the rest of the crew with the Muslims in hot pursuit.

On the way down the ridge-line, he found himself in the company of an old man with an AK slung over his shoulder. For no reason that Glen could see, the old geezer started to laugh. Having narrowly avoided a round of 105mm, Glen found himself suddenly caught up in the joke. The pair arrived back at the Land Rover pissing themselves with laughter.

'What are you so bloody happy about?' Charlie asked him, feeling, no doubt, a little like the only bloke at a stonking good party who's left stone-cold sober.

At last Glen's laughter subsided. Slowly his composure returned. 'I don't fucking know. I'm only laughing 'cos he's laughing, boss.' He jabbed a thumb at the old man, who was now settling down on the grass verge, with his head in his hands.

Charlie whistled for the interpreter. 'Mucky, what's got into the old bloke?'

Mucky went over to speak to him. Presently he returned. Mucky was in his mid-thirties, an officer in the BiH Army, and prone to intense seriousness. 'He just witnessed his farmhouse being blown up by Serb artillery,' he announced. 'He has nothing left any more. His family are already dead.'

That killed the laughter. An awkward silence descended on

the group, broken only by the distant crump-wump of BSA artillery fire and the old man's sobbing. Then, his colleagues caught up with him and gently led him away. The three SAS men and Mucky watched them head back towards the centre of the town.

Suddenly the air crackled and a voice broke through loud and clear from a radio in the Land Rover. Charlie grabbed the set. It was Ray.

'Charlie? Are you there? Glen? Toby?' Ray's voice wavered hysterically. 'I've been hit. I've been fucking hit.'

It turned out he'd taken a shell splinter in the stomach; nothing that serious or he wouldn't have been able to speak, let alone chuck it out fifteen to the dozen. He was babbling like an idiot. 'Shut the fuck up, Ray,' Charlie yelled into his radio. 'You think I don't know what it's like? We just got fucking blattered up there ourselves. Now, tell me, nice and slow. What happened?'

Ray throttled back. 'A round went off close – I mean, real close. Dave's OK, but our interpreter's hit bad. They're shipping him back to the centre of town for treatment. I don't know if he's going to make it or not.' This turned out to be a third interpreter hired that day for the job.

'And you?'

Ray was coming down fast. His voice had just about acquired its normal pitch. 'I'm all right, boss. I'll live, I guess.'

That evening, Charlie filed his sced as usual. At RHQ in GV, his comments were noted down carefully, then committed to a report that was sent post-haste to General Rose at his forward HQ in Sarajevo. If the UNPROFOR commander needed evidence of the Serbs' double-dealing in Gorazde, then Charlie's report had it in spades. Not only were the Serbs advancing on the beleaguered pocket, one of the so-called safe havens, they were now clearly targeting the UN. One of the inescapable conclusions that Charlie had drawn from the Serbian artillery assault on Ray and Dave's position was that they had zeroed in on their white-painted Land Rover, which had been parked up nearby.

That night, General Rose contacted Yasushi Akashi, the UN special representative in the former Yugoslavia, and told him that the attack on his UKLO team in Gorazde, premeditated as it must have been, gave him clear grounds for calling in Nato close air support. He pressed Akashi to get him the permission he needed to attack. Once, previously, when a party of French UN observers found themselves under fire from the Serbs, the UN had given its authority for an air strike against the perpetrators. The attack never took place because the Serb assault was long over and the aggressors dispersed to the four winds by the time the UN had finished umming and ahhing.

This time General Rose was determined not to fall prey to the same mindless bureaucracy.

While the UN slept on it in New York, at Nato headquarters outside Brussels, planners started to plot for this very contingency.

Ray's flesh wound was about to have interesting consequences.

The following morning, the ninth, was the big one for us in Mostar. Keith, Paul, Adrian and I got up early and set out into the city to begin the mapping operation that was the vital prelude to the Muslim and Croat pull-back from the front line. Led by Mohamed, my guide, I walked through the trenches, bunkers and lofts that marked the frontal positions in the centre of the city, plotting their exact locations with the help of my hand-held GPS receiver.

Once I'd got the positions taped, co-ordinates that were accurate to the nearest half-metre or so from space, I jotted them down into a notebook from which I'd later transfer the information to a street map. Not only were we marking locations, we were also numbering the men in the trenches, paying special attention to places where they were congregated *en masse* – the so-called holding areas. Once I'd mapped the 800-metre-long front within the town, I returned to the *basha* and began transferring the data to a master-map. This would become the basis of the legal document that both parties – the Croats and the Muslims – had to agree to and sign, prior to my delivering it to GV by the morning of the eleventh.

Mapping the city centre took the best part of the morning. Everything was going so smoothly that I felt in ebullient mood. It never pays to drop your guard, though. I was in one house, shooting the shit with a bunch of old blokes, who were getting slowly stoned on slivovitz, when I happened to say to Paul, 'It's good, isn't it, this peace thing?'

An old man who'd overheard my remark got to his feet and walked over to where I was standing. He put his arm over my shoulder and took me to a firing slit in the wall of his bunker. He pointed to a house across the way. It was miraculous. All around, the ground had been pummelled by artillery fire. There wasn't a single house that hadn't been hit or half razed to the ground. Except his.

I turned to him and gave him a smile, expecting to see something of it reflected in his eyes. But they remained dull and listless. The booze, I thought.

'The day after tomorrow, when we sign with the Croats,' he said, in a gravelly voice, rich with accent, 'this house, my house, where I was born, and my father and grandfather before me, will be handed over to the Croats. And for nothing.'

He left me staring out over the wasteland. I heard him walk back to his chair and sit down. I wanted to turn, but I didn't know what to say.

Behind me, I heard the chink of bottle against glass. I realized then that this wasn't a celebration but a wake.

Shortly afterwards I made my excuses and left.

Why is it that on some days we are allowed to get away with repeating our mistakes? As someone who believes in no higher authority than the Chief of the Defence Staff, I can only conclude that it is some mechanism of nature, a warning, designed to stop today's idiots from becoming tomorrow's dead idiots.

In the afternoon, after I'd checked that things were going OK with Keith on the Croat side of the fence, Paul and I set off for the countryside to continue the operation there. If anything, the positions outside the city were easier to map as they'd run along relatively clear lines, with none of the crazy zigzagging that took place in Mostar itself. At one point, however, I ran into a problem. I was walking down a long line of trench when it suddenly stopped. About fifty metres forward of the position, I could see a parallel line of trench, running for about thirty metres or so, which then dropped back again, so that the whole thing described a sort of letter U, an unnatural kink in an otherwise blemishless straight line that continued for klicks and klicks.

It made no sense, so I called over the senior Muslim officer for this section of the lines and told him we'd have to join up the dots, so to speak, flatten out the line.

The guy wouldn't wear it. He stood his ground and made it abundantly clear that there was no way they were going to compromise on this funny little bit of salient. I tried to explain to them that if I allowed them this encroachment then I would have to make a similar concession to the Croats somewhere else. This was exactly the sort of tit-for-tat dealing that I wanted to avoid.

Still the Muslim officer shook his head.

Maybe it was lack of sleep, or perhaps it was just plain frustration at the whole Bosnian situation summed up in this single moment of intransigent bullshit, but I flipped.

'OK,' I said, gesturing to Mohamed to start translating, 'how about this? I'm going to whistle up a JCB and we'll simply bury the fucker. If the trench is filled in, it seems like you won't have a whole lot left to argue over, will you?'

I stared at the Muslim officer while Mohamed translated. I watched for his reaction. I expected him to get as angry as I had, but instead, to my embarrassment, his eyes filled with tears. He started to talk to Mohamed in a voice taut with emotion and determination. His pride had suffered and that didn't help.

'He asks me to tell you,' Mohamed said, enunciating slowly, 'that ten of his men died defending this trench during three days of fighting last winter. He wonders what these men will think of him if he gives in so quickly to your demand. He wonders what you would do, Sergeant Spence, if you were in his position.'

It hit me in the gullet. I thought back to the day when all of us, the entire patrol, had been sitting in the classroom with Crusha, mulling over our experiences of Bosnia. A decade in the SAS and I'd seen just about everything: Ireland, terrorists, a full-blown war in the Gulf . . . It had been so easy to say, and I felt justified in saying it because I had the rule-book on my side.

Don't get involved. If you find yourself in a world of shit, skate over it as best you can. Don't let it get to you. That way, you preserve your self-discipline. Maintain self-discipline, and you can get through just about anything. This is what the Regiment teaches you.

This is OK if you're fighting a war. But if you're merely a witness to its atrocities, and its insanity, you need to call on something else, some other kind of reserve. Bosnia didn't require us to be wind-up Schwarzeneggers. It demanded much more of us than that. Charlie, Fergie, Keith and Paul had got the point the moment they arrived. It had taken me a little longer.

I turned to the Muslim officer. 'Let's make sure that your men didn't die for nothing,' I told him. I paused to let Mohamed translate. 'We'll keep the trench the way it is.'

We finished the mapping operation and headed back to town. The next big hurdle was a meeting between the commanders of the two factions at the SPANBAT HQ at 1600 hours. It would be the first time the two sides had had such a meeting since hostilities began; another occasion when we'd need tact and understanding in spades if we were to damp down the tension that hung like fuel vapour in the air around us. The merest spark could set the whole thing off.

The Spanish SF base was located several miles into Croat territory. It had taken a lot just to persuade the Muslim corps commander and his deputies that the whole thing wasn't some giant Croat-UN conspiracy to wipe them off the face of the map. In the end, Paul and I said that the UKLO would take personal responsibility for the safety of the Muslim delegation for as long as it was in the enemy's backyard. It was a pretty worthless reassurance, however: we would have been powerless to have stopped a Croat splinter group, or even a lone guy with an RPG, from taking out the Muslims' vehicle on its way to the meeting. Whether or not my old friend the general knew this, I don't know. Maybe, in the end, like the rest of us, we knew he had to have a little faith. Or maybe the truth was simpler. All of us knew that what Bosnia didn't need, with the Serbs already on the warpath to the east, was another whole section of front plunged back into chaos. Whatever the reason, it worked. Because they came.

The meeting was held in a large conference room close to the SPANBAT commander's office. Four tables were drawn up in a square. Chairs were provided for about twenty people. The Spanish presided on the top table, with the Muslims running down the left and the Croats on the right. Keith, Paul, Adrian and I sat opposite the Spanish. As observers, we could only sit there and watch the proceedings unfold. The Spanish had made it abundantly clear that they were in charge.

The Croats came in first. They looked an arrogant bunch of bastards, an impression not helped by their pristine uniforms and the corps commander's insistence on wearing a clip of rifle ammunition on his chest as if is was a row of medals. Everyone had to surrender their weapons on the way in, but obviously bullets didn't count.

The corps commander spotted Keith and Adrian on the way to his chair and gave them a cursory nod. Via the mechanism of the early-morning meetings, Keith and Adrian had got to know this character as well as Paul and I had come to know General Kislic on the Muslim side.

Two minutes later, a hush descended on the room. It was almost as if the Croats had suddenly sensed the presence of their enemy in the building. The four of us exchanged glances. None of us knew what to expect next.

General Kislic walked into the room with his hawkish aide behind him. He was flanked by four burly-looking blokes with crew-cuts and stubble chins.

Kislic peered at the Croat delegation, then stopped and straightened. He seemed to grow in stature before our eyes.

Then, without warning, he opened his arms, walked straight over to the Croats' table and wrapped himself around his opposite number. I couldn't believe it. They were like long-lost brothers, laughing and chatting and slapping each other on the back.

I found out later that they had been at the same school and had played on the same football team. They had grown up in the same neighbourhood. They had known each other most of their lives. And for the last two years they had been trying to kill each other. It must have been catching, because even the cronies started doing it. It was like watching a Bosnian special of *Surprise, Surprise*.

The meeting opened with an address by the SPANBAT commander. The hippo settled into his chair and cleared his throat. Pausing for his interpreter every few sentences, he reminded both sides that the Muslim-Croat federation had already been agreed to by their respective leaders. It had been endorsed at the highest levels. Right the way across the front, a new *modus operandi* was being plotted out, one that would enable the two factions to resume their lives in peace. It was a shrewd play, because it put the onus squarely on the shoulders of the two commanders. The subtext of the message was: 'Fuck up here, gentlemen, and God help the guilty party.' Mostar was the last gap in the fence. If it couldn't be joined and conflict broke out again as a result, then somebody in this room would take responsibility for it.

It turned out to be the only good thing he did that day – for all I know, it may have been the only good thing he did during his entire stint in the city. But it didn't have any effect. Though both sides accepted the need to move back a hundred metres either side of the divide, the big stumbling block was the holding areas.

For the Croats, finding places to move large concentrations of troops far from the front line wasn't so much of a problem, as West Mostar was hardly touched by the conflict. For the Muslims, it was different; they couldn't move the holding areas further back because there was nowhere to move them to. The place had been flattened.

The one hope was an ex-Croatian Army barracks that the Muslims had captured and which was now several hundred metres from the lines. It was big enough to accept about two hundred troops, which would take pressure off the search for housing. But the Croats wouldn't wear it. They said the barracks were too close to the front for their liking. The Muslims, they said, would have to do better than that.

'There's nowhere else for my men to go,' General Kislic pleaded with his old friend and opposite number. 'If you want us to move into tents, then give us tents. We have nothing. We need shelter.'

'You shell my people and now you ask for shelter?' the Croatian yelled at him.

Jesus, I thought. Less than an hour earlier, they were clapping each other on the back. Now, it looked like they were about to murder each other.

The Muslims were on the defensive. Though it wasn't their fault that there was nowhere to put their troops, technically the ball was in their court. The Croats had agreed to move their troops back. On paper, it looked as if the Muslims were being obstructive.

As an observer, I could see that the Croats had half engineered this. In the artful game of diplomacy, they had just checked their opponents. The Muslims were desperately looking for a way out but all they could see was the old enemy hiding big stupid grins behind their hands.

Now I was getting worried. I could see that we were close to a walk-out. I stared at the SPANBAT commander. If the guy was perturbed by the turn events had taken he showed no sign of it. I watched as he stuck a Biro in his ear, turned it a couple of revolutions, then admired the results. I wanted to jump to my feet and yell, 'Get a fucking grip.' But we were just observers. We had no authority – and he knew this.

Half an hour later, the meeting collapsed. By some desperate last-minute manoeuvring, the SPANBAT boss managed to persuade the two parties to return to the table at two o'clock the following day. Frankly, I didn't hold out much hope that they'd even show, let alone work out a deal.

Talking to the boys back at the *basha*, I asked why the hell the Spanish couldn't get on to UNPROFOR and ship five or six Portakabins into the pocket. These would easily have housed the Muslims – two hundred soldiers who were currently in danger of jeopardizing the entire Muslim-Croat federation and plunging half of Bosnia back into war.

Adrian and I jogged over to the SPANBAT garrison and promptly checked in with the commander's fluttery aide. It was about eight thirty, half an hour after the meeting had broken up. I could tell the hippo was in because I could see shadows moving on a thin shaft of light that was spilling from beneath his door.

'You cannot possibly see him,' the adjutant said. 'He is far too busy.'

'Tell him,' I replied, 'that we think we've got some options for him to play with for the meeting tomorrow.'

'No. This is not possible. The colonel is on the phone to Madrid. He will not be interrupted. Come back in the morning. You tell him then. Please.' He gestured towards the way out.

From the other side of the door came the sound of laughter, loud, belly-shaking laugher. Hardly the sound of a man who was engaged in life-or-death diplomatic discussions. I turned to the adjutant.

'Tell your boss,' I snarled, 'that he'll see us now or I'm going back to the house to put a call through to Sarajevo.'

'I hardly think –'

'Do you want to be responsible for the collapse of the Muslim-Croat federation, Major?'

The adjutant faltered. The look on his face said that he was way out of his depth and he knew it.

'Tell him. Now. Please.'

The adjutant knocked gingerly on the door. There was a growl from within and he stepped inside, shutting the door behind him. A minute later, he was back again. Adrian and I had our audience.

The SPANBAT commander looked like thunder. He said nothing, electing instead to stare us down while tapping his pen on the edge of the desk.

'Look, boss,' I began, 'we're going to lose this meeting if we don't address this barracks business. Somehow we've got to find shelter for these two hundred soldiers.' I started to tell him about the Portakabin idea, but he cut me dead with a wave of the hand.

'Sergeant Spence, I really don't see what this is all about. Now, please, I have some important calls to make.'

'We're supposed to be giving them guidance,' Adrian said patiently. 'They're not getting any, Colonel.'

The commander had picked up his telephone, our signal to leave. But now he dropped the handset back on to its cradle.

'Today has been a good day,' he intoned grandly. 'There are no problems, believe me. Tomorrow everything will be OK. Now, kindly leave. I am busy.' He snapped his fingers and the adjutant came running. Without saying a word, the commander pointed to us, then to the door. Talk about the bum's rush.

Five minutes later, I'm on the satcom to GV. I spoke to Kev first, then James.

'We're losing it,' I told him. 'If we don't do some fixing, and fast, Mostar's going to fold. Someone needs to call that arsehole and make the point or we're all going to be right back where we started.'

'Are you sure?' James asked. 'This is serious shit.'

'If you want to sign that peace deal three days from now, you've got to get to the guy,' I said.

I heard James sigh. 'All right, mate. Leave it with us. We'll sort it out. We'll take it from here.'

I hung up. Three faces stared back at me from the gloom of our makeshift ops room. I could tell from their expressions that they thought I'd overstepped the mark. I knew I had, too. But I hadn't had any choice.

'Is this a winnable stand?' Keith asked, returning a piece of advice I had once given to him.

'I don't know, mate,' I said, trying to rub some fatigue from my face. 'The proof, I guess, will be in what happens tomorrow.'

My first duty on the morning of the tenth was to go and check out one of the weapon-inspection points. I needed to be sure, the closer we got to an agreement, that the Muslims' 81mm and

120mm mortars were exactly where they were supposed to be. Trust but verify, as President Reagan noted once, quoting an old Russian proverb.

The sun was just coming up over the jagged skyline of East Mostar, its rays falling as spears of golden-orange light on a stretch of dead straight road ahead of us, when, *bang!*, a bullet strike kicked up a cloud of dust and grit a few metres in front of the Land Rover. Paul slewed the vehicle to a halt a moment before a second round hit the road, even closer this time.

I skidded across the driver's seat and joined Paul on the leeward side of the vehicle. Paul peered over the bonnet, while I risked a peek around the rear.

'Bloody hell,' I said, catching my breath. 'Reggie wasn't shitting us. The fucker must have been on leave.'

Sure enough, the shot had come from the big derelict block of flats that Reggie had pointed out to us just across the river on the Croatian side.

'Well, there's no doubt that he's back,' Paul said. 'What do we do?'

'There's nothing we can do,' I replied, keeping my eye on the building.

Inwardly, I cursed. We'd already played straight into the sniper's hands by reacting the way we had. If this was the bastard's idea of a game, then he'd just hiked up the score big-time.

I peered across the river, running my gaze in and out of the windows and shell holes dotting the side of the building. But it was hopeless. Without some serious optics we'd never spot him. Which meant that the next time we came by he'd take another pot at us, and then another.

'So what happens?' Paul asked. 'We need to use this stretch of road, Cammy. Without it, mate, our movements are scuppered. Besides, if this fucker misjudges the wind-drift next time he's lining up in front of somebody, we could have a dead man on our hands.'

I nodded. While Paul was talking, I was thinking. He was right, of course: with Mostar on a hair-trigger, this was exactly the sort of thing that could set it off.

'That joker's had it,' I said, gritting my teeth.

'What do you mean?'

'I mean, we're going to get him, mate. Not now. Not today. We've got too much on our plates as it is. But as from now that guy is living on borrowed time.'

We jumped back into the vehicle and drove off. My mind was already working on the sting. Given our limited resources, we'd have to pick our moment, but I reckoned it was do-able. Provided we could clear the Muslim-Croat log-jam over the holding areas, I could see a window of opportunity opening up in around two days' time, just as the two sides were getting ready to withdraw to their new positions.

That, in itself, got me thinking even harder. We'd need to sort this problem before then. The thought of a rogue sniper out there on the day that tens of thousands of men shifted position, each armed to the teeth and filled to the eyebrows with prejudice and hatred, was enough to give me palpitations.

That set the deadline, then. The sniper problem would have to be cleared by the twelfth, the day after tomorrow.

'How are you going to get permission?'

I turned to him. 'We're not. So keep it under your hat. The UN is never going to sanction a premeditated hit. This is one that we're going to do on our own initiative.'

'Jesus, Cammy. You mean . . . ?' He let the words hang.

I shook my head. 'Nothing that drastic, mate. We're just going to give him a bloody good hiding.'

Paul looked visibly relieved. 'And in the meantime?'

'We carry on using the road. I don't want to give this bloke the satisfaction of believing he's got us on the run. Besides, we can't afford not to use it. It's a vital link in our operations here.'

A couple of minutes later, we pulled up at the bomb-site car-park close to the headquarters of General Kislic. We secured the vehicle and set off through the maze of back-streets and alleyways I'd now come to know by heart that led to the Muslim corps commander's centre of operations.

I waved to the guards on the door and marched up the rickety old stairs. We were a little early, but that was because I wanted to talk privately to the general before the main meeting started, as it always did, at 0930. I wanted to see if there had been any movement on the issue of the holding area.

I checked into the hawkish adjutant's office and started to remove my gun-belt.

General Kislic happened to walk into the room at that precise moment. He held his hand up as a signal for me to stop. 'Please, Sergeant, that won't be necessary any more.'

Things had changed.

The general waved Paul and me into his office. There was a map on his desk. In the dim morning light that spilled through the opaque window, I could see that the hollows around the commander's eyes had turned an even unhealthier hue of heart-attack grey. He must have been up the whole night trying to find some way around the stumbling block. He looked like shit, but then again, I hadn't looked in a mirror recently.

I didn't mention the Portakabins. For a start, I wasn't sure that GV had secured them. But, in any case, I didn't want to make things too easy for the Muslims. Peace doesn't come on a plate. If you want it, you've got to strive for it.

We were still five minutes away from the formal, regular meeting, when the general pointed to the map and told me about the remains of an old cement factory. It wasn't much, an old half-derelict asbestos hangar, he said, but it was shelter, some-thing at least for his troops. The problem was, he added, it was far, maybe too far – about forty minutes' drive-time – from the front line. If the Croats attacked, by the time his reinforcements arrived from this place, it would undoubtedly be too late. He looked at me as if to say, 'How the hell would you work this one, mate?' Then, his grim-looking adjutant and the rest of his aides walked in. The formalities started almost immediately.

We talked about a number of things – how many water bowsers should be delivered to the townspeople that day and how we would organize an open event for families on both sides of the divide to meet up in the centre of town on the twelfth.

But Kislic never once mentioned the cement factory and I suddenly understood why. This was something that had been kicking around in his head and nowhere else. It was undoubtedly a move to which his hawks would never have agreed during a debate in open forum. So was that it? Was he just going to bury the idea? Had he told me, simply to say, 'I'm trying, honest, but I'm not getting anywhere'?

I didn't know the answers to any of these questions, but I did see just how far we'd come in the space of a few short days. When Kislic told me I could keep my gun, he'd been sending me a much deeper signal. He'd been telling me that he trusted the UKLO in a way that he didn't necessarily his own side.

I kept my mouth shut.

With my hands tied, I spent the rest of the session wondering what on earth was going to happen at the meeting that afternoon. I just hoped that GV had come up with those Portakabins.

The meeting kicked off, as planned, at two. The Spanish were unbelievably frosty towards us, so I knew someone pretty high up the chain must have chewed them out severely since I'd put the call through to GV about their conduct. Schoolkids the world over are taught how bad it is to snitch on people – and, somewhere deep down, I felt a little bad that I'd caused such obvious suffering to the hippo and his gang. But when I reminded myself just what was at stake here, my doubts evaporated. The

Spanish had got what had been coming to them for some time.

After the SPANBAT commander had finished his address, he turned the session over to the Muslims. He wanted to know if they had made any progress during the night on the issue of the new holding areas. As he did so, Adrian walked in and passed me a note. GV was working on some options. If we could just stall it for a while . . .

I shook my head. We were all out of time as it was.

I tucked the piece of paper into my tunic and looked up just as General Kislic was getting to his feet. The Muslim corps commander glanced down his line of advisers and caught my eye. He held it for a moment, then adjusted his glasses to read some item of text on the table. It was then that I noticed the expressions on the faces of his aides. To a man they looked pissed off. But there was something else there too – resignation, maybe. I felt my heart quicken.

'There is only one place we can find to house our troops and that is the cement factory,' the general began. 'But our objections remain. It is forty minutes' drive away, something that my aides and I are prepared to tolerate, but for one thing. It is also too small. We cannot possibly fit two hundred people in this place.'

At this the hippo stirred. 'Why do you have to put all these soldiers in the cement factory?' he enquired, in a voice that sounded like treacle and gravel.

'We don't have to,' General Kislic replied. 'But my colleague . . .' he paused to deliver a sarcastic, thin-lipped smile at his oppo on the Croat bench '. . . has objected to our siting of any troops in the ex-HVO barracks. He said that so many troops so close to the front lines was too much for his liking.'

I could almost hear the slow grinding of giant gears in the SPANBAT commander's brain. Keith, Paul, Adrian and I looked at each other. It was like watching a game-show on TV when you know the answer but the contestant is just sitting there, lemon-like, staring into space and groping for inspiration.

We were powerless to say anything, but we all wanted to scream out the answer.

The hippo looked left and right, then went for it. 'Surely you could put a hundred soldiers in the cement factory and a hundred in the barracks.' He turned to the Croat corps commander. 'This has to be acceptable, does it not?'

The four of us almost broke into spontaneous applause. The hippo sat back, looking highly pleased with himself. Kislic looked drained. The Croat general crossed his arms and fumed. Now the onus was squarely back on him to come up with an answer.

He held a quick confab with his aides. After a minute of excited whisperings with his countrymen, the Croat leaned forward on his elbows, his fingers crossed, like a judge about to pronounce sentence. 'We could agree to this, yes.'

We all sat back and let out sighs of relief. From there, things moved rapidly. It was as if any diminution of energy at this point might jeopardize all the good work that had been achieved thus far.

Within an hour, the two sides had signed the master-map and its accompanying codicils. This acknowledged the current location of the front-line positions, the new holding areas for the troops and the positioning of the new border. We had our agreement. All that remained was to work out how many troops would be allowed to stay in place along the new frontier, but that wasn't difficult. The hard work had been done.

I looked at my watch. And not a moment too soon.

At five o'clock, when the meeting broke up, I got on the satcom to James at G V. 'James, my old china,' I said, 'mission success! We've got an agreement and both parties are fully signed up to it. All we need now is a chopper to get the map and the documents to you.' I was conscious of the need to get everything to him that night. Tomorrow this map, along with dozens like it, would have to be fed into an even bigger master-map that would draw out the new borders of the Muslim–Croat federation.

The signatures on it had to be inked the day after, on the twelfth. From the unnatural pause I should have known that it wasn't going to be that simple. Bosnia was working its strange magic again.

'What is it?' I asked.

'Slight problem,' James attempted breezily. 'We can't get you a chopper.'

I tried to keep my voice even. 'Come on, James, I'm not asking the fucking Norwegians again.'

'You don't have to, mate. They're not flying either. Nobody is.'

'Why the hell not?'

'Because Nato jets have just launched air strikes against the Serbs around Gorazde. Correction.' He paused momentarily. 'They're actually bombing the bastards as we speak.'

I felt as if I'd just been hit with a double punch to the solar plexus. A dozen questions about the Nato action churned through my head. For the moment, though, I had to put them to one side. The priority here, for me, was the matter of the master-map. If all the UN's helicopters were grounded, there was only one other way to get to GV and that was to drive over during the night.

I told James and asked for his approval in a single breath. I wanted to make damned sure that, if we were to embark on this endeavour, I had the full backing of RHQ. The prospect of a night drive, taking the long mountain route we'd neglected in favour of the ferry crossing on the way over, was risky, to say the least. But I felt I had no other choice. James agreed.

I did a quick bit of mental arithmetic and informed him we'd be leaving as soon as possible. The plan was to be in GV with the map soon after dawn the next day. If we were delayed, or failed to get through, there would be no agreement on Mostar. And the killing would begin again.

NINE

April 10 was the day that Gorazde began slip-sliding, slowly, inexorably towards hell. But a sign, perhaps, of what was in store for the patrol that day came in the form of a strange turn of events that took place the previous night.

A crowd of women had laid siege to the bank where the patrol, the UNMOs and the UNHCR had set up their HQ. The idea of seven SAS men being holed up in a vault with a band of screaming, spitting-mad women outside is bizarre, to say the least; but in truth, there was nothing Charlie and his crew could have done. They sat inside, cradling their rifles, as the women rattled the doors and hurled abuse at them through the windows.

The Serbs had the city held in a ring of steel and now they were beginning to squeeze it tight. Already half-starved to death, the people of Gorazde had watched as the hamlets to the east of the river Drina were picked off one by one by BSA tanks and heavy artillery. All through the night, as Charlie and his men had 'stagged on' on the roof of the bank, looking north and east through their high-power optics, the sky for miles was lit by the flames of burning Muslim villages.

Because all the menfolk were either dead or engaged in a last-ditch defence of the city, it was the women who had come to the bank to register their disgust. While Gorazde burned, all the Muslims' radio signallers could hear was a deafening silence, or a wall of static mush, from a world they thought didn't care. This apparent indifference was communicated to the only people left in the city – its women and children – who took out their anger on anyone they spotted wearing a blue beret.

With Gorazde's outer limits on fire, something almost as bad was happening on the inside. The city was turning in on itself, imploding. And caught between these two dynamics was Charlie's patrol, a handful of UNMOs and some UNHCR reps.

As soon as it was light, the three two-man patrols negotiated their way past the protesters and struck out for the suburbs, leaving Charlie to negotiate with General Rose's headquarters, and the UNMOs and UNHCR reps to deal with the women.

The main barrier to direct intervention was the Americans. Public pronouncements by leading US politicians over the past few days had made it clear that the Clinton administration did not want to involve itself in air strikes. Even the chairman of the US Joint Chiefs of Staff, General John Shalikashvili, had said publicly that air strikes would not take place against the Serbs around Gorazde.

Within the pocket, the news had been greeted with dismay – and not just because it set back the prospect of Nato action. The Muslims and the UKLO knew that the Serbs would take these and other comments as tacit endorsement of their plan to capture Gorazde. The accelerated aggression of the Serb assault over the past few days suggested that this was indeed the Serb interpretation.

As soon as they got to their allotted observation posts, the patrols realized that the battle of Gorazde had entered a new phase. Nick and Fergie took a hill to the north, Ray and Dave an OP to the north-east and Glen and Toby another to the south-east. From these positions, the three patrols could now see for the first time Serb artillery rounds exploding within the old part of the city.

Close to midday, as they reported the tally of incoming rounds back to Charlie, the two patrols to the east saw something that made their blood run cold. The Serbs began to open fire with .50 heavy machine-guns on refugees streaming across the main bridge over the Drina. The advancing Bosnian-Serb Army had infiltrated the forests on the hillsides overlooking the city and were able to pour fire indiscriminately on the outer reaches of the town below. Dave, Ray, Glen and Toby felt helpless. They couldn't see the Serbs to return any fire. All they could do was radio what they saw to Charlie as it happened.

The .50 is a big weapon. The slug is so large it will churn the hell out of bricks and concrete. To be anywhere around one of these machine-guns in a battle is terrifying. The noise it makes, plus its rate of fire, is awesome. As the refugees found themselves coming under attack, they scattered in all directions, seeking shelter. Some ran forwards and some backwards, but whichever way they broke, the Serb gunners seemed to have them covered.

Bullets tore across the road, whipping up a small storm of dust and grit. A handful of women and children were able to make use of the dust-cloud as they clambered on to the wall and dropped over the side of the bridge into the stream below. Those who survived the fall clung desperately to the stone pillars, struggling against the pull of the icy current, as the bullets continued to hammer into the structure above. But for most of the people who had crossed the bridge's threshold before the Serbs opened up there was no escape. Those who tried to hide behind their carts and paltry possessions merely had them shot away by the onslaught of bullets. When there was nothing left to shield them, twenty refugees lay dead or dying, their bodies torn apart by heavy-calibre bullets. Only when the firing stopped did anyone hear the screams.

It was this, more than anything else that day, that helped to focus UN minds on Gorazde.

By early afternoon, the die was cast. General Rose got on the phone to Bosnian-Serb headquarters in Pale and warned Serb commanders that they would be 'bloodied' if they continued their attack. In the meantime, the UNPROFOR commander set about tying up the loose ends with Yasushi Akashi, the UN's special envoy to Bosnia, gaining the necessary approvals for military action.

In Washington, Americans awoke to hear that the Clinton administration had reversed its policy on air strikes. The US Secretary of State, Warren Christopher, was thus able to announce that US warplanes were on standby to hit the Serbs around Gorazde if General Rose requested them.

Slowly – a little too little and a little too late – the world began to rally to the cause of the beleaguered safe haven. Late in the afternoon, when he knew he could back tough words with like action, General Rose faxed to Radovan Karadzic in Pale and gave him the final ultimatum.

He received no response, and detected no obvious lull in the Serbs' attack on the city, so Nato's machinery was activated. US Air Force F-16C fighters scrambled from Aviano in northern Italy to attack BSA targets around Gorazde.

At 1720 hours, the two aircraft carried out a quick recce over the safe haven and designated two targets for impending attack. Having gained the final necessary authority to launch the strike, the aircraft dropped two bombs – one each – and appeared to score hits.

An hour later, the UN in Zagreb recorded the success of the mission. 'Two American F-16s dropped two bombs on two targets south and south-west of Gorazde at 1724 and 1729 BST,' a spokesman announced on CNN, in a listless monotone. 'Authority was given to engage a Bosnian-Serb command post and a tank.'

A couple of hours after the attack, General Rose announced, 'It is absolutely quiet in Gorazde now.'

The Serbs, indeed, seemed to have halted their attack.

In the city, the mood among the population bordered on ecstatic. When they heard what the aircraft had done, the women besieging the bank stopped chanting anti-UN slogans and greeted the three returning SAS patrols as if they were the sole defenders of the city. Far from being lynched, the men were told that a monument would be built to them and erected in the centre for all to see, in perpetuity – a monument for ever more to Rose's men, the seven saviours of Gorazde.

For the patrol itself, it was hard not to get caught up in euphoria. From their OPs on top of the bank, Fergie and Ray reported that the halt in the Serb advance appeared to be holding.

But the rhetoric from Pale did not sound quite so encouraging. Predictably, the Bosnian-Serb Army denounced the air strikes. 'By this act, Nato carried out a clear act of aggression against the Serb people . . . striking at civilian targets far from the front line.'

Intelligence reports coming in to GV and General Rose's headquarters indicated that the air strikes – the first ever to be carried out against ground targets by Nato – had been more devastating to the Serb war effort than had been envisaged. The single bomb that struck the command post had wiped out a number of senior BSA officers – close friends of Karadzic, the Bosnian-Serb leader, and his mad-dog military henchman, General Ratko Mladic.

The UN had at last taken 'necessary measures' to support the UN Protection Force in the performance of its mandate around the safe havens.

The question everyone was asking was, would it be enough?

Driving after dark in Bosnia was a no-no on a good night. On this particular one, we had the added excitement of Nato's air strikes to contend with. Because it was the first time such action had been taken, nobody was too sure what effect this would have on the strategic picture in Bosnia. Would it, for example, inspire the Muslims to launch a counter-offensive against the Serbs? How would the Serbs react to the UN? It was impossible to second-guess how things might develop.

To make matters worse, I didn't have much confidence in our route maps. The cartographic picture of the region shifted almost daily. Just because it said there was a bridge across a river on a map didn't mean it was still there. The ferry was out because of the time: the oily crossing shut down at sunset and it was already getting dark. The alternative, the mountain route out of Mostar, wasn't my idea of fun. At any moment, unless you were paying very careful attention, you could drop into a crater the size of a house – the result of some particularly heavy mortar or artillery bombardment over the past few days. In short, we did not kid ourselves that delivering the Mostar master-map to GV was going to be a fun job. But neither Paul nor I had the slightest clue when we set off that it was going to pan out the way it did.

When we left it was pissing down in Mostar and the wind was rising. I was on first shift behind the wheel, Paul was map-reading. Despite the precious nature of our cargo, we'd elected to make the journey without back-up. Somebody had to stay behind to mind the fort and that job fell to Keith and Adrian.

The only protection afforded the maps themselves was a pair of cardboard tubes, coupled with a hasty effort to hide them under some boxes, and spare clothing we had in the back of the Land Rover. For our own protection we were forced to rely on our sidearms. The SA-80s were an encumbrance up front in the Land Rover, so we left them behind.

As we climbed into the mountains, the weather turned shittier. Freezing rain hampered our vision and the windscreen wipers were working overtime. In our headlights, we could see the wind thrashing the trees. It was one of those nights you wouldn't have dreamed of venturing out in back home. Here, unfortunately, duty called.

Paul had his head down in the map when I noticed something in the lights. I brought the vehicle to a stop, applied the handbrake and got out. Wiping the rain from my eyes, I peered down the beams of the headlights. Up ahead, barely illuminated, was a barrier across the road. It had been constructed from a couple of oil drums with some pine branches strewn between.

I stuck my head into the cabin and had a quick confab with Paul. We could see no sign of anyone, so we decided to push on. Paul slid into the driver's seat, ready to bring the Land Rover through once I'd cleared the way. I adjusted my UN beret and started out for the barrier.

When I reached it, I gave the woods a quick scan, but could see nothing. It was way too dark and we didn't have any night optics. I couldn't believe anybody would be mad enough to be out in this shit so I kept going.

I began to pull and push the oil drums to the side of the road. They were difficult to manoeuvre as they'd been half filled with earth, but I got them there in the end with a bit of huffing and puffing. When there was enough of a gap, Paul eased the Land Rover through. I made sure that I replaced the component pieces of the barricade exactly as they'd been before. Then I jumped on to the passenger seat and we set off again, grinding through the gears on the painfully slow journey to GV.

I looked at my watch. We'd been on the road for two hours, only another five or six to go. Around us, the storm raged with no sign of respite. The irony of it, I reflected, was that all helicopters would have been grounded in weather like this anyway.

A few kilometres on, we encountered another barricade. This

time we drove right up to it and I went through the same rigmarole: dismantling the pieces, Paul driving through, me restoring the barrier to the state in which we had found it, setting off again.

We went through all this twice more. Then, at the next barrier, something a little different happened. I was about to get out of the vehicle when I noticed movement in the trees ahead. Two soldiers stepped out of the forest and into the road. At first it was difficult to tell who they were. They were wrapped up against the cold, rifles slung over their shoulders. The wind whipped trails of condensation from the corners of their mouths. I could see their faces in the side-lobes of the headlights. They looked pissed as hell.

Paul and I said nothing. Each of us was trying to make out what bloody side they were on. We were in a strange pocket of land that was close enough to all three factions for them to have been Muslim, Croat or Serb. Then I noticed a chequered red and white shoulder patch on the soldier in front. At least, I thought, breathing an inward sigh of relief, they're Croatian, not Serb. Explaining our mission to a bunch of hairy-arsed Cetniks would have been interesting with Nato jets buzzing about. And, besides, the Serbs didn't give a shit about peace between their two lifelong enemies. It was in their interest to burn the sodding map we had on us.

The first soldier approached Paul's side of the vehicle, the second swaggered up to mine. I slid back the window, but before I could say anything, he stuck his face in mine and started shouting. 'Who are you? What you do here?' He tapped his digital watch and jutted his chin angrily. I could smell booze on his breath. He looked like a bit-part player in any number of movies I'd seen about crazy in-breeds in swamp-filled US Southern states – hairy, unkempt, and with a gaze that seemed to be focused a few centimetres behind my head.

I explained who we were and where we were going. I did not

mention the nature of our mission. I did not want to reveal the presence of the maps – not unless I had to.

'You no be on this road,' he shouted, sending a gob of spittle on to the inside of the windscreen. 'The barriers – for stopping, not driving.'

I wasn't ready to apologize yet, but I didn't want to antagonize him either. I shrugged innocently.

'What in back?' he demanded, jabbing a thumb towards the rear of the Land Rover.

'Nothing,' I said. 'Just bits and bobs.'

'Bombs?' he shouted.

I cursed under my breath. *Don't try and be fucking clever, Cameron.* 'No,' I said. 'My mistake. Nothing. Really.'

At this, he pulled open the door and was about to grab my jacket and drag me out, when he caught a glimpse of my sidearm. That slowed him down a tad. He took a pace back and gestured to the back of the vehicle again.

'Show me,' he said.

We got out and walked to the back of the Land Rover. Paul dropped the tail-gate and gestured inside. Luckily there was nothing in there to arouse suspicion. We'd left our satcom and GPS gear behind. And, for some reason, they overlooked the maps.

When I turned round, two more Croats were walking towards us in the light of the beams. I threw a glance at my watch. Time . . . marching on. *Come on, you fuckwits. We really don't need this.*

I pulled a face at Paul. He knew what I was trying to say. Somehow we had to extricate ourselves from this situation and get going. There was no room in our schedule for pissing about. If the map didn't make it in time, our arses were going to fry and maybe the Muslim–Croat federation too.

I started back towards the passenger seat. I figured we just had to take charge and move out. Then I noticed the Croats talking animatedly among themselves. They were looking my way and pointing.

'Just keep going,' I told myself.

I opened the door only to have it kicked out of my grasp. It slammed shut, but the wind whipped away the noise. For a moment I felt like I'd stepped into a bad dream – one in which you see everything with the sound turned off. A shrill note sounded in my head as blood pumped into my brain, momentarily throwing me off balance. I had to force my heart-rate down to a steadier pace; one that would work for, not against, me.

I turned and saw my old friend, the hairiest of the four Croats. He had unslung his AK-47 and was pointing it at my chest. Out of the corner of my eye, I could see Paul. A Croat was standing against the door, barring his exit, aiming a pistol at his head. The fucker was grinning, too. I could see his teeth, bright against the darkness.

'You all right?' I shouted.

I heard Paul laugh, a little too shrilly. 'What do you think?'

'Don't make any sudden moves,' I shouted. 'Whatever's ticking them off, I've got a feeling their beef is with me, not you.'

'Silence!' the Croat screamed. He jabbed the muzzle of his gun hard into my shoulder. 'You!' he screamed again, louder this time. 'You no UN! You enemy!'

At first, I wasn't sure I'd heard this right. Then, it started falling into place: my olive skin and dark hair, a handy disguise when I'd been behind Iraqi lines in '91, but not here.

And then it hit me. *Fucking hell, they couldn't – they couldn't possibly think . . .*

I took my memory on a rapid scroll back to my tour of the front-line positions in East Mostar and the moment when Mohamed had begged me to get back under cover, because my jacket looked like his. Jesus, it wasn't just my uniform that made these arseholes think I was their enemy, it was the colour of my skin.

'You!' the Croat shouted again. 'You Muslim!'

I shook my head. 'No, mate. You've got it wrong. I'm a British soldier with the UN.'

I signalled that I wanted to reach for my ID, but at this the Croat went apoplectic. He lifted the muzzle, till I was forced to stare straight down the barrel.

'*Britanac*,' I shouted. '*Ja sam Britanac.*'

Above the howl of the wind, I heard the sound of another AK being cocked, then another. At the edge of my vision, I could just see the third and forth Croatians, standing, legs akimbo, all swagger and arrogance, behind my inquisitor.

'Hey,' I said, mustering as much authority as I could, 'I'm going for my papers, OK? My papers.'

Slowly I reached into my combat jacket. It was as well that I braced myself for the cold touch of an AK because before I could get to my wallet my Croat tormentor had shoved the barrel of his rifle right up against my temple.

In a moment of indiscipline, I revisited the bluebell wood on the edge of Bristol, the endgame scene of our operator's exercise all those years ago. But as quickly as the image entered my head I banished it. Drift in a situation like this, and you're a dead man.

'Cammy,' Paul shouted from the inside, 'what the hell's going on?'

I just managed to shout, 'They think I'm a Muslim,' before the creature from the bayou ground the muzzle of his AK into the thin skin next to my eyebrow.

Gently, I pulled my wallet from my jacket. After a couple of seconds' fumbling, my fingers found my UN ID card. I handed it over. There was an interminable pause while the two Croats to the rear of the vehicle came forward and studied the pass in the light of a headlight beam. Just when I thought we were out of there, I saw one shake his head.

'Liar!' my friend screamed. 'You Muslim!'

I'd had e-fucking-nough of this. 'Paul,' I yelled, 'can you get to the back of the vehicle?'

'I don't know.'

'Take your friend with you and show him the maps.'

'Christ, Cammy, don't you think –'

'Show him the bloody maps, mate. Show him the signature of his corps commander. It's our only way out of here.'

I managed to babble this out under some duress. The other two Croatians had come back with my pass. I was now surrounded by them. For a moment I considered going for my sidearm, but I'm no gunslinger and rapidly rejected the idea. Each had a rifle trained on me. I wouldn't have got a single round into one of the bastards, let alone all of them.

After what seemed like a century, Paul came round the side of the vehicle with his escort's AK in the small of his back. In Paul's right hand was the map, our precious master-map. It was flapping in the wind like a rogue sail on an old square-rigger. Jesus, I thought. Lose that sucker and we're all in the shit.

Paul elbowed his way up to the lights and shoved the map in the beam. More out of curiosity, apparently, than anything else, two of the Croats went forward to see what he was looking at. Paul pointed and their eyes followed. One of the Croats looked from the map to his mate, then went back to the map again.

A chink, a ray of light.

Then, they called over my mate.

While the fourth soldier kept his weapon on me and Paul, the three studied the map. Thereafter, it all happened quickly. We got the map back, slightly damper than when it left the tube, but otherwise none the worse for wear, and I got my pass. There was no hint of an apology from the HVO, but nor were we hanging around for one. We just got back into the vehicle and drove.

I shot a last look behind us and caught the dim red outline of the four soldiers in the reflected glow of our tail-lights. They were standing four-square across the road, watching us go. We left them looking as pissed off as when they'd found us. Then we hit a bend in the road and they were gone.

'Fucking hell,' Paul said, 'what are we *doing*?'

We were well beyond the point of no return. There was no going back. I told Paul this. Besides, I really didn't want to go through that checkpoint again. Nor did he

Paul glanced down at the map on his knees, then looked at me. 'Oh, well, think of it this way,' he attempted breezily, 'another four hours and we're home and dry.'

It actually took us more like seven. Seven long hours, eleven altogether. Though we ran into no more trouble *per se*, the road was much worse than even we had imagined and progress was dire. Some time in the small hours the storm blew itself out and we eventually crawled into GV at close to 0500. As we drove down from the mountains towards the town, the lights of the base were visible for miles. It seemed as if we had our very own beacon guiding us in. I never thought I'd be grateful to see this dreadful place, but it felt like a homecoming.

The plan was to deliver the map, have a quick brew and turn round. There was a lot to do in Mostar still. There were the preparations to make both for the front-line move the day after tomorrow and for a families' day tomorrow. This would, we hoped, oil the springs and cogs for the big move itself.

The families' day would permit Muslims and Croats who had become trapped on the wrong side of the divide to visit their relatives and loved ones. It was to be carried out under strict supervision, but not so much by us, thank God, as the Spanish. We felt it only wise, however, to be on hand to make sure that everything went smoothly. As with so much else in Bosnia, the merest incident could spark trouble. And with things so close to resolution on the broader front, we had to be careful. Which was one of the reasons that made me more determined than ever to take action on the sniper.

We met up with James, Kevin, the scalies and Paul and I handed over the map.

'Any problems on the way over?' James asked.

I threw a quick glance at Paul. 'No, not really,' I told him. We'd agreed not to say anything about the checkpoint incident as it would only become an official drama, something that would have to be resolved with telephone calls and paperwork; and we really didn't have the time.

After a night of no sleep and plenty of eye-strain from map-reading and peering past windscreen wipers, we looked like a couple of booze-soaked down-and-outs. To my great concern, however, James and Kev looked a lot worse.

I asked about Gorazde. James kneaded his eyeballs, taking his time before answering. He told me that things were charging up rapidly on the diplomatic front and not necessarily for the good. The Russians had formally protested to President Clinton about the air strikes, with their foreign minister, Andrei Kozyrev, warning him that 'the world could be dragged into an extremely dangerous series of exchanges of strikes'. Nobody in government or the military was quite sure what that meant. Some media commentators, however, were already counting down to the Third World War.

The hope was, James continued, that the Bosnian Serbs would return to the negotiating table, but the signs from Pale didn't look good. President Milosevic of Serbia had also accused the UN of siding with the Muslims.

'So, in answer to your question,' James said, 'I guess things could be better.' He made his excuses, saying he needed to check with the scalies that everything was all right with the Mostar master-map.

What worried me was that he hadn't answered my question.

When we were alone, I pulled Kev to one side and asked him what the hell was going down in Gorazde. I knew that I could rely on getting the real version of events from him, not the party line. We hadn't served in the same troop for so long for nothing.

Kev sat back in his chair and looked at me. 'We've got big dramas, mate. At first, everyone thought the air strikes had done the trick, but the word out of the pocket this morning is that they've started shelling again, big-style. Intelligence indicates that this isn't some sporadic push on the Serbs' part, it's a major, precalculated offensive, with the specific objective to capture and hold Gorazde.'

'What's going to happen to the boys?'

'The view around here is that there's not a damned thing that can be done about them, mate. We can't get a helo in now, 'cos the Serbs are gong to shoot down anything with UN or Nato markings on it. And they can't drive out for the same reason. They're stuck in there, for better or worse.'

On the drive back to Mostar, I thought about everything I had just heard. With Charlie in charge, backed by the experienced and capable Glen, I knew that the patrol was in the best possible hands. But if the pocket disintegrated, no amount of experience or leadership skills would be enough. What was more alarming was the sense of helplessness in GV. I knew that the problem didn't reside with James or Kev: both were tough, motivated soldiers, with years of special forces training behind them. I felt sure that the flabbiness existed higher up the chain, higher probably than the most senior echelons of the Regiment itself.

The SAS had a long history of delivering the impossible. It was also known for looking after its own. The sense I was getting was that nobody was keeping an eye on either of these two vital facets of our past. Worse, there was a whiff of desperation in the air.

For the sake of those who were fighting for their lives in the besieged pocket, I only hoped that it hadn't been communicated.

Approximately an hour after we set off from GV, Charlie gave the order to abandon the UNHCR outpost next to the main bridge into Gorazde. With refugees streaming in droves from the collapsed pockets of resistance to the east of the Drina, and with Serb artillery shells exploding all around it, the observation post was deemed untenable.

Soon afterwards, reports started coming in that the Serbs had hit a refugee centre in the middle of the city. In the garbled account that Charlie picked up off the radio, it appeared that a single round had inflicted major casualties. He asked Glen and Toby to go and check it out.

When they got there, the two-man patrol reported back their findings. A particularly heavy battle was taking place on the ridge-line above them to the north-east. From what they could tell, many of the Serbs' artillery shells were overshooting their Muslim military targets on the ridge and crashing down on to the city itself. Of course, they told Charlie, it could always have been intentional, but there was no direct evidence of this.

Not that it mattered much either way to those on the ground. One of the shells had come down through the roof of the refugee centre and splintered in two, sending a huge shard of metal into the chest of a man who had already been hit and peppering dozens of others with shrapnel wounds. Even more disturbing was that the shells were still raining down into the area at a rate of six to eight a minute. The refugees had nowhere else to go. It could be only a matter of time before lightning struck again.

Charlie got on the satcom to GV and called for more air strikes. Word came back promptly that they had been approved in Sarajevo, but would require endorsement further up the UN chain of command. Charlie was told to sit tight and wait for developments. Ray, meanwhile, Mr FAC, got up on to the roof of the bank with his 344 radio, ready to talk the jets down on to their targets as soon as they appeared over the city.

Nick and Fergie, watching from a concealed OP way beyond the city limits to the north, told Charlie that they were in a good position to call down strikes on a shedload of Serb tanks and troops that were advancing southwards. But by now a set of rules of engagement had come down that made Nato action against this thrust impossible. For what they were worth, the rules said artillery and tanks were legitimate targets but troops were not. Because they couldn't get a clear shot at either isolated tanks or artillery, Nick and Fergie were told there would be no direct action here, but to keep watching.

In the meantime, Charlie and Glen held a rapid council of war to try to determine which part of the pocket was the next most likely to fall to the Serb advance. Squatting up on the roof of the bank and giving the vista a 360-degree sweep, this was not easy. Fires were burning all around the city, but they appeared most intense in the north-east. To give Sarajevo the accuracy it needed, it was decided that a patrol should get up there to take a closer look. Glen elected to lead it, with Toby, Misha and Carl, the Canadian UNMO, under his wing. It took them a while to get up there, but when they reached the ridge-line, the scenery took their breath away. It had not been possible to see from the city what they saw now, since the bulk of the view was hidden on the other side of the hill.

It was like something out of the First World War. The Muslim trenches stretched away in the foreground, with the Serbs' running parallel around sixty metres beyond. The entire hillside had been stripped of foliage by the intensity of the shelling. The patrol knew it was Serb artillery, because the Muslims had next to no big guns left, let alone the ammunition for them.

The landscape was a sea of brown earth, broken only by the occasional lone-standing tree. These were like spiked guns with their tops all splayed and their branches blown off. There were so many craters that each had merged with a dozen others to turn the place into one giant shell hole.

For whatever reason, however, an unnatural tranquillity had now descended on this part of the battlefield, allowing Glen, Toby, Misha and Carl to navigate their way through the slit trenches to the Muslims' forward positions. Here, they found a single large trench, reinforced in the customary fashion with thick wooden staves.

It turned out to have been a Serbian position only the day before. The smoke that the patrol had observed from the roof of the bank had been the Muslims' counter-attack to capture it. Now, they had filled the trench with all the troops they had – twenty or so young men, who now lay back exhausted against the sides of the position cradling their weapons. Some of the soldiers were on stag, some smoked, some slept. There was a pervasive smell of cordite and rot – rotten wood, rotten clothes, rotten flesh.

Through Misha, Glen introduced himself to the Muslim commander, a haggard-looking captain with a half-smoked roll-up wedged permanently in the corner of his mouth. His straight fair hair flopped over one eye. He looked as if he hadn't slept for a week. He told them that the Serb position opposite was manned by Cetniks – who had the ruthlessness of the Vikings and the Vietcong rolled into one. And these Cetniks were Serbs with a difference. During the night, the Muslims had learned that the BSA forward positions had been filled with ex-convicts – murderers, rapists and child-molesters – who had been promised their freedom in return for results against the old enemy. In the lulls between fighting, the small hours had echoed with the Cetniks' yells of what they would do to the defenders' women and children when they got to them.

The Muslims had counter-attacked because each man in this sector had a house still occupied by his family on the other side of the ridge-line, less than a kilometre away. Making a stand here was the only hope, the captain told them. If they could hold out for a little longer, the captain felt sure that further Nato attacks on the Serbs would force Karadzic and Mladic to call off the attack.

In this, Glen was able to offer them a little hope. Authorization for more strikes had been given. He looked at his watch. It was just a matter of time before the jets came back.

Suddenly there was the distant sound of a detonation. Seconds later, the air filled with the whistle and crack of a heavy-calibre artillery shell rifling through the air above their heads. The UN contingent ducked instinctively as the round detonated forty metres away, sending an enormous cloud of flame and grit into the sky. When Toby looked up, he was ashamed to see that none of the Muslims had moved a muscle, even though other rounds were coming down, straddling the trench in a ground-shaking series of detonations.

Just when it seemed as if the Serb artillery was about to get their range, the shelling stopped and an eerie silence descended again on the battlefield.

The Muslim commander said something slowly and calmly to Misha, then removed a lighter from his pocket and raised the flame to the charred wisps of tobacco spilling from the end of his roll-up. His hand was shaking so badly it took him several seconds to get the thing lit.

'What did he say?' Glen asked Misha.

'He says,' Misha replied, in a low voice, 'that they are about to open fire with an anti-aircraft gun.'

Sure enough, the air split with the boom-boom-boom vibration of a triple-A emplacement opening up on them from somewhere much closer to the Serbs' forward positions. Round after round pummelled the ground in front of the trench. It looked as if the Serbs were using the weapon in an attempt to dig through to the Muslim lines.

Glen, Toby and Carl watched the commander lie back against the trench wall and smoke the remaining stub of his roll-up as if none of this was happening. Around them, his men stirred themselves and reached for their weapons. Some attached bayonets to the muzzles.

His cigarette gone, the captain slapped a fresh magazine into his AK and smoothed his lank hair back from his eyes.

'What's happening?' Glen asked Misha.

The interpreter held a hurried exchange with the captain. Then he turned to Glen. 'He says that the Serbs will attack this position now. He says that we should leave. They will be here in minutes.'

'Tell him we'll do no such thing,' Glen said hurriedly. 'Tell him we'll stand and fight with him. He can do with the extra men. I know he can.'

Misha translated while the captain listened, his eyes closed. If this offer had moved him at all, he showed no sign of it. When he spoke again, his voice never wavered from its regular flat monotone.

'He says he knows that you are General Rose's men,' the interpreter said, more urgency in his voice now. 'He says that it is not your job to be here. Your task is clear. Without you, there will be no one to call down the air strikes. The people of Gorazde need you to stay alive to talk to the Nato planes. He asks you again, in God's name this time, to leave.'

Glen looked at the captain. He guessed that they were about the same age. The Muslim gave him a half-smile, then a final, weary, dismissive wave. 'Go,' he said, in heavily accented English. 'Go now. Please.'

Three minutes later, two hundred metres below the position, Glen, Toby, Carl and Misha heard the screams of the Cetniks as they went over the top and dropped down into the Muslim trench. There was a brief exchange of small-arms fire. The four stood rooted to the spot as they stared back up the hillside. Each knew in his heart that the position had gone. The two SAS men confessed later that it was the most gut-wrenching moment of their professional lives.

Not long afterwards, two US Marine Corps F/A-18s flew over Serb artillery positions to the south of the city. They turned and swept low over the guns again in an attempt to warn the Serbs to stop their shelling. But the guns carried on firing. A little later, with no let-up in the bombardment, the two US fighters returned. By now, Serb tanks and armoured personnel carriers were advancing in a column along an approach road to the main bridge over the Drina. This time, the US pilots were guided all the way in by Ray, who had a clear view of the advancing armour.

At 1419, the aircraft attacked the armoured column with bombs and 20mm cannon. Two minutes later, three APCs were burning out of control, the tanks scattered every which way in their effort to escape the onslaught. It was later discovered that only one of the four bombs 'dropped' actually did what it was supposed to. Of the others, two failed to explode and one got 'hung up' – it never left the pylon.

So much for technical superiority.

Within half an hour, Charlie was able to report that the Serb attack had been halted; that the only shelling now was sporadic, the shells falling well outside the main part of the town.

He also told GV that with the Muslim positions overrun on the north-eastern ridge-line, the Serbs now had an almost clear route into the city.

In the evening, from the roof of the bank, he was able to watch the Cetniks digging in around the ridge-line they had recaptured from the Muslims.

It was just a matter of time now, Charlie told the group, before the pocket fell.

*

The following morning, an hour before daybreak, we slipped Keith into position on the long straight stretch of road in front of the derelict block of flats. I had to trust that the sniper was either asleep or not using night optics. His MO suggested that this was idle recreation for him so I was almost certain he'd still be snoozing off the slivovitz from the night before. But I couldn't be 100 per cent sure about this and told Keith, since he was the bloke in the firing line. Keith knew and understood the risks, but wouldn't have it any other way. On our drive back from GV the previous day, the sniper had taken a pot-shot at him and Adrian as they'd driven to the weapon-inspection pit. Like an animal that develops a lust for human flesh, it looked as if our man's taste for action was growing by the day. It was just a matter of when, not if, this bastard killed somebody.

Keith slipped out of the back of the Land Rover and dropped down into some dead ground beside the road. Over the course of the next hour, he would manoeuvre himself into a firing position. He had his SA-80 plus KITE-sight with him, which would provide clear magnification of the target area by day and night.

We knew the sniper was operating from the derelict block of flats across the river on the Croat side. Reggie had tried sending his men in on the odd occasion, but every time they'd searched the place, the sniper had vanished. Now that I was a believer, I'd decided that conventional pest-control methods weren't going to work. If we wanted to catch our rat, we were going to have to play it his way, nice and dirty. Which is just the way we like it.

It was the families' day, and the Spanish had already set up the facilities for this operation down by the river in the centre of town. To give the sniper plenty of opportunity to have a crack at us, we motored several times up and down the straight stretch of road, taking our time and talking our moves through with Keith over the radio.

Thankfully, the Spanish seemed to have the families' day

under control. They'd set up some large marquee-type tents on either side of the bombed-out Bailey bridge spanning the river. Over the course of the day, people who wanted to visit their relatives and friends on the other side would report to the SPANBAT officials in charge and then proceed from the tents in carefully controlled dribs and drabs to the meeting point: the crippled girders of the bridge itself.

It was a bizarre sight to witness people who hadn't seen each other for perhaps a year or two meeting on this twisted piece of military engineering. The Bailey bridge was a replacement for the town's old stone bridge, an early casualty of the conflict. Then the substitute bridge was hit – though it was still navigable by pedestrians – and the repair work stopped. It was here that people hugged and held each other, some in silence, some weeping, some in groups and some in simple one-to-one reunions. Even from afar, I found the sight, much to my surprise, intensely moving. It made me realize that, somewhere along the line, Bosnia had worked its way under my skin – which, just a few short weeks ago, I'd sworn it never would do. Unsure of this discovery, I returned to something I knew and understood. I got on the radio to Keith and asked him if there was any sign of the sniper. 'Negative,' came the reply. Not a damned thing was stirring in the derelict building. All my instincts told me that the bastard would have had a go at us by now if he was there – we'd certainly given him enough opportunity. It was pointless keeping Keith there any longer. It was time to go back and bring him in.

Paul and I stopped the Land Rover half-way along the straight stretch of road and got out of the vehicle. We pretended to give the building a scan. Putting the Land Rover between him and the sniper's line of sight, Keith scrambled across the dead ground where he'd concealed himself all morning, jumped on to the road and under the vehicle's tarpaulin. He was pissed off, but otherwise none the worse for wear after his five hours down in the weeds. Once our quarry was safely aboard, Paul and I got back in and drove off, frustrated that our plan had come to nothing. I was beginning to think we were dealing with a phantom here – or else that the son-of-a-bitch was even more wily than we'd thought and had known what we were up to all along.

No sooner had we moved than Paul brought my attention to some smoke rising above the skyline on the eastern edge of town. When I looked through my binos, I realized that what at first we'd thought was a single fire was actually several. We decided to go and investigate.

When we got to the area, an outlying part of the Muslim side of town, the fires had spread across the divide into the Croat sector, which was an interesting phenomenon in itself since there was a wide swath of devastated no man's land between them, making it impossible for the fire to have got there by itself. When it became obvious that no one was lifting a finger to stop these fires, I finally got the message. They had been started deliberately, at first by the Muslims and then by the Croats, because these houses were due to be swapped under the handover agreement tomorrow.

I thought back to the meetings we'd attended. There were the Muslims, wringing their hands over the lack of housing in which to shelter their troops – or anyone, come to that – and now they were torching them. I leaned back against the Land Rover's grille and watched the flames licking through the shell holes in the roof of what had once been an ordinary suburban house in an ordinary suburban street. It didn't make any sense. The only thing that mattered in this place was an eye for an eye and a tooth for a tooth. Never mind that homeless Croat children might have found shelter from the cold and rain under some undamaged part of this roof tomorrow night. The important thing, if you had vengeance on your mind, was that no one should have this place if you couldn't have it yourself. I thought back, too, to the way the two opposing commanders had greeted each other like long-lost brothers and wondered what the arsonists would have made of it. Would they have seen things with the same clarity that I felt I now saw them? That Bosnia was a sick game, fuelled by the basest of emotions, and played out on a giant, incomprehensible scale. As the thought tumbled through my head, the exasperation and sadness I'd felt welled in the pit of my stomach as anger. I jumped back into the vehicle, calling Paul and Keith after me. There was only one way to put a stop to this and that was to solicit assistance. I set up a rendezvous with Adrian, dropped Keith off so that the two of them could pay a visit to the Croat boss, then tore off with Paul to visit my old friend General Kislic.

When we reached his headquarters, Paul and I were told that he was out. When we asked where he had gone, nobody seemed to know. It was a classic fob-off. I knew now that these fires weren't sporadic outbursts of local pique or anger, but a manoeuvre carefully orchestrated at the top. It registered as a real slap in the face: I'd felt that Kislic and I had established a rapport built on a modicum of trust. Was I to believe that, like everything else about this place, this, too, was a sham?

We spent the rest of the day chasing fires. Whenever we reached one, we found no evidence of the perpetrators, of course, just a small crowd of onlookers who denied all knowledge of how the blaze had started. More galling still, just as we got to one fire, another would start up somewhere else, proving that the whole thing had been intricately planned and run on careful, split-second timing. No doubt a bunch of people somewhere were pissing themselves watching us dart from one blaze to the next. Even though Bosnia itself was always the loser, the hard core of its lunatic fringe couldn't have given a toss.

That night, exhausted and depressed by our runaround, I got on the satcom to GV and told them the news. In return, I learned that the fighting in Gorazde had eased somewhat. Not that anyone thought this was evidence of a lasting swing-shift in the situation, simply one of those lulls that you often get in a protracted battle. The Serbs had been attempting to storm Gorazde for over a week. They could be seen digging in in the heights above the city, regenerating themselves for the next round of fighting. In the meantime, diplomatic efforts were continuing to stop the violence. There had been no more Nato air attacks.

Despite the tension in Mostar, the movement of front-line troops and civilians would go ahead tomorrow as planned. Being a single piece in a much bigger jigsaw, we had no choice but to go along with this. There was nothing we could do about the ethnic burning, as I called it. I just hoped it would fizzle out during the night.

I put the satcom handset down and thought about what tomorrow might bring. At daybreak, thousands of people would be on the move in this sector alone. The potential for disaster was breathtaking.

TEN

For once, there was no chat, no banter, as we rose from our beds and made ready for the day's work. The four of us went about our preparations in a purposeful silence. There was much to reflect on. April 13 was the day to which all our preparations as a patrol in Bosnia had been leading. Today was the day when tens of thousands of Croat and Muslim troops would either move back peaceably from their forward positions or decide that to fight was better than to withdraw and send the only part of the country that wasn't in flames back into the devil's kitchen for another grilling.

I don't eat much at the best of times, but today I felt the need of even less fuel than usual. A piece of bread to line the stomach, a cup of thick, strong tea in my trusty old metal mug, a couple of fags to get my lungs started and I was ready to go. As we RV'd outside, I did a quick 360 to see if I could see any flames on the horizon, but the line where earth met sky seemed impossibly dark, except in the east, where there was a faint pre-dawn glow. Mercifully, the spate of ethnic burning from the day before seemed to have a snuffed itself out. It was time to move.

While Adrian saddled up and drove for the Croat side, Paul and I headed in the opposite direction, ready to deliver our cargo, Keith, to his position on the straight stretch of road in front of the derelict block of flats. To ease the tension a little, I tried to persuade our 'jackal' that there had to be a reason why the sniper hadn't shown the day before.

'Like what?' Keith asked. He clearly wasn't in the mood for talking.

'Like maybe you were sunbathing out there or something. Maybe he caught sight of your lean masculine physique and you scared the fucker away.'

The Racing Snake was unmoved. 'Piss off, Cammy, and watch the bloody road. It's bad enough getting caught between the Croats and the Muslims in this place, but when you're not even sure whose side your own troop sergeant is on . . .'

I got the message. Since Paul had spilled the beans about our encounter at the Croat checkpoint I'd been wondering how I was going to live down the quips back at Hereford about my new affiliation to the Muslim brotherhood.

When we reached the run-in to the drop-off point, Keith gathered up his rifle and I slowed the vehicle to a crawl. There was the merest ripple of canvas as he slipped over the side of the still-moving vehicle and jumped down on to the road. Then he was away and into the thicket of weeds and tall grass that characterized the dead ground in front of the sniper's building.

As I drove away, I did a quick radio check. Keith came back, loud and clear, on the 349.

At around 1015, Paul and I headed back towards the sniper's beating ground on the pretext – real, as it happened – of heading to a part of the Muslim lines where the withdrawal was taking place. I dipped the transmit switch of the 349 just to check Keith was still awake. 'We're about two klicks from you,' I informed him. 'Any sign of X-ray, over?'

I received a brief crackle of answering static, then, 'No, mate. Not a fucking sausage. Over.'

'Keep scanning, Keith. Maybe he'll show as we drive by.'

He didn't. With Paul doing the driving and me scanning every nook and cranny of that building with the binos, we pottered by feeling slightly stupid for ever having believed there might be a way we were going to get this bloke.

We headed for the Muslim lines on the edge of town, dismounted and jumped down into the maze of trenches, holding areas and sniping lofts that snaked across the front. We walked past scattered groups of soldiers making their way back to their new positions. There didn't seem to be any bitterness or resentment on their faces, just a kind of resigned weariness, the same kind of look you get on a captive who's just had the stomach for a fight knocked out of him.

Also to my satisfaction, I noticed that the SPANBAT troops, kitted out from head to toe in Kevlar, were monitoring exactly where they were supposed to be. I put a quick call in to GV that, so far, the withdrawal was going like clockwork.

Paul and I put in another deliberate pass down the sniping alley, our minds and bodies relaxing by the second as the whole journey took on a kind of routine mundanity. It was like going to work on a bus every day with only the merest suggestion – a kind of thousand to one shot – that this might be the day of all days that some terrorist just happened to put a bomb on it.

We inspected another part of the lines and observed that things appeared to be happening here much as they were in the previous area. This time, I moved deliberately to some large holding areas I'd plotted on the maps, keen to check that the Muslims weren't hiding troops who could move forward swiftly to occupy the vacated Croat front lines. They were clear as a bell, empty.

My faith in the peace process was building by the moment.

As we drove back again, Paul behind the wheel, me in the passenger seat, I radioed Adrian to see if things were going as well on his side of the fence as they were on mine. While I was waiting for him to get back to me, I called Keith to tell him we were a kilometre out on the approach to the sniper's initial eyes-on.

'Quiet as the bloody grave,' Adrian said, as soon as I went back on to 'receive'.

'They're moving back?' I asked.

'Meek as you like,' he answered. 'Just a thought, mate, but maybe your sniper's been withdrawn. Maybe he's been pulled back along with everyone else.'

'Yes,' I said. Part of me actually felt disappointed. 'The thought had occurred to me, too.'

We were barely another three hundred metres down the road, when a slightly breathless-sounding Keith came on the line. 'Cammy?' I reached for the radio. As I did so, he called me again. 'Cammy?'

I was about to tell him to stop fussing like an old woman, when I realized that there was an urgency in his voice I hadn't heard since we'd been in Norway on the Mainwaring job. I dipped the transmit switch. 'Yes, mate. What is it?'

'X-ray visible. I repeat, X-ray visible. Got 'im, Cammy. Over.'

I felt a surge of adrenaline. *Bingo.* 'Gimme the rundown.' I looked at Paul. We were about five hundred metres now from the moment when we moved into the sniper's line of fire.

Keith's voice came back at strength three, which is workable, but I had to strain to catch each word. 'He's in the block of flats, all right. Top floor, third shell hole from the right. Over.'

'What's he doing?'

'Lying prone. The fucker's got himself a damned good position. I can just see the barrel of his rifle and the top of his head. The rest of him is concealed behind the rubble. Over.'

'What are his intentions?'

'He looks like he's readying for a shot. Over.'

I sat back and took a long, deep breath. I noticed Paul's knuckles whiten on the wheel. It had never occurred to me before, but it did now. Maybe this guy wasn't playing. Maybe he'd been shooting to kill all along, but hadn't quite got it right. Well, he'd had plenty of practice over the past two weeks. His luck could only improve.

We were now two hundred metres from when we broke cover. Keith needed silence to concentrate on the task in hand. I just needed one last exchange of information before committing ourselves once and for all.

'Keith, confirm one X-ray. Over.'

'One X-ray, confirmed.' His voice sounded strangely detached, almost robotic. 'What do you want me to do with him? Over.'

'I don't want a body-bag on this one. That understood?'

'Not a problem, mate. How close do you want it?' Again, the mechanical voice. I could picture him squinting down the sights, getting his breathing right down to the point where he was almost flat-lining.

'Just scare the crap out of him, mate. Over.'

'X-ray's moving, Cammy. He must be able to hear you. Confirm that. I can hear you now. Nice and slow as you drive. I've got him in my sights. Here we go . . .'

I put the radio down and picked the binos up just as we cleared our last piece of shelter and trundled out on to the stretch of road in front of the block of flats.

I took a quick squint through the optics but could see nothing. If I was looking for a rifle and the top of someone's head, there was a fuck-all chance I was going to spot it with the Land Rover dipping in and out of the pot-holes.

Only now did I realize what a long shot this was. Four hundred metres for the sniper, five hundred, maybe, for Keith . . .

We were now at the half-way point in the road. The tension was killing me. Why didn't Keith shoot? What the hell was he waiting for?

As I stared at the building, my eyes half closed in expectation of the shot I was about to hear from Keith's rifle, I saw a tiny puff of smoke from the third shell hole from the right on the top floor.

A fleeting expletive went through my head at the precise moment the sniper's round of high velocity exploded in the road. Since light travels faster than sound, the crack of the sniper's shot reached me at the same moment. At the second the round hit, Keith let loose a corker with his SA-80, sending a bullet into the brickwork right by the sniper's head.

I watched what happened next through the binos. The sniper got to his feet in a mad panic and started to leg it to safety – or what he thought was safety. The shot had been so close, maybe he thought there was someone right there in the building with him.

As he ran past the next shell hole, Keith, still concealed in his patch of dead ground, sent another round thumping into the brickwork just behind him. The sniper reacted as if he'd been stung by a hornet; stumbling, falling, picking himself up again and running on to the next shelter. As he headed blindly past one last piece of exposed wall, Keith anticipated his trajectory and sent a final round crashing into the ceiling, bringing a cascade of plaster on our man as he barrelled past.

I radioed my congratulations to Keith as Paul and I jumped back into the Land Rover, ready to pick him up. In case we needed to go through the procedure again, we went for the same covert method of collection, putting the Land Rover between the sniper and Keith and scooping him up under the canvas.

Later, in my regular evening sced to GV, I was able to tell James that the movement of troops in Mostar was 75 per cent complete and had gone through so far without major incident. He, in turn, told me what had been happening in Gorazde, which, for once, wasn't much. The Bosnian-Serb Army commander, General Mladic, had repeated his threat to shoot down Nato aircraft and the Russians had delivered further warnings to

Nato about the danger of a wider conflict if the air strikes continued.

While Gorazde was relatively quiet, the situation there was still desperate as more refugees streamed into the town and food stocks dwindled to nothing. Relief had been promised in the form of the eight hundred Ukrainians we'd run into earlier in the month, but given the state of them and their equipment, I didn't put much faith in the scheme. Neither did James.

Before I signed off, I gave James a warning order on our future intentions. We'd continue to monitor the final part of the Muslim–Croat move the following morning but, if all went to plan, we expected to be out of the city and heading back to GV by around midday. Between the lines, I was hoping that James might read this as evidence of our availability for deployment to Gorazde to lend assistance to Charlie's half of the troop. But if he got the hint, he didn't show it.

While the world's major powers argued over the fate of Gorazde – and the Serbs, in deference to the wishes of their allies the Russians, put their offensive on hold – the patrol took advantage of the lull in the fighting to do a little reconnaissance.

Ever since the Cetniks had overrun the Muslims' positions in the north-east, for Charlie, at least, the writing had been on the wall.

It seemed sensible to put in some serious preparation for a helicopter extraction while they had the chance. When Gorazde fell, as it had to soon, Charlie reasoned, the end would be swift. There'd be no time to dick around looking for ways out. They had to have their escape options ready.

But they also knew they had to be damned careful how they went about it. The mood in the city had turned against them once and it might again. For the moment, while the Serbs held back and the memory of the air strikes stayed in the defenders' minds, the patrol's stock was high. But if the Muslims detected that they were plotting an escape, they'd take them hostage before any of them got anywhere near a helicopter landing site (HLS).

On the day after the F/A-18s attacked the Serbian armoured column, Charlie and Glen headed for an area to the north-east of the city about three klicks from the bank. Fergie and Nick, who had come to know the area from their observations of Serb movements another four klicks to the north, had mentioned that it looked promising as an HLS. There was flat ground here, as well as a number of large buildings in the vicinity, which would offer some protection from Serb and Muslim gunfire for a helo touching down, albeit briefly, on the ground.

They spent the initial part of the morning surveying a patch of pastureland close to a stream. The area was eerily quiet and bordered on three sides by woodland. It had looked ideal as an HLS on the map and even better now that they were here. But something was not quite right, Charlie and Glen agreed, and they couldn't quite put their fingers on it. If anything, the place was too bloody quiet.

While Glen swept the edge of the forest with his SA-80, Charlie scouted the ground one last time before making up his mind.

Suddenly he called Glen over to the middle of the clearing. There, in the long grass, was a wooden pallet, the type the RAF or the Americans used to load kit on to and then chuck out the back of a C-130. They walked on a little way and found another, then another. The wooden planks were still relatively untarnished – the very fact that they were here at all and hadn't been snaffled by the local population for firewood said they hadn't been here long.

'Fucking hell,' Charlie said, 'you know what this is, don't you?'

Glen glanced skyward. 'I'd say, on the evidence, boss, that Air America's alive and well and still very much in business.'

'And after the bloody locals refused permission to us.' Charlie shook his head bitterly. 'Come on, let's get out of here. If they catch us in this bloody place, they'll probably shoot us.' He told Glen about our patrol's experiences in Tuzla, when the Norwegians had been prevented from flying us into Maglaj by the mysterious no-fly order and yet during the night the air had reverberated with the drone of high-flying C-130s. It looked like Tuzla hadn't been the only pocket to be benefiting from the covert US weapons-delivery programme. The CIA had been busy here, too.

What galled wasn't that the Yanks' dirty tricksters were engaged in the great game in Gorazde – Charlie and Glen figured that the Muslims needed military assistance from somebody just to hang on in the face of the Serbs' well-oiled war-machine. What got up their noses was that they'd requested an air-drop from the Muslim commander a few days earlier and he'd turned them down. If they, the Muslims, couldn't get supplies, the commander had told Charlie, then there was no reason why the UKLO should either. Everybody would be in the same boat. But evidently they weren't in the same boat as the Muslims, Charlie told Glen, as they jogged back to the Land Rover.

They were driving towards the centre of town when Charlie slowed the vehicle to a halt. Up ahead was what looked like a factory; a large, low-lying building that was relatively intact but apparently deserted. What the factory was, or had been, mattered less to the boss than what was in front of it: a large area of flat concrete car-park that was delightfully free of overhead obstructions. If a helicopter were to touch down here, it would be relatively easy to secure as the whole area was ringed by a substantial-looking chain-link fence.

They got out and clambered over the fence to take a look around. No sooner had they touched down on the other side than a military vehicle screamed up. A couple of Muslim militia-men got out, pistols drawn.

'Get in the vehicle,' one of them yelled.

Charlie and Glen looked at each other. Then Charlie turned to the senior of the two Muslims. Drawing himself up to his full height and brushing back his blond hair, he started to bluster in his best Hugh Grant.

'Now, look here. *Ja sam britanski oficir. Mi smo sa UN. Na sta se zalite?*' I am a British officer. We are UN personnel. What seems to be the trouble here?

The accent was atrocious, but it seemed to have the desired effect. The Muslims holstered their weapons as Charlie burbled his excuses. He managed to convince them that he and Glen were just out for a stroll, taking the air, that kind of thing. Maybe they truly believed that this was what British military officers did all the time in a major fucking war-zone. Maybe they really thought that British Army officers were cut from the same cloth as Alec Guinness in *The Bridge on the River Kwai* and Michael Caine in *Zulu*. Whatever they believed, it worked. Twenty minutes later, Charlie and Glen were back in the bank and grilling Misha, the civvy interpreter, about what they had tripped over on their excursion to the north-east.

Misha was embarrassed. At first he was reluctant to say anything, then it all came out. It transpired they'd tried to recce a part of the town where the Muslims had set up well-concealed ammo factories and depots. The building they'd seen was given over to the manufacture of grenades and shells. This, for the Muslims, was a major strategic secret. If the Serbs got wind of it, all they had to do was lob a shell through the roof and – *boom* – that would be it. The fact that the district was so quiet was a clever deception. It made the Serbs believe there was nothing worthwhile to shoot at.

Between the Yanks' covert air-drops and this factory, Charlie and Glen couldn't have picked two worse places to go looking for an HLS.

They sat back and laughed about it, leaving Misha to walk

off scratching his head, wondering about the eccentric behaviour of the British.

That night, the patrol drew up plans for the next few days' activities. Nick and Fergie were to drive to the north to check out Serb activity in the high ground. Ray and Dave were to go south, to a district in the southern part of the city called Binarici, where they'd picked up persistent reports of a female Serbian sniper who was spectacularly good at her job. How the Muslims knew it was a girl doing this deadly work was never ascertained, but whoever was behind the trigger was a master or mistress of their trade, regularly pulling off fatal shots at distances in excess of a thousand metres. Glen and Toby, meanwhile, were to be used as sweepers, roving from place to place with a dual responsibility: looking for signs of renewed Serb military activity and keeping their eyes peeled all the while for that HLS. Without one, escape would be impossible.

On the morning of 14 April, I turned up unannounced at the office of the Muslim corps commander. I told General Kislic our mission was complete and that we were going. It seemed churlish now to mention his behaviour over the ethnic-burning incidents. He knew I was pissed off about it and it hadn't happened since – which was what mattered. The movement of troops had resumed again this morning and was likely to be complete by midday, which was when we were due to ship back to GV. We shook hands. I like to think I saw a look of genuine regret in Kislic's face, but who knows? Things are hard to read in Bosnia, especially faces. I'd learned not to go too much on appearances. In the final analysis, I kept telling myself, results were the only thing that mattered.

'Perhaps you would be good enough to pass on my congratu-lations to General Rose.' Kislic gave me a half-smile. 'Who knows? We may even have a little peace around here. Will we be getting any more UKLO in Mostar, Sergeant?'

I knew the answer to this was no, but I kept it to myself. The UKLO was overstretched as it was. I told Kislic that unit members would probably be back in the near future but I couldn't say when. It seemed to pacify him a little.

Just before we were due to leave, I put in a call to James in GV. 'Well, that's us all wrapped up,' I told him. 'We should be with you in four to six hours.'

'There's been a change of plan, Cammy,' he said suddenly.

I felt a stab of adrenaline. 'Gorazde?'

'No, mate. Gorazde's gone quiet, thank God. We want you to get down to Split.'

'But what about Charlie's mob? I bet he could do with all the help he can get.'

'That's as maybe, but the pocket is closed. The reality is we couldn't get you in there without a major fucking shindig. Charlie was lucky . . .' He paused, no doubt a little stung by the irony of his choice of words. 'Charlie was fortunate in that he got into Gorazde via a unique set of circumstances. To be honest, you'll be of far greater value to us after you've rested up in Split for a few days. You guys have done a bloody fine job. Well done. But get some rest, mate. We've got our eyes firmly on the situation. We're taking care of it as best we're able.'

We reached Split without encountering any problems. It was dusk when we arrived and we headed more or less straight for our pits. I didn't really know how knackered I was until the pressure eased. I slept like a baby for damn near ten hours.

The following morning I met up with some senior NCOs from B Squadron who'd just arrived from Hereford to have a look around. They were led by their sar'nt'-major, a big guy called Frank who took no prisoners and had a curious habit of eating garlic raw, in much the same way the rest of us might have a fag or chew a stick of gum. He maintained it was good for the heart, but it couldn't have done anything for his social life.

The presence of Frank and his mates in Split told me that there'd been a sea-change in the relationship between Bosnia and the Regiment. D Squadron had been the first to come out in any significant strength. We'd been the bridge between them and B Squadron, which would be arriving in force in the next few weeks. It was almost as if Bosnia had become part of the circuit, like doing a stint in Northern Ireland.

'You busy?' Frank inquired, as soon as we had a moment alone to chat.

'You could say that,' I replied. 'I dare say you've heard about the situation in Gorazde.'

Frank gave a minor snort of triumph, sending a garlicky blast past my left ear. 'Yeah, well, B Squadron'll be here shortly. You guys have done your bit, but you can relax now. We'll take it from here.'

I looked at him and said nothing, but inside I felt a little bit sorry for the guy. He didn't know what was about to hit him. None of them did.

While I continued to show the B Squadron NCOs around, Keith and Paul took it in turns to man the radio in our ops room. This was twenty metres or so from our dormitory. It was much like the ops room at GV. Half the space was given over to planning and tactics and half was used for storage. Given the situation in Gorazde, we thought it best to have someone permanently on hand, in addition to the resident scaly, to man the comms links. We even decided it would be wise to put a bed in here, so that we could give the Gorazde pocket the round-the-clock attention it deserved.

Around mid-afternoon, I'd just finished giving Frank and his mates the low-down on Mostar, when the door of the briefing room opened. I looked up and saw Keith. He beckoned me away from the group. 'Cam, you'd better get on the blower to GV and quick. I just had James on the horn. He sounded like grim fucking death.'

'What's happened?' I asked, taking the stairs to the top floor three at a time.

'I don't know. But, by the sound of the bloke, whatever it is it ain't good.'

The satcom was too difficult to set up in a hurry, so I got on the landline instead. Straight away, I hit the scrambler, a little button on the side of the handset that allows you to talk securely. I felt this might be our call to go to Gorazde. I didn't want to take any chances.

'Cammy?'

There was something in his voice, a tautness I'd never heard before. 'What is it, James?'

'There's no easy way of telling you this, mate. We've just got word from Gorazde. Fergie's been shot in the head. They're trying to get a chopper in to reach him, then fly him to Sarajevo. There's word, too, that Nick Evans, the D Squadron captain, has also been badly injured. We're not sure what happened but it seems the Serbs opened fire on them. I'm sorry, mate, but that's all I've got at the moment. Obviously we'll keep you posted, but I gotta go. There's all shit busting loose here.'

And that was it. It took me a moment, sitting there alone in the darkness of the ops room, to come to terms with the message. The details were so sparse. I had to fight to stop my imagination working overtime to fill in the gaps. All I knew for sure was that Fergie had taken a round in the head and that was bad enough. I felt shattered. A round in the head. My God, it was what all of us dreaded. Was he already dead? Was he alive, lying out there in the field somewhere, waiting for the chopper? If they got him to Sarajevo, would the doctors be able to save him? A bullet to the brain. Jesus, nobody survived that, did they? And even if they did . . .

I sat there with my head in my hands, groping for answers.

*

Glen was perched around fifteen metres up the TV mast at Salihoba-Raban, focusing his binos on a developing skirmish in the hills four klicks to the north. Toby was making non-vital repairs to the Land Rover below him. They were reliving an incident a few days earlier when a Serb shell had screamed in and exploded in a thicket just beside the path they were walking along.

It had become something of a routine among the seven of them to indulge in a little 'chicken' during such moments. Even Charlie had joined in. Once, when a particularly large shell had whistled over, Glen and Toby had gritted their teeth and stood their ground. When they turned, Charlie was lying flat on his stomach, inspecting the ground and pronouncing on the rare beauty of Bosnian grasses and weeds. He professed to know nothing about any shells.

On certain days in Gorazde you needed a dry sense of humour just to get by.

When the shell had exploded in the thicket, Glen's nerves shredded and he threw himself on to the path and spun round, expecting to see Toby down in the weeds beside him. But Toby had remained on his feet; the guy was just standing there, ramrod straight. The shrapnel had barely finished rattling through the trees and pinging off the buildings all around them when Toby looked down at Glen and said, 'You wanker!'

'What do you mean?' Glen asked, incredulously. 'Didn't you hear that?'

Somehow, in the intervening seconds, Toby managed to regain his composure. 'Hear what?' he replied blithely.

The remark had earned him the nickname Iron Balls.

The two of them were still laughing about this when the radio crackled inside the Land Rover. Glen's attention was still fixed on the fighting. It had been quiet for the past couple of days, but now there were signs that things were hotting up again.

Nick and Fergie had gone even closer to where the skirmishing was taking place to try to get more information.

The radio crackled again. Then, Nick's voice burst through at high volume: 'Contact! We've had a fucking contact! Fergie's taken a round in the head. I've been hit, too. Glen, Toby, if you can hear this, they're steaming past here and heading for your location. Get the fuck out of there or you're dead. I repeat, they're pouring past us for your position. Over.'

Cetniks. Jesus.

The power of the message – with its heady mix of warning and catastrophe – put the equivalent of a small bomb under Glen in his eyrie. He tried to do a fireman's shimmy all the way down the metalwork, but ended up falling the last six metres. The thought of mixing it with a band of stinking, battle-hardened Serbs fought with the knowledge that two men had been hit, one seriously. He never felt the ground that rushed to meet him.

Within seconds, Toby had the bonnet down and the Land Rover ready to move. Glen was already on the radio to Charlie in the bank. 'What are you going to do?' Charlie demanded.

Glen and Toby knew roughly where Fergie and Nick had gone, but it was a big area and there was no way of knowing precisely. They'd tried to raise Nick again without success. Glen did some hard thinking.

If they stayed, with the Serbs streaming towards them, there was every chance that four men would go down, not two. If they left, two colleagues – two friends – would die, no question. One at least, from the sound of things, might already be dead.

It was one of those life-or-death decisions that had to be made in a nano-second. Glen dipped the transmit switch. 'What the hell?' he told Charlie. 'We'll go in and get them.'

Two minutes later, they re-established contact with Nick. He was able to tell them the grid reference where he and Fergie had been attacked. They'd been in the Land Rover at the time, edging forward slowly along a track in the foothills. He supplied one other vital recognition detail before the radio went dead again. The Land Rover, he told them, had been attacked on an S-bend.

They headed out on foot, following a slope that led to the area indicated on the chart. Suddenly, five silhouettes appeared on the ridge-line two hundred metres ahead. Glen and Toby froze.

'Now what?' Toby hissed. He was standing a foot or two behind Glen, staring at the silent, immobile figures up ahead. 'Serbs or Muslims?' he whispered.

Glen screwed up his eyes against the light. The sun was directly behind their reception committee. Swift recognition was impossible.

'Your guess is as good as mine,' the senior NCO answered quietly. He took a deep breath and added, 'Stuff it, we haven't got all day. Here goes.'

He held up his right arm.

'*Ne pucaj.*' Don't shoot.

More figures appeared on the ridge-line. They did a quick head count. There were about twenty in all, bristling to a man with AKs and heavy machine-guns and ringed with bandoleros stuffed full of ammo.

'If I get shot,' Glen said, out of the corner of his mouth, 'you fuck off and head for the vehicle, got it?'

Expecting some kind of acknowledgement, and getting none, he flicked a glance over his shoulder. For a moment he thought Toby had legged it.

But Iron Balls was sticking to him like glue. He managed a smile. 'Sorry, mate,' he said. 'We're both in this up to our ears. Thanks, though. I'll buy you a pint if we get out of it alive.'

Glen gritted his teeth. 'Make it slivovitz,' he replied, even though he hated the stuff.

The sun dropped below the ridge-line and Glen suddenly saw the faces of the men on it. He was greeted with the dead stares of people who knew they had had it, their minds filled with the certain knowledge of what would happen to them and their families when the Serbs swept into the town.

The party trudged past without giving them so much as a second look. Glen grabbed one of the stragglers, a kid still in his teens, and almost had to shake the answer out of him, using a mixture of broken Serbo-Croat and mime.

His accent must have given him away. There was a momentary flicker of recognition behind the kid's eyes. 'Ah, British . . .'

He turned slowly and indicated an area over the ridge-line.

The two soldiers started up the slope again. When they looked back, the Muslim party had vanished into a thin line of smoke that had drifted up from the scattered hamlets below.

They now saw the extent of the Serb advance. The morning's skirmish had been the prelude to a full-blown assault. This time, they knew, the Serbs would make it their last push to capture the town. Now, though, it looked as if the Muslims were just managing to hold them a kilometre from the T V tower.

Glen tucked in behind a scattering of boulders and tried to call Nick on the radio, but got nothing back, which led him to suspect the worst. He reported this to Charlie.

Comms on the radio were now getting difficult. To hear anything Glen had to turn the volume way up. As a result, anything Charlie said was accompanied by a deafening blast of static.

Both men agreed to press on, but from now on they would abandon the radio and stick to a Motorola mobile phone that Glen had brought with him. In the high-threat scenario into which they'd tumbled, all the radio noise succeeded in doing was drawing the attention of anyone nearby.

Remembering the incredible accuracy of the sniping they'd seen in Bosnia, Toby said, 'You don't think she's out here, do you?'

'Who?'

'The thousand-metre girl.'

'Ta, mate,' Glen panted. 'Like, I really needed that now.'

They hit the ridge-line and crouched down behind some rocks. Stretching away below them was a slope littered with stumps of trees and craters. It was a replica of the scene they had visited a few days earlier. A few pines had survived the relentless artillery bombardments but they were stripped of all greenery. Under the rolling clouds gathering from the east, it was a grim scene.

From their vantage-point, Glen and Toby made out the demarcation lines between the Serb and Muslim positions. Roughly a klick away, in a zone that constituted a kind of no man's land, they were able to make out the kink in the road where the white-painted Land Rover had come to grief. But of the vehicle itself there was no sign.

Despite sweeping the terrain with their optics, neither man was able to spot a trace of Fergie or Nick.

They'd been there no more than a couple of minutes when a gaggle of Muslims came up the ridge-line behind them. A minute later, Glen and Toby were standing before the commander in a semi-reinforced trench. The Muslim officer was a tall, thin man with two weeks' worth of growth on his cheeks. He listened as they told him about Fergie and Nick.

The commander knew all about the Land Rover. He claimed that the Serbs had fired on it, knowing that it was a UN vehicle. He also maintained that the two UKLO men were lying in a trench still tenuously held by Muslim forces. It was, he said, indicating a position close to a break in some rising ground below, just a few metres from the Serb lines. He had lost communication with the trench some time back, he said, and he no longer knew whether those within it were alive or dead. Despite the threat of an imminent assault by the Serbs, he allocated a three-man detail to take Glen and Toby down to Nick and Fergie's last-known position.

They were about to set out along the criss-cross grid of

interlocking slit trenches when a Serb triple-A battery opened up on them. Glen was on the Motorola to Charlie when the first shell struck. There was an explosion of dirt as the whole of one side of the trench blew in. Incredibly, all eight people inside escaped injury. Another string of triple-A fire pummelled the side of the trench, forcing everyone to move into an adjoining position.

Glen, Toby and their escort kept going until they reached a trench around three hundred metres short of the one in which Nick and Toby were supposed to be located.

Glen poked his head above the parapet. A burst of heavy machine-gun fire raked the ground a metre or two from his face. In his snatched view of the ground ahead, he saw that their objective was cut off from the rest of the trench network, but still holding out against the Serbs.

A little way to the left were the remnants of a wood. They worked their way around to it, were spotted by the Serbs and received mortar fire. Airbursts exploded above their heads. As the shrapnel zinged down around them, they made their way back to the trench and got on the Motorola to Charlie.

With the batteries failing, Glen informed him that the only way they would be able to get to Nick and Fergie was by mounting a night assault on the Serb positions, removing the threat of their mortar and machine-gun fire, then going in and doing a Casevac. The Muslims, he said, had already agreed to it and were assembling a strike force as they spoke. It was simply a matter of sitting it out – and praying that in the meantime the Serbs didn't mount their own attack – till it got dark. Then they'd go in and hammer them.

They never did catch Charlie's reply because at that moment the batteries gave up the ghost and an American A-10 tank-buster flew over.

By the time Charlie had re-established comms using the radio, the Serbs had stopped firing, knowing that the A-10 was prowling for targets. Apart from the strange, high-pitched whine of the twin turbofans as the aircraft circled above them, the battlefield had fallen eerily quiet.

'Glen,' Charlie's voice crackled, 'we don't have the mandate. The UN'll crucify us for this.'

'To hell with the mandate,' Glen told him. 'We've got to get them out of there, boss.' He looked at his watch. It had been over an hour since he'd received Nick's first message up the TV tower.

'Listen,' Charlie replied, 'hold your positions while I get on to RHQ and call down an air strike.'

And then the radio went dead.

They watched the A-10 in the dwindling light as it circled above the battlefield. They waited for the strike to come down, but it never did. Fifteen minutes later, to their deep consternation, the aircraft dipped its wings and headed for home.

The Muslims went apoplectic. Fuck it, thought Glen. There goes the prospect of any help. If they were going to get to the two injured men, they would have to do it on their own.

Glen tried to get Charlie on the radio, but couldn't get through. 'Bollocks,' he said to Toby. 'We'll wait till it gets dark, then we'll go in tactically.'

An hour later, they got on their stomachs and crawled the remaining three hundred metres to the trench. They were able to cut through some of the darkness with the image-intensifying KITE-sights on their SA-80s. Both men were aware, however, that what was good for them was good also for the Serbs. They hugged the ground and prayed that a Cetnik with a thermal-imager hadn't picked them up and was homing in on them for a shot.

A few metres from the trench, Glen checked it out with the sight, then dropped into it, as quiet as a panther, his SA-80 at the ready. Toby slid in behind him. They combed the moon-shadows with their sights, scarcely daring to breathe. It took them a moment longer than it should have to grasp the truth because neither man wanted to believe it.

The trench had been abandoned.

Glen fell back against the side wall. He stared at the night sky. Occasional cracks of rifle-fire rose up from the valley. Otherwise it was strangely quiet.

Toby hunched down beside him. The only other sound they could detect between sporadic bursts of gunfire was the Cetniks talking and laughing in their trenches. They were that bloody close.

'What now?' Toby whispered.

'We've come this far. I'm going to shout to them. They've got to be somewhere close.'

'Don't be an idiot,' Toby hissed. 'The Serbs'll drop down on us like a ton of bricks. Listen, Glen, we've done everything we can for Nick and Fergie. They're not here.'

Glen lapsed into a moment of introspection, then pushed himself away from the trench wall. 'You're right. Let's get the fuck out of here,' he said. He swept the ground between them and the Serbs with his KITE-sight. Then, he slithered over the top of the trench.

They left the way they'd come in, crawling through the freezing dirt on the road. Then they got to their feet and marched back down the track using the same tried and tested method as before – Glen in front, then Toby.

To the repeated refrain of '*ja sam Britanac*' they walked all the way back to the Land Rover, found to their amazement that it was still where they had left it, then drove fast to the bank. It was a tactic born of desperation. There were pockets of fighting all around them as Serbs and Muslims engaged in house-to-house warfare.

Back at base, they discovered that Fergie had been airlifted out of the pocket by helicopter, thanks to a twenty-minute ceasefire organized by the UN. He and Nick had been found by a Muslim platoon and driven in their own Land Rover to the hospital on the outskirts of the city. Amazingly, it was still in the defenders' hands, but only just.

The doctors had stemmed the flow of blood from Nick's injuries, which were serious, but not life-threatening. He had been shot in the shoulder. Fergie, though, was in a dreadful mess. The Serbs had fired two shots as they'd been driving forward to inspect the edge of the battlefield. One round had come in through the back and hit Nick, the other had punched through the windscreen and hit Fergie in the head. His only chance of survival, the doctors had said, was to get him on to an operating table, preferably at a UN facility where they had the requisite skills and all the right drugs and equipment.

By an incredible process of shuttle-calling, Charlie had contacted Sarajevo, and Sarajevo the Bosnian-Serb headquarters at Pale. The Serbs agreed to a short ceasefire to enable a UN helicopter to land in the football stadium to the south of the city and airlift Fergie out.

By a quirk of the local topography and the prevalent weather conditions, neither Glen nor Toby had heard the chopper come in or out. It had snuck in under top-cover from the A-10 that had patrolled the sky above them, seemingly in such a detached and callous way. When the chopper left, the A-10's job had been over and it had turned for home.

Glen and Toby gave their report to Charlie, who listened appreciatively, then told them to get some rest. But sleep would not come. Everyone was thinking about Fergie. All military units are close-knit, but I know of few that look after their own like the SAS. While Fergie's life hung in the balance, there would be no rest for anybody.

Charlie forced himself to focus on the Serb assault that was now overwhelming the Muslims' defences in the north and east. Like a faithful old oiler, Gorazde, battered and holed in multiple locations, was about to give up the fight and slide into oblivion.

But Charlie refused to give up.

He got on the radio and told G V that there was only one thing now that could possibly save Gorazde from a bloodbath as the Serbs swept into the centre of town. At daybreak the next morning, they needed air strikes. And they needed them in spades. Force was the only language the Serbs understood.

Tomorrow, he said, neither the UN nor Nato should pull any damn punches. He asked GV to gain the necessary clearances for the Serbs to be hit and hit hard – for Ray, for Nick, for Fergie and for the thousands of people that would otherwise die in this unholy tragedy.

Three hours later the phone rang again, and I got the news I'd been expecting against all hope. The chopper had airlifted Fergie to Sarajevo and they'd managed to get him on to the operating table, but even Fergie's big heart had not been up to the last great fight of his life and he'd died in the midst of the doctors' struggle to save him. His injuries had been too severe. It was astounding he'd survived so long.

I received the news in the darkness of the ops room. The scaly who'd been there when the call came in got up and made himself scarce. I don't know how long I remained by the radio with the lights off. It was only when it crackled – I'd left it on to monitor the other half of the troop's transmissions from Gorazde to G V – and I heard Charlie checking in again, that I remembered that this thing wasn't over yet, not by a long way.

A voice in the back of my head kept telling me that we had to put this behind us and concentrate on the difficult hours ahead. We owed Charlie and the others that much – and we owed it to Fergie, too. As I made my way down the stairs, I became aware of all the UN clerks, drivers and pay-wallahs moving to the side of the stairwell to make way for me. I never found out whether they knew about Fergie or whether it was just my imagination, but it seemed suddenly as if the whole world had zeroed in on our small community. It was an uncomfortable feeling. As a unit, we're not used to attention. I felt the shadows pulling me back, but first I had to break the news to Keith and Paul.

I found them in the mess-hall. As new recruits, they hadn't known Fergie long, but they were gutted all the same. Fergie had been a highly popular member of the squadron. It was hard to believe he was gone.

I told them I'd be in the ops room if they needed me.

Back in the darkness, with only the red and green diodes of the radio and the tac-sat for company, my mood shifted from sorrow to anger. By now, it was obvious that Gorazde had all the ingredients of a Saigon in the making, but all I saw and heard was the UN's inaction.

The BBC World Service, quoting American officials, said that the Serbs had captured every strategic point in the town and were now within five hundred metres of the hospital where Nick and Fergie had been taken after the attack. This turned out to be a little pessimistic, but it reflected the desperate nature of the situation. Serb Army chiefs were calling on the Muslims to surrender and for all citizens to take shelter behind Serb lines.

Haris Silajdzic, the Bosnian prime minister, had gone on air blaming the UN for 'the people who are dead and those that will be killed tonight and tomorrow'. He concluded his address by saying: 'We do not know what more the Serbs have to do to be punished.'

For their part, the Serbs had given a clear indication that Fergie's death might not have been altogether an accident. The propaganda machine in Pale said that the 'two UN soldiers' had been too close to the battle lines. 'They were not supposed to be there,' a spokesman said. 'They were supposed to be in the town. We suspect they were forward air controllers.'

Wrong, you fuckers. That was Ray's job. And Ray, despite the frag wound, was still in the frame.

In Sarajevo, the UN special envoy, Yasushi Akashi, said that air strikes had been considered during the day, but rejected because of the temporary halt in the fighting to allow Fergie – the 'wounded UN soldier' – to be airlifted out. Well, the airlift had come and gone. And now Fergie was dead. So what the hell were they going to do about it?

I got on the satcom to GV. 'Kev, when are they going to pull in some air strikes, for God's sake?'

There was a terrible weariness in Kevin's voice. 'We're doing all we can, Cammy. It's just not that easy, mate.'

'Try telling that to the blokes in the pocket.' I put the hand-set down and took a moment to knead my eyes. Then I picked it up again. I was surprised to find Kev still there. 'Look, I'm sorry. I know RHQ is doing everything it can. It's all this goal-post changing. It's driving me fucking spare.'

Kev was about to say something when Charlie came through on the radio. His transmission to GV was weak. I got off the line so that Kev could deal with it. Charlie asked to speak to James just as Paul and Keith entered the ops room. We sat and listened to the exchange that followed.

'James, listen to me,' Charlie said urgently. 'The Serbs are in the city. The Muslims are fighting for every house and every street. It's like the last days of the Reich and Beirut on a bad night rolled into one. We're taking a shitload of incoming. The defenders are holding out, but only just. And, to cap it all, we're running out of battery power.'

'Can't you recharge them?' James asked. He was shouting to make himself heard. Charlie's signal was now even weaker.

'The generator's gone, mate. Everything's bloody gone.' There was a momentary pause, laden with the hiss and moan of atmospheric distortion. 'The pocket has gone, James. It might not fold tonight and it might not fold tomorrow. But the pocket has fallen, mate, believe me. The Serbs will be here any –'

'Wait a minute! Hold it!' An unfamiliar voice had burst through on the radio. I looked at Keith and Paul. This wasn't James talking. It didn't even sound like GV on the horn. If it hadn't been delivered with all the crustiness and sharpness that some officers muster with ease I might have thought it was the Serbs jamming the transmission with one of their own.

I recognized the voice now. It belonged to a major, a member of the Regiment on Rose's staff in Sarajevo. Just as we were monitoring the transmissions in and out of the pocket so, of course, was UNPROFOR's forward headquarters. This major, I remembered now, was a liaison officer, an LO, on the general's staff.

'Charlie, this is Richard at headquarters. Watch your choice of words, man.'

'What the hell do you mean?' Charlie said. Despite the frailty of the signal, you could hear the mixture of astonishment and indignation in his voice.

'I'm saying that you should think before you speak. This isn't just a military situation that we have on our hands here. The whole thing is highly politically charged. Gorazde has not fallen. It will not fall.'

As I listened, my anger returned with a vengeance. I wanted to pick up the handset and give this guy the chewing out of the century. What was this arsehole accusing Charlie of? Defeatism? Who were they afraid of in Sarajevo? A bunch of appeasing politicians in Brussels or some mealy-mouthed bureaucrats at UN headquarters in New York?

Thankfully, Charlie was a big boy. He knew the score. If he said that a safe haven was falling, then it was falling. The last thing he needed was a lecture from his own side on political etiquette. 'Listen,' the LO said. 'Hang on for a bit longer. We're trying to call down air strikes just as soon as we can. If you can hold on until first light, Charlie, the jets will come. Have faith, lad. With fighters overhead, the Serbs will back down or, at the very least, hold off for a while. Then we can all think again.'

By the time he had finished talking, Charlie had gone off the air. Evidently, his batteries had just given up the ghost.

ELEVEN

Daybreak came with no sign of a Nato jet. The patrol took it in turns to go on watch on the roof of the bank. As the sun rose over the hills, it was possible to see how the battle had developed during the night. The sound of fighting was omni-directional. There were fires everywhere, too, some of them very close.

Dave and Ray, who took the first stint on stag, reported that the Serbs were less than a klick away to the south and the east, their advance checked by the mother of all Muslim counter-attacks. No one was under any illusion as to how long the defenders could hold out.

In the north and west the picture was more confused. From the smoke that could be seen rising from houses on the edge of the town, it looked as if the Muslims still held some land as much as three or four kilometres out. It seemed scarcely possible, but somehow Gorazde was hanging on by the fingertips.

When he focused in on the TV tower with his optics, Dave saw what he took to be Muslims with their shirts off half-way up the super-structure. They were waving flags in what appeared to be an insane act of zeal and defiance. He called over Mucky, their military interpreter. Mucky took a look and announced sombrely that the flags bore the emblem of the double-headed eagle. Those weren't Muslims, he told Dave, but Cetniks.

'They're high as kites,' Dave said, as he held the image of the tower in his binos. 'I've never seen anything like it.'

Ray adjusted the focus of his optics in time to see a Serb scale the pinnacle. The semi-naked figure proceeded to spray the ground with machine-gun fire in a wild 270-degree arc that must have taken in elements of his own side as well as Muslim positions.

'Jesus Christ,' Ray said, peering through his own binos, 'they're gone, absolutely gone.'

When the Cetnik had expended all his bullets, he dropped his trousers and urinated into the wind. From the roof, it was possible to see that he was laughing his head off. The men below him were showered with piss, but none of them seemed to notice, much less care. Whether they were drugged up to the eyes, orgied out on war, or a combination of both was impossible to tell.

For the past two weeks, this unit had probably done little but kill, loot and rape its way across the outer limits of Gorazde. The human decency these people had been born with was now lost in a heady collective blood-lust that nothing but well-aimed bullets could cure. For Ray and Dave, it was a sober portent of things to come. No Cetnik hell-bent on eating the flesh of his vanquished enemy was ever going to pay attention to a piece of paper signed in New York or a light blue flag draped over the door of a bullet-spattered bank.

'I'm telling you here and now, mate,' Ray said, fixing Dave with a stare, 'that I am not going to be taken by those fuckers.'

Mucky, who was still watching the tower through his binos, suddenly gave a cry of hope. 'Look,' he shouted, 'now we counter-attack.'

The three men watched as twenty Muslims charged up the road in a frontal assault that bore all the hallmarks of a suicide attack.

They hadn't got fifty metres when the Serbs realized what was happening and turned all the small arms they had on them.

A moment later, half of the Muslim counter-attacking force had been cut down. Those who could still hold a weapon lay where they had fallen in the street and returned fire. The strikes sparked their way up the metalwork as the Muslims raked the tower with bullets. The deranged idiot at the top could be seen desperately trying to pull a new magazine from his thigh-pocket as bullets pinged and ricocheted off the superstructure around him. Suddenly, a brilliant red flower bloomed in the middle of his chest and he spread out his arms. There was a moment at which he stood stock-still on the second rung from the top, his arms stretched wide, like a high diver preparing for the big one. Then, a further two rounds punched into his upper body and he pirouetted off the apex, spiralling down like a sycamore seed, head-first into the concrete below.

Several other Serbs fell to the ground before the Muslims were overwhelmed by superior firepower. The battle for the TV tower had been short and bloody, but it was finally over.

For Charlie, the priority of the day had been to get Nick out of the hospital and returned to the temporary sanctuary of the bank. Toby and Glen were dispatched to collect him in a Land Rover. The hospital had been ringed by defenders, who were having some success in holding off the Serbs. But it was still coming under sporadic mortar and artillery fire, some of it pretty heavy. After a horrendous trawl through the bloodsoaked corridors and wards, wall to wall with the bodies of the injured and the dying, they found Nick. He was drugged to the eyeballs, but still in a lot of pain. Despite the terrible working conditions, the hospital's desperately overworked doctors had done a good job of patching him up. The bullet had entered his arm just below the shoulder joint and shattered the bone in a dozen different places. The entry wound wasn't too bad, but on its way out the bullet had torn a sizeable hole through Nick's flesh. To reset the bone, the doctors had had to pin it together with an array of bolts held in place by what looked like a Meccano exo-skeleton on his upper arm. This unwieldy arrangement stuck out from his body at an improbable-looking right-angle.

When they had had time to take in the state of him, Glen and Toby were struck by the full implications of Nick's injuries. Apart from the fact that he still needed serious medical attention, they both realized he should never have been here in the first place. Looking at him, they were openly sympathetic, but inside both men shared the same thought: why the hell hadn't he left on the chopper flight that had casevac'd Fergie out of the pocket?

Nick greeted them with a dumb, happy smile. He was clearly delighted to see them, although Toby and Glen weren't convinced that he knew who they were. On the way back to the bank, sandwiched awkwardly on the front seat of the Land Rover between his two colleagues, Nick asked them about the state of play on the tactical front and about Fergie. Glen and Toby exchanged brief but meaningful glances. There was no sense in telling Nick how it really was. The guy was in no condition to be told the truth: that the patrol was half fucked and that Fergie was dead. When the drugs cleared his thinking, he'd learn the truth soon enough. If they didn't then he was probably the lucky one.

As soon as Nick came in, Charlie needed only a glance to take in his grey, drawn complexion and the spacy look in his eyes. He ordered him to go to the vault and stay there.

Charlie's second priority had been to recharge the batteries for their radios. Someone eventually found enough spare petrol to get the generator running for long enough to give the batteries some more juice. To preserve power, Charlie spoke to GV and gave RHQ set times when he would radio in with updates on the situation. For their part, RHQ told Charlie to stand by for another air attack.

Charlie promptly ordered Ray over to the Hotel Gradina, another tall building two hundred metres to the west, with a commanding view of the town. Here, Ray had height, space and solitude, three ingredients that allowed him to concentrate on his job as patrol forward air controller.

The only person to go up there regularly, he had so far managed to avoid the attentions of Serb snipers. He was anxious to keep it that way. Being an FAC is demanding anyway. Having bullets pinging all around you when you're trying to do your thing doesn't help concentration. It can even wind up causing you to direct bombs on to the wrong place. And the last thing any of them needed was for Ray to dump a whole load of HE on the Muslims.

Back on the roof of the bank, the rest of the patrol *was* coming under sniper fire. Glen, Dave and Toby decided to remove some bricks from the metre-high surrounding wall; something through which to direct their optics and weapons without getting their heads shot off every time they glanced over the parapet.

Unknown to them, on top of the building that, together with their own, dominated the skyline of the town, Ray had just made contact with a pair of Royal Navy Sea Harriers from 801 Squadron, operating off HMS *Ark Royal* in the Adriatic.

His radio crackled again. 'Four Zero Alpha, Four Zero Alpha, this is Foxtrot Zero One Tango. Radio-check. Over.'

Ray felt a surge of adrenaline. He always did at the moment of first contact. The lead aircraft was stooging at five thousand metres over the initial point, or IP, some thirty kilometres to the north-east. The IP is always a clearly recognizable feature – in this case a tall factory chimney outside Serb-held territory – from which the pilot begins his run-in to the target. The second the aircraft leaves the IP, Ray's job begins. The speed at which the aircraft flies has to be matched by the FAC's lightning ability to direct it to the target, in this case a clutch of Serb armoured personnel carriers that he'd spotted earlier moving reinforcements to the front.

The APCs had come to rest a kilometre or so to the east of

the TV tower and were clearly visible through Ray's optics. To get the pilot to pick them up, which is not easy from a height of around seven hundred metres at close to the speed of sound, Ray had to lead him in via a set of carefully selected, easily recognizable way-points. The pilot's job is to put the whole thing together under the expert guidance of the FAC, flying down the way-points – turning with them, this way and that – in an aerial, high-speed equivalent of join-the-dots.

'Four Zero Alpha, Roger,' Ray acknowledged. 'Read you strength five. Are you ready for orders?'

Economy with words becomes second nature to Ray as he girds himself for the roller-coaster ride to come. Once the aircraft leaves the IP it will be flying too fast for the pilot to absorb anything but the briefest of details. But that's the trick. Somehow, Ray must deliver the goods without overburdening the pilot's senses, maxed out as they are on flying the aircraft and scanning for trouble. It's an art that Ray's learned from months of training in Hereford and weeks of freezing his arse on remote bombing ranges in the UK and elsewhere. But still he doesn't find it easy. Few FACs ever do.

After an interval of several seconds, during which he takes a quick, familiarizing look at the map on his knee, the pilot replies, in an eerily calm voice, 'Roger, send now.'

Ray now gives the pilot a complete talk-through on what he is likely to expect on his way to the target, a condensed version of the course that he will begin to fly for real in a matter of seconds. He gives the pilot a bearing and a grid reference to the first way-point, then a brief description of what he will see as he screams overhead. This is followed rapidly by another bearing and grid reference to the second way-point, coupled with a description, then a final bearing to the target, which, by now, should be very close. Finally, he advises on the nearest location of friendly forces – by which he means Muslim troops – so that the pilot is well aware of the potential of blue-on-blue 'confliction', a jargon term that means knocking the shit out of your own side. In the Gulf War it also came to be known as 'collateral damage'.

The pilot reads the information back and Ray confirms that it is correct.

'Roger, wait out,' the pilot responds, as he feeds the information into his navigation and weapon-aiming computers. There is another crackle on Ray's speaker as the pilot's voice comes over the radio one last time before the aircraft leaves the relative sanctuary of Croatian air-space. 'Four Zero Alpha, this is Foxtrot Zero One Tango. Leaving IP . . . wait, wait, wait . . . now!'

Ray knows that this is where it all comes together or falls apart. He feels a momentary stab of self-doubt, then just as quickly kicks it off as he turns in the direction the aircraft will be coming from. A ball of tension in his stomach twists rapidly into a hard knot as he looks down the flight heading and scans the horizon with his binos. There is high cloud cover above the pocket, making it difficult for him to see anything. Then, suddenly, a thumb's width above the skyline, he spots the Sea Harrier.

'Foxtrot Zero Tango, have you visual now.' Short, sharp and to the point. Ray's training takes over. He doesn't have to remind himself of anything any more. It's like he's spoken this way all his life.

The pilot, his voice muffled by the background rush of slipstream, his breath fast and reedy in the confines of his mask, acknowledges, 'Roger, out.'

Ray switches to his map. He knows the aircraft is where it should be. The rest is down to his ability to convey a real-life image to the pilot from the two-dimensional world of the map pinned down by stones on the roof beside him.

'Two kilometres, twelve o'clock, bridge over the river Drina,' he barks.

A slight pause, then: 'Contact bridge.'

'Go nine o'clock, one kilometre, lone copse, one hundred metres across.'

Ray hears the pilot grunting against the onset of Gs as he goes into the turn, then: 'Roger, contact copse.'

'Come right five hundred metres, three o'clock. Tracked APCs at road junction. Target.'

'Contact target.'

'Target – destroy.'

Ray put the mike down, his job done. The adrenaline had turned his throat dry and injected a slight shake into his left hand. But, as FAC jobs go, he knew this had been a good one and raised his head above the parapet just as the lead Harrier swept over the outer edges of the town.

Back on the roof of the bank, Glen, Dave and Toby were still chiselling their way through the wall when they heard a high-pitched whine.

Everyone turned as the two Sea Harriers screamed over the pocket. They came in at seven hundred metres. Through their binos, the men on the roof could clearly see the bombs slung on weapons pylons underneath.

The Sea Harriers made a dummy pass, dropping flares as they went. The patrol had observed this tactic when the F/A-18s came over. It was meant to serve as a warning, a final message to the Serbs: desist offensive action or be attacked. The implication was clear. Next time around, there'd be no flares, but a couple of half-tonne general-purpose bombs instead.

The three patrol members and Mucky braced themselves for the Sea Harriers' second and final run-in. The targets appeared to be a huddle of APCs they'd spotted in the vicinity of the TV tower earlier. Because the sky was overcast, Toby was surprised to see a glint, a flash of what looked like sunlight on metal to the north, where the hills met the flat land on the edge of the town's outer limits.

By the time he realized what it was, any thought of a warning was too late.

'Jesus Christ,' he managed to blurt to the others, 'missile launch.'

After the initial flash of the rocket ignition, the SA-16 shoulder-launched missile moved faster than the eye towards its target. There was no indication that the Sea Harrier pilot had the remotest idea he was under attack when it hit amidships and exploded in a flash of flame and debris.

The aircraft wobbled, flew on a little, then was rocked by a second explosion. For a moment, the watchers on the roof thought that the pilot had had it, but then they spotted a lick of white against the grey clouds. The second explosion had been the plume of the ejector-seat's rocket ignition as the crewman had abandoned his stricken plane.

As the pilotless Sea Harrier flew on to the south, trailing fire, the parachute descended behind a pall of smoke. The poor bastard had fallen into the thick of a battle in the north-east quadrant of the city. Glen got on the radio to Charlie and called in the grid reference in the vain hope that someone, somewhere might be able to send a chopper to get him out. There was nothing else they could do.

The other Sea Harrier egressed rapidly to the south. Within thirty seconds, the sky was clear again. It was as if nothing had ever happened. No bombs had fallen. The Serbs fought on and the city still burned. There would be no more air strikes that day; no more air strikes, in fact, in defence of Gorazde at all.

News of the missile attack flashed around Nato lines of command. People in charge, no doubt recalling the images of pilots held captive by Saddam Hussein during the Gulf War, decreed that no further Nato jets would be sent to defend a city that was, in any case, doomed.

On the radio and TV, the UN announced that there was nothing more it could do to protect the enclave. Officials were forced to confess for the first time that the Serbs could capture Gorazde whenever they wanted.

In Washington, President Clinton said that further air strikes to defend the enclave were unlikely because it would no longer have the 'desired effect'. From now, for defenders, attackers and observers alike, it was a case of every man, woman and child for him or herself.

Moments after the second Sea Harrier had disappeared from view, the Serbs celebrated by whacking the roof of the bank with a concerted burst of heavy .50 machine-gun fire. The punch of this weapon, used earlier to deadly effect against the refugees on the bridge, is so powerful that it succeeded in blowing a hole right through the wall where Dave had been trying to dig his observation post. Everyone scattered as the bullets pinged and ricocheted in all directions. The four men pressed as hard as they could against the roof as the bullets tore into the brickwork. The air crackled with the whizz and whine of large-calibre rounds above their heads. They could clearly feel the vibration as the .50 chiselled out great chunks of building several levels below them.

'Fucking hell!' Glen shouted. 'Where's that lot coming from?'

Nobody replied, because nobody heard him. The noise was deafening. A .50 round will go through the engine block of a truck and stop it dead. Aimed in the right place for long enough it can also collapse a building. It was only by a miracle that nobody was hit.

Glen had seen enough. As soon as the shooting stopped, he told everyone except Toby to get down to the vault.

Clutching his SA-80, Iron Balls was put on picket duty by the main door. His job was to keep out unauthorized personnel and to listen for the first approach of Serb armour. If the wind's in the right direction, you can generally hear a tank when it's several klicks away thanks to the throaty revs of its engine. Closer still, and you can pick up the terrifying clank-squeak of the tracks. The blokes on the roof had earlier seen tell-tale exhaust plumes belching into the air as Serb tanks negotiated difficult obstacles or sharp inclines five to ten klicks distant. No one had any doubt that, before long, the Serbs' T-55s would be inside the town itself, shooting the hell out of anything that moved with their armour-piercing shells and heavy machine-guns.

Charlie gave the order that no one was to step outside the building unless he had to. He also told Ray to pack up the radio and get his arse back from the Hotel Gradina.

On the return journey, Ray observed a small army of dispossessed citizenry, many of the same women and children who had laid siege to them several days earlier, marching on the bank. There were hundreds if not thousands of them. After the failure of the air attack and the UN announcement about the imminent collapse of the pocket, the mood of the defenders had again turned ugly.

Ray only just made it into the building. Seconds after Toby had locked the door, the crowd arrived, surged forward and began to chant.

Toby, manning the shadows inside the entrance way, was unable to understand, but he got the gist readily enough. The women of Gorazde were directing their hatred at the patrol for the failure of the air strikes, but they still looked on it as their last and only hope. The Serbs were coming because their husbands and sons were dead. When the Cetniks arrived, they would be raped and tortured, then killed. But even then it wasn't over, because God only knew what the Cetniks would do to their children in the days and weeks that followed.

Toby listened to the slogans, the wails and shrieks of hatred and supplication, in silence. As much as he was tempted to fear for his own safety, he knew that no one in the bank had it half as bad as these people.

A little after nine, a couple of hours after it had first got there, the crowd's mood lapsed into one of despondent resignation. Toby was beginning to allow himself to believe that everyone might just disperse and head back for their basements, when he noticed bustle and movement at the back of the gathering.

A ripple ran through the sea of heads. Then the crowd parted. A moment later, there was an angry rap on the door as an AK-47 butt was beaten against the toughened glass.

Iron Balls suddenly found himself staring through the plate window at half a dozen hard-arsed Muslim soldiers. He recognized some from the meetings they'd held over the past ten days in the briefing room upstairs. He pulled back the bolts and let them in, then shut the door firmly again. The leader, whom Toby knew to be a local army commander, demanded to be taken to Charlie.

It was only when they entered the candle-lit area downstairs that Toby noticed the man in the midst of the Muslim delegation. He was dressed differently from the others and, judging from the cut on his lip and the black rings around his eyes, looked like he'd been roundly beaten up within the last couple of hours.

Before Toby could say anything, Charlie appeared and shook the hand of the Muslim commander. Then he looked at the stranger with the cuts and bruises.

The guy stepped forward and smiled. 'Christ,' he said, 'am I glad to see you guys.' The voice was so clipped and affable that Charlie was poleaxed.

'I'm sorry,' the Englishman continued self-deprecatingly, 'I really should have introduced myself. I'm Lieutenant Nick Richardson. That was my Sea Harrier that got shot down.'

I set my alarm to wake me early the next morning, a few minutes before Charlie was due to call GV with his first sced of the day. I'd hardly pulled on my combats when he came on the air. He sounded tired, but upbeat, considering the circumstances.

We'd followed the shooting down of the Sea Harrier the

previous day and knew from the patrol that the pilot was safe. By a stroke of good fortune he had bailed out over the last quadrant of the city still in Muslim hands. Apart from a few lacerations and bruises from the ejection he was in pretty good shape. They'd given him Fergie's rifle and sat him down in the basement of the bank. I knew that Charlie would welcome his arrival as an extra pair of eyes and hands.

Although a pilot lacks a member of the Regiment's combat training, he does a four-week course that teaches him how to live off the land if he ejects behind enemy lines. And while the emphasis of this combat survival course is on navigation and map-reading as well as trapping and snaring, part of it is also given over to weapons instruction. Richardson knew how to handle an SA-80, which was just as well. The way things were going down, he'd be using it before long. Everything was pointing towards a last-ditch defence of the bank. But there was one last alternative. 'James,' Charlie said, 'we discussed our position during the night. It's time to go, mate. There's nothing more we can do here. What are our options?'

'Hi, Charlie, Richard here. I've moved to GV specifically to monitor and advise on your situation. I'm talking to you from the ops room with James.'

I turned to find Keith and Paul in the room. They, too, had set their clocks for Charlie's sced. You could almost feel the temperature drop. Richard had been the LO in Sarajevo who had told Charlie, as the fur was flying all around him, that he was forbidden to allude to the fact that Gorazde was falling.

'Morning, Richard,' Charlie said a little testily. 'What's happening?'

'We've given a lot of thought to your position, Charlie,' Richard replied. 'This may seem a little harsh but we really believe it's your best shot. We think it would be wise for you to stay where you are. At the very worst you would be treated as prisoners-of-war, but – and you've got to trust us here, Charlie

– we'd fight for your early release. It might take a few months – three or four at the most – but you'll be free before the summer is over, I guarantee you. How does that sound to you, Charlie? Talk to me.'

'For crying out loud,' Paul said, 'is that the best they can do?'

'It's a sell-out,' Keith said.

I, too, couldn't believe what I was hearing. This was not the Regiment I knew. This wasn't the Regiment at all. It was as if I'd slipped into a parallel universe. I found myself staring into a strange, dark corner of the profession that had nurtured me, and that I in turn would have died for – many times. It was a place that, until now, I hadn't realized existed.

'Don't, Charlie, for Christ's sake,' I found myself shouting into a dead receiver. 'Break out, do it!'

After an interminable pause, Charlie gave his reply. How he managed to maintain any evenness in his voice, I don't know. I would have been spitting blood. But that was Charlie, cool and unflappable to the end. 'Listen, Richard, if it's all the same, we'd like to give this some thought. After the air strikes, the Serbs aren't going to look on us too kindly. They know there are special forces in the pocket. They've already alluded to it in their broadcasts. If we get caught, I don't rate our chances. We're already prime candidates for retribution. I think our only hope lies in doing an E and E.'

Keith, Paul and I looked at each other. I wondered how GV would react. The term E and E – escape and evasion – had its own peculiar resonances. Whatever the circumstances, it always made you sit up and listen.

'How are you going to do it?' Richard asked. The inflection in his voice conveyed a sense of hopelessness.

This was not what Charlie needed. 'To be honest, I don't know.' Charlie's voice trailed away momentarily in the weakening signal. 'There aren't any HLSs left in the town. We've recced the entire area. Any that there were have now fallen to the Serbs. But if needs be, Richard, we'll walk out of there. We'll do it without a helicopter. We'll walk all the bloody way to Sarajevo if we have to.'

'With two injured men and a pilot who's just ejected from a blown-up plane? Come on, Charlie. You've got to be realistic, man.'

'Believe me, I am. The alternative – your alternative – is no alternative at all.'

That seemed to do the trick. When the LO responded, it was as if somebody else had stepped into his shoes. 'What do you need from us?' he asked.

'Your support – and a little time. I need to put this to the Chinese Parliament. This should be everyone's choice, not just mine. We'll get back to you in a couple of hours.'

'OK,' Richard said. 'Whatever you decide, we'll run with it. Just let us know and we'll start the ball rolling this end.'

'Wilco. Over and out.'

I waited five minutes before calling GV on the landline. I told Kev I needed to speak to James.

'Christ,' I said, when he came on, 'what the hell was all that shit about staying in the pocket for a couple of months?'

'I know, Cammy, I don't like it any better than you do. All I can say is, don't lose sight of the big picture, mate. There's a lot more at stake here than the safety of a single patrol, as hard as that sounds. Besides, if Charlie does decide to do a walk out, he's going to have his work cut out for him. The Serbs have got the pocket sewn up pretty tight.'

I nodded in silence. In a sense, James was right. I didn't have access to the big picture so it was always possible that there were diplomatic options for getting the patrol out, options of which we – myself and Charlie included – were as yet unaware. But, all things considered, I knew Charlie's assessment was bang on. His best hope lay in getting out of the pocket, whatever the risks. You couldn't negotiate with the Serbs, not after Nato had just tried to bomb the hell out of them.

It was time to go.

'He'll have to do it tonight,' I said. 'Any later and the Serbs will have consolidated their gains. After tonight, there won't be any more chances. They really will have the place sewn up with new minefields and Christ knows what.'

James agreed. But, in the end, it was the patrol's shout. We weren't there, so we couldn't make up their minds for them.

The Chinese Parliament was a tried and tested method that the Regiment had perfected and relied upon since its inception. They would gather in a pow-wow and mull over their options collectively. Though Charlie was the boss, he would listen to the advice of his men and, if necessary, when all was said and done, wade in with his casting vote. It was something you'd never find in a million years in the green army, but in the Regiment somehow it worked.

It seemed strangely appropriate, too, that today each member of the patrol would decide his own fate, not leave it in the hands of cold logic that had been cooked up in some nameless HQ far from where the action was taking place.

Moments after Charlie signed off, there was an almighty ruckus as the Muslim delegation arrived for its regular morning meeting – a somewhat quaint procedure, given the state of the city, but necessary none the less. Charlie moved upstairs from the basement in time to find Toby struggling to get the bolts across the doors with the crowd pressing against them on the other side. He only just made it in time. The boss then invited everyone up to the big briefing room on the next floor.

As delegates, patrol members, UNMOs and UNHCR reps settled into their seats, it was obvious that there had been some change during the night in the relationship between the local commanders and those who wore the blue beret of the UN. To anyone who didn't pick up the vibe, the crowd outside provided a vocal reminder. The angry chants carried from the street, through the lobby, up the stairs and into the briefing room.

'They hated us at the beginning and they hate us again now,' Charlie said to himself. *Only in the middle, when we dropped a couple of bombs, did they ever let themselves believe that we were their friends.*

The Muslim commander of the sector opened the bidding with a shot from the hip. 'You! You Rose's men!' he boomed, waving a finger at those members of the patrol who were in the room. 'You stay in Gorazde or you go now?'

Some sixth sense kicked in at the back of Charlie's exhausted brain. Even though he hadn't had time to fully formulate the permutations, he knew that to delay, to show any lack of resolve here, could be fatal. He began to understand that he was staring at a potential hostage drama; one in which the Muslims would hold them as a bargaining chip against the advancing Serbs. If they stayed, either way, they were in a lose-lose situation. It helped to stiffen his resolve. They had to get out and get out fast.

Charlie's eyes remained fixed on the Muslim commander. He let none of his thinking show. 'We stay,' he said, staring at him squarely. 'Of course we do.'

As the Muslim commander sat back and watched him, Charlie found himself thinking about the UNMOs and the UNHCR contingent. These guys were unarmed, so the Serbs would spare them, no question. If they could make the Muslims believe that the UNMOs and UNHCRs had no knowledge of the break-out, then they would be safe from that quarter, too. Charlie would put it to Carl and the others that they were free to try to bust out with the patrol if they so desired, but he would put it to them also that their best bet was to stay.

Without a safely reconnoitred HLS, Charlie had no choice but to authorize a walk-out across eighty kilometres of rugged, hostile terrain to Sarajevo, with not just the Serbs at their heels but the Muslims gunning for them as well. The likelihood of them making it was piss-poor. No one could call them a proper fighting unit, not with Ray nursing his frag wounds and Nick barely conscious from the pain of his shattered arm and the drugs.

And then, of course, there was the pilot, who, capable and likeable as he seemed, was scarcely familiar with the hard-won skills of a combat exfil.

And then it hit him.

Christ, Richardson.

Richardson, the pilot. Maybe, just maybe . . .

A couple of minutes later, the Muslims broke up the meeting, satisfied for the time being that the patrol was staying, and marched from the room. As Toby opened the front door to let them out, there was a surge from the crowd, which poured into the reception area of the bank. Charlie was forced to put thoughts of escape to one side as he ran down the stairs, determined to find out what the hell was going on.

As he pounded into the lobby, he found women dropping to their knees, many clutching babies. They were begging Toby for sanctuary.

'Tell them they can go on to the intermediate levels,' Charlie told Toby and Glen. 'Not the basement or the second floor and not the roof, 'cos otherwise they'll get their arses shot off by the Serbs. But anything in between is OK. On one condition. No weapons in the building. No weapons at all except ours. Is that understood?'

The two men nodded and got to work. Charlie ran back up the stairs to the conference room. There, he zeroed in on Richardson, who was deep in a discussion with Ray about their options. He led the pilot downstairs, past the crowds streaming up the steps, and into the basement. Charlie invited him to step into the kitchen and shut the door behind them.

'What's up?' Richardson asked.

'Nick, what would it take to get a chopper into the pocket? You're a flyer. You know all the latest threat assessment intel. Is there any way a helo might be able to land somewhere around here?' He pulled a map from his jacket and unfurled it across the draining board.

Richardson held his gaze. 'The Serbs have got the medium altitude environment pretty well sewn up with their SAMs,' he said. His finger rubbed the cut on his lip from the ejection. 'I found that out the hard way.' He paused for a moment, before adding, 'But at low level, somebody might be able to sneak a chopper in. It'd have to be real nap-of-the-earth stuff on full NVGs, but provided the guy's good ... yeah, I'd say it was possible.' Night vision goggles were a chopper pilot's best friend on a low-level mission in the night skies of Bosnia.

Charlie nodded and moved on to the next question. 'If you were that chopper pilot, Nick, where would you try to land?'

Richardson was up to speed on the tactical situation. He knew where the Serbs were and where they weren't. He bent over the map, studying the topography in silence for several moments. Then he pointed to a patch of flat land in a valley about five klicks to the south of the bank.

'On the evidence, I'd say that's your spot. It's in a valley, so the sound of the ingress would be shielded. It'd also be difficult for anyone with a shoulder-launched SAM to get a seeker lock. Any closer to the town and you'd stand the risk of picking up a load of small arms. But in the darkness of this valley, five klicks out ... well, it could be a goer.'

Charlie had heard enough. He wrote down the map reference and folded away the chart. Then he clapped Richardson on the back, stepped into the main area of the vault and called on the members of the parliament to meet him upstairs in five minutes.

They pulled Carl into the meeting and gave him the option to come with them, but the Canadian chose to stay with his colleagues. In an amazing act of self-disregard he offered to do a bit of diversionary work as the patrol slipped away. This was welcome as the Muslims had just posted armed sentries outside the main door of the bank as extra insurance against the patrol changing its mind.

The plan was to wait until dark, then go about things as normally as possible at the end of another day. Thanks to the Hotel Gradina, which had become an alternate observation post now that the roof of the bank was off-limits, they had the excuse they needed. The difficult bit would be persuading the guards that all seven of them needed to leave the building at the same time.

This was where Carl's offer would come into its own.

The next decision was what to do with their kit. Briefly they considered torching the Land Rovers, but reasoned in the end that it would be a bit of a giveaway. The vehicles stayed.

They decided to take as much of their comms gear and GPS kit as they could manage, paying special attention to the sensitive ancillary items, which could never be allowed to fall into the wrong hands.

They then discussed what to do about the guards. If they were challenged, the textbook said they'd have to be killed on the spot, no dicking around. But the textbook didn't take into account the precarious nature of their situation. It was entirely possible that they'd break out of the city, get so far, then find that escape was an impossibility; that there was simply no way past the Serb positions. That being so, they'd have no option but to hand themselves in, either to the Serbs or the Muslims, or return to Gorazde. Better, therefore, that the guards were simply rendered unconscious. That way, they might all just get a second chance.

Richardson seemed troubled.

'What's up, Nick?' Charlie asked.

'Stupid question,' the pilot said, 'but what's the best way of "rendering someone unconscious"? I mean, I've got my own ideas, obviously, but I wondered whether you guys get taught some magic way of decking somebody at Hereford.'

Charlie paused. He nodded to Toby. 'Iron Balls, why don't you fill in the flyboy here on some of our more classified techniques?'

Toby coughed and got to his feet. He walked over to where Richardson was sitting and gestured for him to stand. 'It helps to appreciate first off,' he started, 'that your average Muslim ain't that big and he's been physically weakened by lack of food these past months. This means that if you hit him in the right place, and you hit him hard enough, with any luck he'll go out like a light.'

'With any luck . . . ?' The Navy officer looked unimpressed.

Toby manhandled him by the shoulders until he was standing square on, no more than an arm's length away. 'Yeah, well . . . a little luck always helps. But if you get it right and you're exactly on-target, he'll go straight at the knees. Boom. On the floor. Out for the count.'

'So where is this magic bloody G-spot?'

'Jaw-bone,' Toby replied, mimicking a punch to the pilot's chin. 'A good punch on the jaw and it's all over. More'n likely you'll bust the bastard – and it'll hurt your hand like hell – but if you hit it square on, the transmitted shock up into the brain does the trick every time.'

Richardson frowned. 'That's it? I learned that stuff at school.'

'What were you expecting, mate? The Vulcan death-grip? Phasers on "stun"?'

Everyone laughed, including Richardson. It helped to purge the tension.

'What do we do with Mucky and Misha?' Charlie asked, getting back to basics. 'Do we tell them? Or do we piss off without saying a word?'

'I hate to leave Mucky behind,' Glen said. 'Misha should be all right as long as he can convince the Serbs he's with the UNMOs and the UNHCR types. He's a civvy, after all, so it shouldn't be too hard. Mucky's different, though. He's Army. You saw the look on the face of his commander back there in the briefing room. He'll kill the guy when he discovers we've gone. And, if by some miracle he doesn't, Mucky'll die at the hands of the Serbs, for sure. I think we should take him with us, boss, give him the option. Besides, we can do with an interpreter. You know we can.'

Charlie sucked his teeth. Mucky had served them proud these past two weeks. He deserved something in return. 'Make an approach,' he told Glen, after a brief moment of reflection. 'You're right, we can do with the help. But stick to him like glue, Glen. If he shows any sign of wavering or blabbing, deck him or tie him up or something. Is that understood?'

'Perfectly, boss.'

Charlie looked at each of them in turn, then said, 'Right, we meet in the basement at eight, ready for the off. I'm going to get on the horn now for that chopper. We'll set the RV for 0500 tomorrow morning. Between now and then we'll go into radio silence. There'll be no going back. Once we go out that main door tonight, we're committed 100 per cent. We'll give GV one last check call at 0445 hours just to let them know that the LSRV is clear of enemy military activity. But other than that, we'll maintain radio silence all the way. We don't have the battery power for any more chit-chat, so it's not like we have a whole lot of choice.'

Charlie stopped to look at his watch. Then, he added, 'If we miss the call, I don't want any of you to be under any illusions. We'll be walking the rest of the way out. And Sarajevo is a long way from here. The alternative is staying in this bloody bank and getting blatted by the Serbs, the Muslims or both of them.'

He gave the assembled company one last penetrating gaze. 'Any questions?'

There were none, so Charlie got up and made his way down to the basement to make his sced to GV for the last time.

Paul, Keith and I were glued to the satcom when Charlie made that call. He went straight into the option. I could hear his resolve. There's something indefinably different about a bloke who knows he's committed to combat. I heard something of that in this young rupert's voice and found myself sharing his anticipation.

'We've talked among ourselves,' Charlie told James. 'We're all decided. We're going now because if we don't we'll never get out. I'm as sure as I can be, too, that those we're leaving behind will be all right. In fact, they're probably a whole lot better off without us.'

Right call, I thought. James, too, gave this his full support. I waited for some interjection from Sarajevo, but there was none. Charlie carried on. 'James, here's the gen on the HLS. It's approximately five, repeat five, kilometres to the south-west of the town, co-ordinates eight, six, seven, three, nine, one. We'll be there at 0500, but I'll call you fifteen minutes beforehand at 0445 with our final go/no-go decision. The direction we're heading in looks like it's the least sewn-up part of the pocket, but there's still a strong possibility that the HLS is occupied with, or close to, enemy forces. So, I repeat, stand by to hear from us at 0445 with a status check on the HLS.'

'You know that the helicopter will have to be in the air at that point,' James said. 'And that there'll only be one shot at this.'

'Roger that.' Charlie paused. 'There'll be eight for the ride, James – the six of us, plus the pilot and, most likely, one of the interpreters. A guy called Mucky. Can you pass that on to the chopper pilot. I don't want them sending a two-seat bloody Gazelle for this job.'

'Understood, Charlie. Don't worry, we'll take care of everything. The French are handling the extraction. It looks like they're going to send a Puma.'

'Good. Line up those beers because I'm telling you now that if we make it out General Rose is doing the bloody buying. You can tell him that from me.'

And with that he was gone.

Keith was ahead of me. He passed me a map and pointed to the co-ordinates. Then I got on the satcom to GV.

I asked James if Keith, Paul and I could make the call for the chopper ride.

James hesitated. Then he explained that the French wanted to keep the loading as light as possible to allow the pilot maximum manoeuvrability on the way in and out. The memory of our flight in the Bell over Maglaj was still fresh in my mind. The Puma was a big machine. It had room for around twenty fully armed troops inside. Less than a half-load gave the pilot more than a bit of scope for chucking the helo around the sky in case they got locked up by Serbian radar. As we knew from our own experience, it was pretty desperate stuff, but desperate is better than nothing and James understood this. He told me that there'd only be room for one other member of the Regiment this time, but he thanked me anyway.

'So, who gets to go?' I asked.

James held off a beat before replying. 'I figured it'd better be me.'

I caught the edge to his voice – that same mix of tension and excitement I'd heard in Charlie's – and was pleased for him. He'd been owed this one for a long time. Though the decision was his, and his alone, it was clearly the right choice.

*

The patrol announced its intentions to the assembled group of UNMOs and UNHCRs in the vault. The small gathering did not seem overly troubled by the news. Perhaps they had been expecting it for some time. People outside the eight members of the break-out team had too much on their minds to worry about developments inside the bank. Everyone was now focused on the bigger picture of what tomorrow would bring.

Moments earlier, a shell fired from a Serbian tank a quarter of a mile away had driven a two-metre-wide hole through the middle of the eighth floor. Only by a stroke of good fortune had no one been anywhere nearby when it exploded. Equally gratifying was the absence of panic among the refugees, who were now sheltering on other floors of the building.

This was because the women, it seemed, were now resolved to their fate. From the sound of the mumbled prayers that drifted down the stairway, it was obvious to Charlie and the others that they had finally committed their lives – and those of their children – into the hands of Allah.

Prior to the off, Dave and Toby went around the vault attending to one last detail. Dave topped up the kettle and set it on the stove while Toby dispensed tea-bags and coffee into their cups. It wasn't much, but it might just buy them a few extra minutes of getaway time if the guards came downstairs after they were gone and found a scene of near-normality; one that looked as if it had been only temporarily abandoned.

At ten minutes to eight, Glen and Mucky moved up to the roof, giving the Bosnian the chance to take one last look across the city. The others, meanwhile, lined up in twos on the stairs leading up from the vault, ready to make their way out.

There'd been no time to say a proper goodbye to Carl. Charlie offered to buy him a bottle of slivovitz next time they met and the Canadian managed to laugh. He promised to take them up on it, then marched upstairs to go shoot the shit with the two Muslim guards outside the main doors. Following the strike by the tank, the sentries had been visibly less preoccupied with what was going on inside the building and much more concerned with what was happening down the street. This, at least, was something in their favour.

Glen and Mucky arrived on the roof a few minutes after sunset. As he swept the skyline with his binos, Glen asked the Muslim if he had any last-minute regrets about his decision to go with them. Mucky shook his head. Most of his friends and family were dead, he explained. For the few who were left, he vowed to come back as soon as he could. But, in the meantime, Gorazde needed a spokesman, someone on the outside who could plead for it in the face of the disinterest that had led to its downfall. Mucky was determined to take on this task. First, however, he considered it his moral duty to act one last time as the patrol's interpreter and guide.

If he had ever doubted it, this was the moment at which Glen became convinced they could all count on Mucky. The bloke was definitely on-side. As for Misha, the civilian, he'd left them earlier to join his family. This was fortunate, as it allowed them to continue their escape plans without fear of compromise from the inside.

From the roof, under a clear sky, the flames of burning buildings and the Serbs' campfires were visible in a near-perfect circle around the pocket. There were odd cracks of gunfire, but for the most part, the town was silent.

Glen had few illusions as to what this meant. The Serbs were rallying for their last offensive. In the hours before dawn, there would be time for the attackers to eat, drink, talk, brag and sleep. Finally, in the small hours, the artillery and mortar barrages would begin all over again.

Half an hour before the assault by Serbian shock-troops, the Bosnian-Serb Army gunners would triple their rate of fire. This is the darkest moment for a defender, who, already exhausted and weakened, is now at his most run-down and vulnerable.

For the few remaining Muslim soldiers, the battle options that had sustained them over two weeks of heavy fighting were all used up. There was nothing they could do except wait for the Serbs to arrive in force. The Muslims had already retreated to their fall-back positions. There was nowhere else to go.

Glen took a last look through the binos to the south-west, the vector that would lead them towards the HLS, then he signalled to Mucky that it was time to leave. They moved downstairs, past women and children sleeping in the corridors and the stairwell, until they reached the lobby. It was empty.

Through the double doors, Glen could just make out three silhouettes. Carl was chatting to one of the guards. The other sentry was sitting on the top step, puffing furiously on a cigarette. Glen could see the red glow of the tip through the smoke-brown glass.

For better or worse, the other six members of the patrol were committed to the streets between here and the first rendezvous, a patch of dead ground on the edge of the town. The two of them would have to move fast to catch up.

Glen pulled open the door and gestured for Mucky to head on out. Then he followed suit, stepping as nonchalantly as he could into the cold evening air. Carl and the two guards turned towards him.

A voice at the back of Glen's head told him they'd never buy eight of them all leaving the bank within twenty minutes of each other, but he smiled all the same.

'Hey, Glen, I'll catch you later,' Carl said, as the senior NCO moved past him. 'Big day tomorrow, huh?'

Ahead Mucky was already making for a break in the houses on the opposite side of the street. All his instincts made Glen want to up his own pace, accelerate towards the shadows, but with a supreme effort he forced himself to stop and turn.

'If you're making coffee, I'll be back in a couple of minutes,' he called to Carl. 'I'll even take a shot of slivovitz, if you've got any left.'

Carl grunted, gave him a wave of acknowledgement and turned back towards the guards. He offered the one on the steps another cigarette. For an instant, Glen was left standing there, watching them, feeling detached, almost as if he wasn't there. Then the moment caught up with him and he turned and headed for the alleyway down which Mucky had disappeared.

He found the Muslim waiting for him half-way to the Hotel Gradina. The threat of compromise on this part of the journey was relatively low, as the short distance between the bank and the hotel formed a part of the patrol's regular M O. But the two men kept their senses peeled for trouble.

The next five minutes held two big potential dangers: the moment when he and Mucky deviated from the normal route to the Gradina; and the possibility of discovery at the R V where the others were waiting. At any time, in effect, the balloon could go up. The trick was to keep going, but at a speed that would not draw undue attention to themselves.

The point of no return came quickly.

Emerging from the alleyway, they saw the blacked-out façade of the hotel. A quick glance up and down the street and Glen led the way across. Then they were into another alleyway, even darker than the first. They moved purposefully, past shattered houses and shell holes. They peered through the gloom for the merest sign of activity ahead, but seeing anything was difficult. This, thankfully, cut both ways. All it would take, Glen knew, was for an old lady or a kid to shout a warning that the U N was leaving, and that'd be it. The Muslims' last remaining defenders would be on them in seconds. They would then face the stark choice of surrendering or fighting their way out. Either way almost certainly spelled death.

They slunk past a ground-floor window, the panes of glass

blown in from a shell's near-miss, and heard a low growl from inside. *A dog. Fuck!* No one had considered the impact of dogs on their escape plan. The two pressed into the shadows as a hand drew back a blanket that had been hung across the window against the cold. A narrow sliver of yellow candlelight fell across the alleyway as the dog gave a series of barks, each louder than the last. Just when it seemed as if they would have to break cover and run, they heard a rasped admonition and a whimper from the animal as its owner cuffed it into silence. Then the makeshift curtain fell back into place and the light went out.

A whiff of boiled vegetables and woodsmoke wafted past them as silence returned to the alleyway. Then they were on their way again, maintaining the pace, scanning ahead, looking round, hugging the shadows, until they reached the patch of dead ground where the others were supposed to be waiting.

They ducked down into the long grass and weeds. The area had once been a recreation ground for a large block of flats 150 metres to the east. Like the apartment building, the little patch of parkland was a bombed-out shadow of its original existence. Scanning the area, however, Glen could just make out the silhouette of a swing frame. His bearings confirmed, he moved a little deeper into the interior, urging Mucky to stay close. He was cursing his lack of night-vision equipment when he heard a low whistle a few metres to his left.

Glen edged forward, his SA-80 at the ready. Then he parted a clump of grasses and saw the other members of the break-out team lying prone in a slight dip ten metres in front of him. One bloke – it looked like Toby – was squatting on his haunches, beckoning them over. He gave Mucky a half-triumphant nudge in the ribs.

So far, so good, he told the interpreter. From now on things would be a lot simpler: it wouldn't just be the Muslims but everyone who was out to kill them.

*

271

They cammed up and arranged themselves into a semblance of a fighting orbat – Mucky in front, Dave next to him, then Toby, Nick Richardson, Nick Evans, with his shattered arm, Ray, Charlie and Glen at the rear. The idea was for Mucky to do the talking if they ran into anyone. If that didn't work, they'd resort to plan B: banjoing anything or anyone that got in their way.

The rest of the orbat had been just as carefully considered. Dave and Toby were fighting fit and thus capable of laying down a lot of firepower if they needed to resort to their weapons. Richardson was fit but not a soldier, hence his position in the middle where he could rely on some good protection from the front and rear.

Nick, too, needed protecting in the centre because of his injuries. His metal frame had been adjusted to allow his arm to be temporarily positioned in a sling, which was less likely to catch on obstructions as they worked their way through the darkness. He was drugged as far as anyone dared, short of putting him into a stupor. Next came Ray, whose stomach injuries weren't too bad, then Charlie, in the ideal spot for directing a fight if it came to it, and finally Glen, the most experienced member of the team, bringing up the rear and watching their six o'clock.

With Gorazde quietly dying behind them, Mucky and Dave led them out. They spaced themselves around ten metres apart, far enough not to be tripping over each other, but close enough to hear whispered warnings or to read hand-signals.

They got off the road as quickly as they could and into the surrounding countryside. Everyone knew about the risk posed by mines, but there was nothing to be done about it. Each man tried to banish the thought, but it wasn't easy.

No one place is safer than any other in respect of mines, especially in former Yugoslavia where nobody gives a toss about the Geneva Convention. Swaths of countryside are ripe for wide-area mine coverage, while tracks are exactly where you'd expect to find individual, but highly unpleasant, anti-personnel devices. These are many and varied and come in all shapes and sizes. Some are as big as your hand and will take off your leg and maybe an arm at the same time; others amount to no more than the combined size of your index and middle fingers, but are still quite capable of vaporizing your foot or removing your face with a thousand tiny pellets, optimized specially for maiming. The worst type of mine is one that activates as you step on it, delays a few seconds, then pops out a fist-sized anti-personnel grenade that explodes at a height of around two metres behind you. If you survive this onslaught, chances are it's just the beginning of your troubles, because minefields and GPMGs go hand in hand. Pop off a mine and a dozen machine-guns will pin you down in the general area of the minefield and hold you there, until you're either dead or you wish you were.

I hate mines almost as much as I hate snakes.

It was close to midnight when they hit the base of the heights that surrounded Gorazde. Nick was having a lot of difficulty cross-graining the steep terrain. Cross-graining is not easy at the best of times: it's a technique that's designed to keep you off ridge-lines and valley-floors, places where typically you find pathways and, *de facto*, people. In rolling country, cross-graining usually means trekking over the steep terrain that exists between the top and bottom of a valley – a no man's land that, by its very nature, is devoid of habitation but difficult to negotiate. The sides of this particular valley were characterized by a never-ending series of tributaries and ditches bringing rainwater down from the ridge-lines. These are difficult enough to spot, but for a man with a badly broken arm, they can be a nightmare. Nick kept falling over. Without the use of his arm, he fell awkwardly – and often Richardson and Ray were too far away to catch him. But on the couple of excruciating occasions that he fell on the metal exo-skeleton, he managed somehow to keep the pain to himself. Not once did he cry out. For this, he won everybody's respect.

It was almost three o'clock, with a little over two hours to go to the helicopter rendezvous, when Charlie and Glen called the patrol to a halt. The two leaders were starting to get worried. The terrain was not corresponding to what they'd expected to find when they'd plotted the break-out on the map.

Charlie tabbed up to the front and confronted Dave, who'd been navigating using the time-honoured map-and-compass method. This entailed stopping every so often, placing the compass on the chart and checking terrain against bearing. Dave had been doing this regularly, but to Glen and Charlie it still didn't feel right. The valley should have been flattening out below them, but it wasn't. If anything, it was getting steeper.

'Dave,' Charlie whispered, 'where the fuck are we?'

'South,' Dave replied, a little indignantly. 'We're heading south. Bang on course.'

'I don't know,' Charlie said. 'We should be in sight of the chopper's set-down point by now. But this doesn't look like it at all.'

The boss asked Dave for the hand-held satnav set. The GPS has an internal light so it can be read in the dark. Charlie dipped the switch and cupped his hand over the illuminated read-out.

There was a moment of silence as the enormity of the error sank in. Then Charlie said it. He meant to keep it low, but everyone heard him. 'My God, we're going the wrong way.'

'*What?*' Dave rasped. His tone conveyed something of the thousand and one things that must have just powered through his brain like an express train.

Some of the others took up the refrain.

'Christ,' Ray said, 'we're never going to make it.'

'You know what this means, don't you?' Toby added, trying to keep the bitterness out of his voice. He knew – they all did – that it was a mistake that could have happened to anybody.

But, given their circumstances, he could have done without it happening here, now. 'We're going to have to hole up by day and just pray that the Serbs don't find us.'

Ray held his head in his hands. 'Or the Muslims.'

'And with failing battery for the radio,' Mucky added dejectedly. 'Maybe we cannot contact helicopter now. Maybe that's it. *Kaput.*'

At this Glen and Charlie, who'd been busily poring over a map and checking their real position, had heard enough.

'Fucking listen, all of you,' Glen snarled, keeping his voice low, but still managing to maintain enough depth and authority for all of them to sit up and shut up. 'Get this into your heads. We are fucking committed to this. It's like Charlie said. We're going to make it out. All of us. Tonight. I don't want to hear any more of this shit. From any of you.'

'Right,' Charlie said, driving his fist into the palm of his other hand to make the point. 'We've got a couple of hours left. We've fucked up once. We can't afford any more mistakes. Nick, how's the arm?'

'OK,' he replied groggily. 'I'll make it.'

'Good, 'cos you're gonna have to, mate,' Glen said uncompromisingly. He turned back to Charlie. 'We're going to go back the way we came and start all over again. This time, though, we do it at the double. And this time, we double-check our position on the GPS.'

That had been their downfall. In their haste to get to the HLS, Dave had not thought to take this precaution. Technically he should have verified their course with regular spot-checks on the GPS. This is best done when crossing streams or tracks or other fixed features marked on the map.

But Charlie also knew that Dave wasn't the only person to blame. The Regiment told you from day one, the moment you entered Selection, that you were in charge of your own destiny. In some respects, this meant unlearning everything you'd been taught in the green army. If a green army rupert told you to stick your head in an oven and turn on the gas, you were expected to obey orders. In the SAS, everyone is taught to think for himself, not rely willy-nilly on the bloke who is leading from the front.

There was no time to dwell on the error. Having checked that Nick was still with them, Charlie scoured the darkness for Richardson. The pilot was kneeling on the ground close by, staring at the ground. His breath was coming in sharp, reedy gasps. Charlie patted him on the shoulder. 'You still with us, big man?' he asked.

Richardson nodded.

'Good,' Charlie said. 'Then, let's fucking go.'

Shortly after three, I got on the satcom to Kevin to find out if there'd been any news. He'd heard nothing, which was a good sign at least, though deep in my bones I was filled with a sense of foreboding.

After the SA-16 attack on the Sea Harrier, there was a general feeling that any flight into the Gorazde pocket was a suicide job. I prayed the French knew what they were doing. It was a brave call, no mistake.

'Let me know as soon as you've got anything,' I said.

'Sure,' Kev acknowledged. 'The chopper's due to send a signal from the LSRV. I'll call you the moment I hear the news.'

Keith, Paul and I tried to rest, but sleep would not come to me. Charlie's patrol into Gorazde had been determined by the bunch of us sitting down and drawing lots. It had been supposed to be a breeze, a simple monitoring job. Instead, it had turned into a nightmare.

Crusha, our teacher back in Split, whose concern for us had seemed so needless, had been right. She'd crystal-balled the whole thing dead-on.

*

After the set-back, the break-out team made marginally better progress. Charlie and Glen had found a path through a wood that allowed them to shortcut the route that would otherwise have taken them all the way back to their initial rendezvous on the edge of the city. They kept going, cross-graining over more difficult terrain, the fitter ones cajoling those less able to maintain the relentless pace. They knew they were taking risks moving fast across countryside they did not know, but the imminent arrival of the helicopter gave them little alternative. The chopper was due to land at the LSRV in just under an hour.

They stopped to catch their breath in a ditch by a semi-paved track. Glen and Charlie held a hurried confab. Fires were burning inside the shells of buildings on both sides of the valley. They looked like campfires. In the flickering light they could see that the track curved away from them in the direction of the LSRV. The two men studied the buildings in their optics. The Serbs had to be close. A campfire in the ruins of a building could hardly be the Muslims, not with their lifelong enemy breathing down their necks.

Both men appreciated that these positions didn't pose too big a problem. If you could see a threat, you manoeuvred around it. It was always the ones you didn't see that got you.

Charlie was fighting to catch his breath. They were still a klick and a half, maybe more, from the LSRV. At the pace they'd been moving they were never going to make it.

'The road,' Glen said, reading his thoughts. 'We're going to have to use the road.'

'Right,' Charlie said. 'Hang the risks. We're all out of time.'

Moving along a road, at night, in the teeth of the enemy's forward positions, without first having carried out any kind of recce, broke just about every rule of special operations. All Charlie's instincts told him not to do it. But his head said he had no choice.

Glen looked at his watch. The helicopter touched down in

twenty-six minutes. Fifteen minutes before that, they were due to call GV with a status report on the HLS. He didn't say anything because he knew it was nothing that Charlie hadn't already considered. They'd just have to wing it, calling in as soon as they had eyes-on, praying in the meantime that GV didn't scrub the mission.

Charlie called the others around him. Everyone moved close.

'Listen up,' he whispered. 'We're going to have to use the road. I don't like it but, shit, we've broken so many bloody rules tonight there's no point stopping now. When we're a couple of hundred metres from the LSRV, we'll stop and whistle up GV on the tac-sat. From the map, the track should take us to within a few hundred metres of the touchdown point. In the meantime, there's a very real danger of ambush, so keep your eyes peeled. OK, let's move it.'

They edged into the road, keeping the same orbat as before, though with less of the earlier discipline. There was no point in maintaining the ten-metre spacing any more. Everyone needed to keep their eyes on Dave and Mucky out front. If there was a problem, then these two would be the first to spot it.

Seconds after they set off a series of lightning-like flashes lit the sky behind the hills. Then the air reverberated with the crump-wump of shell and mortar explosions as the Serbs began softening up the centre of Gorazde in preparation for their inevitable dawn offensive. The timing couldn't have been worse. If the Serbs in the surrounding area ever had been asleep, they certainly weren't now.

Charlie was just wondering how much more bad luck they could absorb when, twenty metres ahead, he saw Mucky and Dave drop down on to one knee in a synchronized move that meant only one thing: danger.

Charlie's pulse hammered in his ear. He could see Dave's clenched fist, with the thumb pointing to the ground, moving up and down behind his back. The signal reinforced the original message: they had a problem, and it was coming this way.

Everyone else dropped to the ground. Then they closed up on Dave and Mucky.

As Charlie dropped down into position behind the interpreter, another round of detonations lit the sky behind them. It was at that point that he glimpsed movement on the road two hundred metres ahead. Then the sky went black again and he lost his night vision.

In his mind's eye, Charlie replayed the image that had just burned itself on to his retina. 'Mucky,' he whispered urgently, 'who are they? What are they?'

'I don't know,' the interpreter shot back. 'Too far to tell.'

Charlie didn't hesitate. He'd already heard more than enough. 'Immediate ambush! Everybody get off the road. Move it!'

It was a drill that all except Mucky and Richardson had practised dozens of times. On a mission 'immediate ambush', or IA, is something you never, ever want to hear because it means that all your best-laid plans have just turned to rat-shit.

Charlie threw a glance to his right, remembered a barbed-wire fence he'd clocked moments earlier, and dived over, dragging the pilot with him.

Without saying a word, Ray and Glen lifted Nick to his feet and half-pushed, half dragged him over the fence. By the time they'd got him a few metres back from the road – Glen's hand across his mouth in case he screamed – the rest of the patrol had taken up position.

Everyone lay prone. There is a drill for an ambush that's designed to ensure that all the guns on your own side don't take out the same bloke, leaving the others to get a hold of themselves and return fire at you. Rather than marking individuals, you concentrate instead on a piece of territory that corresponds with your position in the ambush team. Anything or anybody that enters this 'box' is yours – and, if push comes to shove, hopefully dead.

Dave, at the front, trained his SA-80 on a patch of ground approximately thirty metres forward of his position. Toby, the next in line, took a bead on a portion of roadway a few metres further on. And so it went, all the way back to Glen, the tail-end Charlie.

The one thing you don't do is track a target in your sights. This close, he'll almost certainly clock the movement in his peripheral vision and start shooting at you first. The order of the day in an IA is to let them through at all costs. Everybody in the team knew that if they were forced to open fire, the enemy would be on them in the blink of an eye. And, even though Charlie was committed now to fighting his way through if necessary, if the helicopter pilot caught sight of a raging gun-battle as the Puma dropped down towards the LSRV there was no way he'd land.

Charlie turned his head slowly in the direction of the men moving along the road.

He could see light from the hillside fires catching on the barrels of their rifles. He counted six of them.

The sound of their voices drifted across the field. For men heading into battle, they seemed to exhibit a remarkable disregard for their own safety. It was only when one of them started singing that Charlie put it all together.

They were pissed. Totally rat-arsed. Quarter to five in the bloody morning and these troops – he still didn't know if they were Serbs or Muslims – were heading off to fight the enemy with slivovitz coursing through their veins.

He held his breath as the first soldier entered Dave's killing zone. Then the next man crossed into it and the next.

Charlie thought the tension would kill him. All it would take was for a member of the team to *think* he was compromised and that would be it. The rules of an IA in this respect are clear: anybody has the authority to release his weapon and start firing if he even so much as suspects the game is up.

In the chill of the pre-dawn, Charlie could hear the crunch of gravel under their boots and the chink of bullets chafing on their ammo belts. He tracked them with his eyes as they moved past three, maybe four, metres away.

A groan from Nick or a rustle of indiscipline from any of them now and the firing would begin. He wondered if Glen still had his hand clamped over the injured man's mouth, but he didn't dare look. He didn't dare breathe.

To come this far to get sprung by a bunch of piss-heads was the cruellest irony imaginable. Only in Bosnia, his mind kept telling him, only in bloody Bosnia . . .

And then, as quickly as the crisis had come upon them, it was over. Charlie realized that all six soldiers had moved past their position. They were gone.

The relief was temporary.

With barely fifteen minutes to go before the helicopter landed, Charlie couldn't afford to wait for the soldiers to get out of earshot.

He moved forward, checked that the coast was clear, then waved everyone back on to the track.

There was now only one thing left to do and that was hoof it down the road – on, on, on, until they reached the LSRV.

With Toby supporting Nick by his good arm, they ran as fast they could.

It was Glen who was the first to hear it. Indistinct at first, the sound muffled by the surrounding terrain, the note of the engines and rotors soon became unmistakable. Suddenly, about a kilometre ahead, the helicopter broke cover from behind a hill and started its descent into the LSRV. Though it was flying lights-off, it was big enough just to be visible as an indistinct shape against the hillside.

With or without their confirmatory signal, the French had decided to do their own thing and set down in the valley anyhow. Worse, they were bloody early.

Before the disbelief sank in, and before the full impact of the development had time to flatten his own resolve, Charlie called everyone around him.

With the noise of the descending helo as his backdrop, Charlie unfurled his map in the middle of the road and called Glen forward. Then he yelled for Richardson.

Another time and place, the pilot might have hesitated, but Richardson knew what he was being called upon to do. He didn't hesitate.

Charlie played the beam of his penlight over the map. 'We've lost this one,' he shouted over the noise. Somehow, he managed to maintain the semblance of an even tempo to his voice.

'Nick,' he said, cupping his hands over his mouth so that the pilot could hear him, 'look at the map and check the terrain immediately around us. Pick an alternative landing site. Somewhere much closer to our position. Somewhere that you, as a pilot, might just be able to land, however bloody tight the thing looks on the map. I don't have to tell you that we've run out of time, Nick, so make it fast, mate. Real fast.'

Talk about pressure.

All eyes swung on to the pilot. Richardson, who'd never flown a helo on active duty but who knew all about the dizzying effects of a heat-homing missile exploding in the underbelly of his aircraft, forced himself to focus on the dimly lit topography of the chart.

There was panic in the air now, but controlled panic. The kind that beats around in your brain like a bird in a greenhouse. Richardson felt it. They all did. The easy option would be to sit down, say, fuck it, then head for the nearest wood, praying you could find somewhere to lie low until the following night, and then the next and then the one after that.

But a lot of people had put their necks on the line to get them out tonight. You didn't need to be an archbishop or a veteran of Britain's premier special forces unit to clock that one. Richardson knew that the situation called them to go that one last step –

the step that the Regiment always asks of you, when your mind and your body scream that you can do no more – if they were to stand the remotest chance of making it home.

Behind him, there was a flurry of activity as Ray began to assemble the main components of the satcom.

Toby unfurled the antenna and angled it skyward. He had to position it spot-on to pick up the satellite, but the bearing and elevation, even at dead of night, were etched as permanent fixtures on the back of his brain.

For a moment, the noise of this activity threw Richardson off his stride. But then he found some inner reserve. 'Give me a couple of seconds,' was all that he said.

'Zero Bravo, Zero Bravo, this is Zero. Radio check, over.'

It was a minute before five when the radio crackled into life again. The 0445 deadline had come and gone with no word from the patrol, leaving Keith, Paul and me with no alternative but to mull over the worst. There were no end of potential scenarios to choose from, all bad: maybe somebody had stepped on a mine or they'd had a contact; maybe there'd been a firefight and they were all dead.

It was then that Kevin's voice jolted me into action.

I picked up the handset. 'Zero Bravo, Zero Bravo. Roger, strength five.'

'Cammy,' Kev said, 'we've got a problem, mate.' His voice drifted in and out of the distorting effect of the ionosphere, which is always at its worst just before dawn. 'The patrol's not at the landing site.'

I fought to control my voice. 'What the fuck's happened?'

'I don't know, mate. Charlie did as he said he would. He kept radio silence all the way out of Gorazde. But he's not called in to say he's got eyes-on at the HLS. Any number of things might have happened to them. Making the journey in the first place was always going to be a tough one.'

283

'Where's the Puma?'

'It's in the valley now, approaching the HLS. The pilot's going to take a look-see. Maybe he can get a visual of them. It's always possible that their radio's out.'

I prayed that that was it.

'And if they're not there? Will it wait?' I knew the answer to this as soon as I opened my mouth, but I was clutching at straws.

There was a pause as a babble of indistinct radio-traffic filled the earpiece of my handset. A message I couldn't begin to hear was coming in over another channel in the ops room at GV.

And then I heard Kev's voice again.

'Cammy, bad news, mate. The pilot's just taken off again. He's heading out of the immediate area. There's no sign of them at the HLS. That's it. We'll have to try again tomorrow night.'

I brought my fist down hard on the table and swore. I felt sick. In my bones, I knew that they'd never survive a day out there, however good a lying-up position they had prepared for themselves in the meanwhile. With the Serbs moving forward all around them, there were no hiding places within a fifteen-kilometre radius of Gorazde. That was the God's honest truth of the matter.

But Kev suddenly came back on the air. 'We're getting another signal,' he yelled, a note of clear excitement in his voice. 'Gotta go, mate,' he said. 'Things have just gone ballistic around here.'

It was then that I heard Charlie's voice, weak but unmistakable, on the ether.

The helicopter was in the air and heading for home when Charlie fired up the satcom, praying that the batteries had enough power to make the call to RHQ. The lights on the dials flickered into life. Charlie didn't lose a moment.

'One Zero, One Zero, this is One Zero Bravo. Can you hear me, over?'

Their low batteries and the sound of the helicopter, invisible to them a kilometre away, made the response difficult to hear. From the tempo of its engines, they could tell it was climbing fast. In a second or two, it would be out of the valley and lost behind the mountains.

'One Zero Bravo, this is Zero. Receiving you strength two. You're very weak, Charlie, over.' The acknowledgement from GV was equally indistinct.

'Request change of landing site, over,' Charlie yelled into the handset. 'Repeat, new HLS. Grid: seven – six – nine – two.' He paused momentarily. 'Five – one – zero – four.'

Before RHQ could respond, he repeated the reference again. It was a set of co-ordinates for a field that Richardson had pinpointed barely seconds earlier.

The new HLS wasn't perfect – a slope made it somewhat hazardous – but it was something, the only possible thing left.

'Roger. Stand by.' This was Richard, the LO from Sarajevo, now at GV. He needed the interval to flick on to another frequency to talk to the pilot.

Charlie made his decision. He couldn't hang around for Richard's answer. They had to commit a whole lot sooner than that. Even before he told them what to do, Ray was disassembling the satcom and cramming it back into his day-sack.

'Follow me,' Charlie said, turning to the rest of the patrol. 'Let's go. Fast!'

It took them three minutes to reach the spot pinpointed by the new grid. The field looked impossibly small. It lay in a remote area between a copse and the western side of the valley. The slope was also much more pronounced than it had appeared on the map.

They left Nick in the middle of the field and spread out. A light wind was blowing up through the valley. Everyone strained for the sound of a helicopter, but they heard nothing.

Suddenly, there was a deafening blast of rotor wash as the Puma swept round a bluff a few hundred metres away. The pilot bled off his airspeed and brought the large, twin-engined helicopter to a juddering hover before it touched down fifty metres down the hillside from where Nick lay exhausted. In a superb display of skill, the pilot crabbed sideways up the slope, keeping his right wheels on the ground, the left set hanging free in the downwash of his main rotors.

The patrol pulled back from their perimeter positions around the field.

A shadowy figure was beckoning from the open door of the helicopter. A shout, barely audible above the din, confirmed him as one of their own.

It was James.

Dave and Toby picked Nick up and hurled him on board. Seconds later, they were scrambling through the open doorway themselves. Ray, Nick and Mucky were only moments behind.

Glen and Charlie took a last look over their shoulders, sweeping the hillside with the muzzles of their SA-80s. Then hands reached down and pulled them into the cabin of the helicopter.

There was a roar from the Puma's twin exhausts as the pilot throttled up in the thin atmosphere. Then the big helicopter clawed slowly into the reddening sky.

EPILOGUE

A week later, we flew out of former Yugoslavia as covertly as we'd flown in, a handful of anonymous-looking signallers on our way home with only ourselves and a coffin for company.

As the C-130 climbed out of Split, I took a last look at the ground below, searching the horizon for a glimpse of the country that, in spite of all my efforts, had ended up ingraining my skin like dye.

I picked out Diamond Route – the Ho Chi Minh Trail – and the mountains and the hairpin bends that Dougie had negotiated so expertly a little over a month before. The bulk of Bosnia remained hidden behind the clouds. I know in my bones I will never see it again.

Over the Adriatic, I got up to move aft to spend some time with Fergie, my last chance before his body was handed over to his next-of-kin at RAF Lyneham. But the Air Force loadmaster wasn't having any of it. Rules were rules, he said. The coffin stayed behind the curtain that had been drawn across the back of the aircraft and only RAF personnel could move beyond it. And that was that.

He ushered me back to my seat.

I was tempted to tell the officious oaf that this man had died trying to save a place that nobody had heard of a month ago and in another month everybody would have forgotten. But I ended up biting my lip. We'd broken enough rules in Bosnia to last us a lifetime. For once, I decided to go with the flow.

Fergie's sacrifice had left the rest of us wondering what, if anything, his death had achieved. As I sat on my canvas seat, the noise of four giant turboprops threatening to drive all rational thought from my head, I saw a bunch of way-points on a map – Split, GV, Tuzla, Maglaj and Mostar – and began to see Gorazde and the wider operation in a different light.

From the look on the faces of the other blokes, I could tell that they, too, had not considered it a total waste. It hadn't all been about petty bureaucracy or the failure of politicians to act decisively when decisive action was needed. As quasi-military operations went, we'd learned a lot. But there was also much that still needed to be absorbed. I only hoped to God that somebody somewhere, with the right clearances and a bit of influence, was reading the file and paying attention.

Bosnia had been a million miles from the roles for which we'd trained since the Regiment had come into being a half-century earlier. In a sense, it had been its ultimate post-Cold War test. It had shown that the SAS could perform with considerable effectiveness in the peacekeeping role. With the skills it had learned for war, along with its kitbag of comms, recce and medical tools, the Regiment had proved it could adapt to the humanitarian mission. This is just as well, since the pointers are that this kind of deployment will be on the increase in the early years of the twenty-first century.

With the end of the Warsaw Pact, the Regiment has been reinventing itself to stay with the times. We'd proved our worth in the fight against Saddam Hussein, but the world was moving so fast that even that operation belonged to a different military manual.

The punk soldiers I'd seen on the streets of Prozer, with their Mohicans and shoulder-launched SAMs, were just as likely to be our enemies in any future conflict as the troops of some deranged dictator. It's when these creatures acquire laptops and drift into cyber-terrorism that things will get really interesting.

Fortunately, the Regiment is pacing these developments. It's just too bad I can't be there to give them a hand.

Bosnia was my last active deployment. Along with our operation in the Gulf, I found it the most challenging – and, it's true, the most frustrating – mission of my career. The memories of the bitterness and the despair, not to mention the wanton destruction of such a beautiful country, will stay with me for the rest of my life.

Amid all the carnage, however, one miracle still strikes me as an apposite testament to the man from our ranks who gave his life for it. A week after Charlie took the patrol out of the pocket, as our C-130 headed home, Gorazde's defenders were somehow still managing to keep the enemy at bay. Three days later, they were rewarded when the Serbs agreed to meet a Nato deadline for the withdrawal of all their heavy guns and armour.

Against all expectation, Gorazde was reprieved. But the cost in human life had been immense.

The same, of course, can be said for the Balkans as a whole. Though the fighting formally ended with the Dayton Peace Accord in late 1995, its echoes have been heard in rumbles of discord since. And no one is under any illusion that the tensions that have beset the region for centuries have finally gone away. The Regiment has reportedly been back there since the dark days of 1994, more often than not to look for the perpetrators of the horrors committed during that time. Occasionally, as another war criminal is brought to book, their exploits have made the headlines.

From time to time, I see some of the lads who made the UKLO deployment. All bar a handful are still serving with 22 SAS. The exceptions are Charlie, who is now a civvy, plus Nick and James, both of whom are back in their parent regiments.

Keith and Paul, the two rookies of the mission, are now highly experienced members of the Regiment. On a personal note, my most sobering lesson of the deployment was that, through them, this old dog finally learned some new tricks. Involvement and professionalism needn't be mutually exclusive. You can be involved and give 100 per cent to the task in hand at the same time.

As the aircraft droned westwards, chasing the setting sun, I felt I had learned this lesson the hard way.

GLOSSARY

203	M 16 rifle with 40mm grenade-launcher
2i/c	second-in-command
319	main high-frequency (HF) radio
349	small individual radio
A-10	US ground-attack aircraft
AFV	armoured fighting vehicle
Air America	secret airline run by the CIA during the Vietnam War
Airburst	artillery shells designed to go off over the heads of troops out in the open to inflict maximum casualties
AK-47	Russian semi-automatic rifle
APC	armoured personnel carrier
Bell 412	US-built troop-carrying helicopter
Bergen	Army backpack
BG	bodyguard
BiH	Bosnian Army in Herzegovina (the Muslim forces)
BMP	Soviet-designed reconnaissance vehicle
BRITBAT	British peace-keeping contingent
BRITFOR	British contingent of the Bosnian peace-keeping force

Browning .50	heavy-calibre machine-gun
BSA	Bosnian-Serb Army
BTR	Soviet-designed armoured personnel carrier
C-130	veteran four-engined transport aircraft, built in USA
cammed	camouflaged
Casevac	casualty evacuation
chaff	strips of metallic foil designed to confuse SAMs
CIA	US Central Intelligence Agency
CO	commanding officer (e.g. of the Regiment itself)
comms	communications
crap-hat	Para nickname for infantrymen
CS gas	non-lethal toxic gas, also known as tear gas
CT	counter-terrorist
Diamond Route	official term for one of the Bosnian MSRs (*q.v.*)
DPM	disruptive pattern material; camouflage
Dragunov	Russian snipers' rifle
E&E	escape and evasion
EMU	electronic module unit, part of the 319 radio
ESM	electronic surveillance measures
exfil	exfiltration
F/A-18	US carrier-based multi-role fighter aircraft
F-16	US multi-role fighter aircraft
FAC	forward air controller
FIBUA	fighting in built-up areas
frag	shrapnel
G	measure of gravity; i.e. at 3G, in a manoeuvring aircraft, for instance, one's body weighs three times its normal weight

G222	Italian transport aircraft
GPMG	general-purpose machine-gun
GPS	global positioning system; satellite-based navigation aid
green slime	slang for Military Intelligence
GV	Gornji Vakuf
HE	high explosive
HF	high frequency
HLS	helicopter landing site
Ho Chi Minh Trail	slang for Diamond Route
HVO	Croatian Defence Council; HV was the Croat army in Bosnia
int brief	intelligence briefing
int sums	intelligence summaries
IR	infrared
KITE	individual night-sight for a weapon
KL43	an attachment to the secure comms radio
klick	kilometre
LO	liaison officer
LS	landing site
LSRV	landing site rendezvous
LTD	laser target designation
M16	semi-automatic rifle
MALBAT	Malaysian peace-keeping contingent
Medevac	medical evacuation
MILAN	European-made anti-tank missile
MIRA	Milan infrared attachment; special night-sight for the MILAN missile
Mk19	grenade-launcher
MO	*modus operandi*, method of operation
Motorola	mobile phone
MP	Military Police
MP5	Hechler and Koch 9mm machine-gun

MSR	main supply route
NATO	North Atlantic Treaty Organization
NBC	nuclear, biological and chemical
NCO	non-commissioned officer
NORBAT	Norwegian peace-keeping contingent
NVGs	night vision goggles
OC	officer commanding (e.g., of a squadron or troop)
OP	observation post
Orbat	order of battle
OTP	one-time pad (key pad for special forces secret codes)
Parker L52	snipers' rifle
Pira	Provisional IRA
PNG	passive night-vision goggles
Puma	Anglo-French troop-carrying helicopter
Quad	four-barrelled anti-aircraft gun
R&R	rest and recuperation
RCT	Royal Corps of Transport
REME	Royal Electrical and Mechanical Engineers
REMF	rear-echelon mother-fucker, slang for non-frontline troops
RHQ	Regimental Headquarters
RN	Royal Navy
RPG	rocket-propelled grenade
rupert	lower ranks' nickname for officer; somewhat derogatory
RV	rendezvous
RWR	radar-warning receiver
SA-80	standard British Army semi-automatic rifle
SA-13	Russian SAM
SA-16	Russian SAM
SA-3	Russian SAM
SA-6	Russian SAM

SA-7	Russian SAM
SA-8	Russian SAM
SA-9	Russian SAM
SAM	surface-to-air missile
satcom	satellite communications
scaly	slang for a member of military intelligence
sced	the sending/receiving of signal data
Scimitar	British tank
Sea Harrier	British carrier-based multi-role fighter aircraft
Sea King	British troop-carrying helicopter
Sig Sauer 9mm	German pistol
slivovitz	powerful Bosnian alcoholic spirit
smart bombs	laser-guided bombs
SP	special projects (normally referred to as SP team, for anti-terrorism training)
SPANBAT	Spanish peace-keeping contingent
squaddie	Army slang for lower ranks
stag	sentry duty
Stinger	US-made shoulder-launched anti-aircraft missile
Stirling Lines	SAS headquarters in Hereford
TAOR	tactical area of responsibility
Triple A	anti-aircraft fire
U-2	US spyplane
UKLO	United Kingdom Liaison Officers
Ultimax 100	lightweight automatic machine-gun
UNHCR	United Nations High Commission for Refugees
UNMO	United Nations Military Observers (unarmed)
UNPROFOR	UN Protection Force
Walther PPK	German pistol
Warrior	British armoured personnel carrier